D0396569

No Longer Property of
ANYTHINK LIBRARIES/
RANGEVIEW LIBRARY DISTRICT

TRAGEDY, HOPE AND TRIUMPH
IN TUSCALOOSA

THE STORM

AND

THE TIDE

LARS ANDERSON

Also by Lars Anderson

The First Star

Carlisle vs. Army

The All Americans

The Proving Ground

Pickup Artists:
Street Basketball in America

TRAGEDY, HOPE AND TRIUMPH

IN TUSCALOOSA

THE STORM

AND

THE TIDE

LARS ANDERSON

Copyright © 2014 by Lars Anderson

Published by Sports Illustrated Books,
an imprint of Time Home Entertainment Inc.

Time Home Entertainment Inc.
1271 Avenue of the Americas, 6th floor
New York, NY 10020

Book design by Stephen Skalocky
Map illustration by MacNeill + Macintosh

All rights reserved. No part of this book may be reproduced in any form or by
any electronic or mechanical means, including information storage and retrieval
systems, without permission in writing from the publisher, except by a reviewer,
who may quote brief passages in a review.

ISBN 10: 1-61893-097-4
ISBN 13: 978-1-61893-097-2
Library of Congress Control Number: 2014933893

Sports Illustrated is a trademark of Time Inc.

*In memory of the 53 lives lost in the
Tuscaloosa tornado, and for those who still suffer
from the tragic events of April 27, 2011*

Contents

Contents

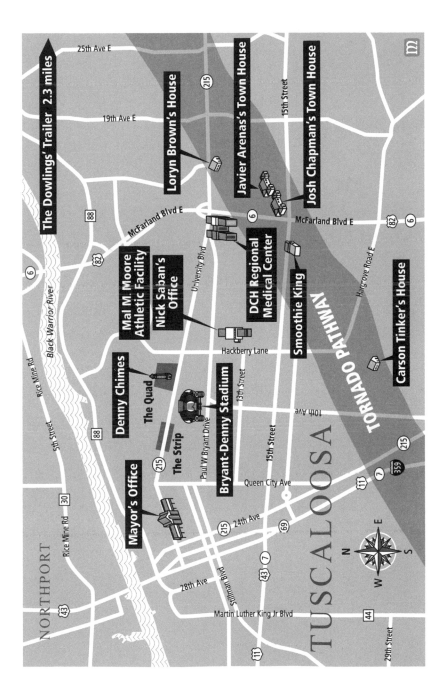

CHAPTER 1

An Ill
Wind

A SHARP CRACK of thunder startled Carson Tinker from his sleep. He peered through the west-facing window of his wood-frame house in Tuscaloosa, Alabama. It was 5:30 in the morning, April 27, 2011, and flashes of lightning fractured the dark sky. He watched mesmerized as the bolts danced and skittered.

The storm passed quickly, though, and soon the air outside turned quiet and calm. The 21-year-old Tinker, a junior at the University of Alabama, began his morning routine. He left his house, a four-bedroom rental at 611 25th Street, and headed for campus, where he attended class, then met up with his girlfriend of 11 months, Ashley Harrison, a senior honors student. The two had been introduced at a party in Tuscaloosa the previous spring, and Tinker's immediate thought was that he had no chance with this girl, a lovely, brown-eyed brunette whose soft smile made him weak in the knees. But soon afterward he asked Harrison out, and it wasn't long before the two of them were constantly at each other's side, hand in hand, flush with happy romance. They enjoyed doing everything together, whether making sushi in the kitchen or spending time outdoors with their dogs. Carson's dog was Josey, a German shepherd mix, and Ashley's was Ms. B, a black Lab.

Ashley and Carson were in love, both knew it, and they talked of a future together. She prophesied to Carson that in several months, in January, on the day before they would celebrate her 23rd birthday, she would watch him play for the national championship in New Orleans. She was a football fan, if not an aficionado—when Carson told Ashley that he was a long snapper on the football team, she had called her father in Texas and asked, "Dad, what's a long snapper?"— and she would be there in the Superdome, seated close to the field, her eyes locked onto his every step as her Carson would help lead the Alabama Crimson Tide to the title. It would be glorious fun. That was Ashley Harrison's vision.

ASHLEY HAD happily watched the beginnings of her dream scenario coming to life just recently; she was one of 92,310 fans who had filled Bryant-Denny Stadium on the Alabama campus on April 16, 2011, to watch the Crimson Tide play their annual spring football game. Traditionally called the A-Day game, it was really just a scrimmage between the first string (the Crimson team) and the second string (the White); as much as anything, it was an exhibition for the fans. But there is no such thing as an unimportant football game in Tuscaloosa, and so the largest crowd in the school history of A-Day was humming with excitement before kickoff.

A gravelly voice thundered from above, God-like, rumbling down from the afternoon sky to fill every inch of the stadium. The craggy image of Paul (Bear) Bryant appeared on the video boards at each end of the towering grandstands, and in a bass-thumping Southern drawl the words from the legendary Alabama coach poured out of the P.A. system: *I ain't never been nothin' but a winner.* The crowd erupted in a kind of rapture.

The voice of the Bear before any Alabama home game is a crowd-stirring tradition, spring game or not. (Former Florida coach Urban Meyer once said he didn't feel like he'd arrived in the Southeastern Conference until he heard Bryant's booming baritone minutes before kickoff in Tuscaloosa.) It didn't matter to the Tide fans, here on April 16, that the start of the 2011 season was more than four months away. It sounded and looked and felt like game day.

As Bryant's voice faded into echo, Nick Saban stood in front of a cluster of players who were jumping up and down in the north end zone portal. Dressed in a gray suit, white shirt and crimson tie, the coach led his first-stringers, in crimson jerseys, onto the field while *Sweet Home Alabama* blared from the stadium speakers. Seen from almost any distance, the 59-year-old Saban, at 5' 9", 180 pounds, hardly cut an intimidating physical figure; but he was clearly the center of energy on the field, and to those in the stands he was the bull's-eye of interest. Fans stood on the ramps and squatted in the aisles, everyone straining to see the coach, the man who had ignited this great revival of football faith in Tuscaloosa.

Before Saban had arrived at Alabama, the attendance record for any SEC spring game was believed to have been 73,000, at Tennessee in 1986; Alabama fans had now shattered that mark multiple times. (For comparison, the second-largest spring-game crowd in the country in 2011 was 66,784 at Nebraska.) And now the roar of the 92,000-plus could be heard for blocks and blocks outside the stadium, where many fans stood on apartment balconies and backyard decks just to let that joyful noise wash over them.

It was only a glorified practice, yes, but Saban was intense as always, standing on the field 20 yards behind the offensive line, clapping his hands after nearly every play, slapping the pads of a player in appreciation of sound fundamentals or jumping in the face of a player who committed a blunder. He was not going to let the failures of the previous season happen again.

After winning the 2009 national title in just his third season at

Alabama, Saban had spent the ensuing summer and fall exerting all of his persuasive powers to try to keep his players from tasting the forbidden fruit of complacency. He warned them in the locker room, warned them on the practice field and even warned them through the media. (At press conferences, whenever he wants to send a message to his team, Saban likes to look directly into the cameras instead of at the reporter asking the question.) *Success doesn't breed success, only hard work does,* he told the players a thousand times.

During many autumn afternoons in the 2010 season, Saban, wearing his customary straw hat at practice, unleashed profanity-laced tirades at any player he believed was giving less than full effort, screaming that if things didn't change, losses were certain to follow. Saban's temper had become legendary on campus—even student workers on the team tiptoed in fear of falling target to one of his rants. But his warnings and pleadings hadn't worked that year. The Crimson Tide, who began the season ranked No. 1, lost to South Carolina, LSU and Auburn and stumbled to a disappointing 10–3 season.

Now during the spring game, Saban was back at it: yelling, praising, barking, instructing. He was paying especially close attention to quarterback AJ McCarron, a redshirt sophomore from Mobile who was competing with redshirt freshman Phillip Sims to be the starter. Neither one had yet stood out, but late in the fourth quarter McCarron, number 10, wearing a black jersey to signify to defenders that he was not to be tackled, led the second-string offense on a long drive. He displayed a nice touch on sideline throws and repeatedly checked down to running backs when the defense dropped seven players into the secondary. He moved the White squad to the Crimson's 28-yard line with seven seconds remaining. Trailing 14–10 McCarron flung a pass into the end zone for wide receiver Kevin Norwood. The ball fell to the ground, incomplete. The game clock expired. McCarron, indeed the entire team, was still a work in progress.

The two squads met in the middle of the field, hugging and high-fiving. Senior noseguard Josh Chapman gathered with several defensive teammates and took the opportunity to remind the younger players that it was the defense that would have to lead this team in 2011—and that the players would take no summer vacation. "We win national championships in the weight room," Chapman told them. "Now it's time to get serious."

Nearby, junior Barrett Jones, a third-team All-America as a right guard who was now moving to left tackle, spoke with other offensive linemen. Jones believed this unit could be the best in the country, but it wasn't yet. "Our chemistry has to improve," he warned his mates. "We've got to keep trusting each other."

Carson Tinker looked up into the crowd and spotted Ashley Harrison. They pointed at each other, smiling, practically disappearing into each other's eyes. Later that evening they would join other players and friends at the bars near the stadium. High spirits were everywhere; football was in the air in Tuscaloosa.

LESS THAN two weeks later, after their classes on April 27, Carson and Ashley went to Carson's house, where they spent the afternoon building a flower bed, digging into the rich Alabama soil in the front yard; above, bright springtime sunshine now prevailed. At lunch they ate leftover ham-and-potato salad that Harrison had prepared for Easter three days earlier, then settled into the living room couch to watch *The NeverEnding Story,* a movie from the '80s. It wasn't Tinker's kind of flick and, soon restless, he took the two dogs to a large, grassy open space across the street. On the mowed field, he hit golf balls with his pitching wedge, blasting them high into the April sky; Ms. B and Josey fetched.

This field, framed by towering oaks, pines and pecan trees, was one of Tinker's favorite places in Tuscaloosa. He felt peaceful here; aside from the occasional bark from one of the dogs, the only sound he heard was that of the wind strumming the leaves in the tall trees. He often told friends that whenever he could spend time in the field with the dogs, it was "one of the highlights of my day."

Carson walked back to the house an hour later. The sky had turned gray again, but there was no rain. After taking a shower he returned to the living room and saw that Ashley and his two roommates—Alan Estis and Payton Holley—were fixated on the TV screen. But it wasn't the movie they were watching. It was a weatherman declaring in a heightened voice that a tornado was bearing down on Tuscaloosa.

It was just after five o'clock when Tinker and Holley stepped onto the front porch, looked upward and searched for a funnel cloud; all they saw was a darkening sky. Seconds later, while they were still standing on the porch, Tinker's cellphone rang. It was his grandfather Jim Cartledge, calling from Hoover, Ala., about 50 miles northeast of Tuscaloosa. "Carson, you need to take cover *now!*"

"Yes, sir," Carson replied.

Tinker and Holley dashed inside. What they didn't see was the danger lurking four miles to the west of their house. The most powerful long-track tornado ever to descend on Alabama was on the ground—a huge twister with winds of 190 mph, now roaring toward Tuscaloosa. Quickly the four students, with the two dogs, wedged themselves into a walk-in closet in Estis's bedroom. Carson wrapped his 6' 1", 220-pound frame around Ashley. "We're going to be O.K.," he whispered into her ear.

It was 5:13 p.m.

LORYN BROWN was about to step into her Crimson-colored dream. Ever since she was a three-year-old girl growing up in Tuscaloosa, Loryn had wanted to attend the University of Alabama, and soon it was actually, finally, going to happen.

On the morning of April 27 she was in her rented three-bedroom house at 51 Beverly Heights in Tuscaloosa, a house shaded by oak and pine trees that stretched 80 feet into the sky; Loryn shared the place with two roommates. Her final test of the semester at nearby Shelton State Community College was later that evening. Loryn, 21, wanted to become a sports broadcaster and she had already been accepted at Alabama, where she intended to enroll the coming fall, her lifelong ambition realized at last. Her plan for today was to study in the house, then drive the two miles to the Shelton State campus for her 6:30 exam.

The crimson ran deep in Loryn's blood. Her father, Shannon Brown, had been a backup defensive lineman on Alabama's 1992 national championship squad and was a team captain on the '95 team. Little Loryn, who'd been born when her father and mother, Ashley, were students at Stanhope Elmore High School in Millbrook, Ala., never missed a home game. Wearing her daddy's number 93 jersey (then number 75 after he switched numbers), she'd sit on her mother's lap in Bryant-Denny Stadium and point excitedly at her father on the field. After the games she'd wait outside the locker room with her mom and run into her daddy's arms as soon as she spotted him. He was her hero.

During the championship parade in Tuscaloosa in January 1993, two-year-old Loryn had a crimson ribbon tied in her ponytail and wore a button on her white turtleneck that read, MY DADDY IS NO. 93. With her mother watching, she ran excitedly in small circles around the players as they waited to board a float that would ferry them down University Boulevard and past the soaring stadium. "Mama," Loryn said, "*I'm* going to go to school *here.*"

Loryn, with her dark curly hair and dimpled cheeks, even melted the heart of Alabama coach Gene Stallings, a notorious curmudgeon. Before the Sugar Bowl game against Miami that would decide the '92 national title—underdog Alabama would defeat the No. 1 Hurricanes 34–13—Loryn dined with the team at the pregame meal in their New Orleans hotel. Loryn had just learned the "show-your-food trick," as her mother called it, and midway through the meal she stood on her chair and yelled out, "Hey, Coach Stallings!" Once she had the coach's attention, Loryn, dressed in an Alabama cheerleader's outfit, opened her mouth wide to show the piece of steak she was chewing. The coach nearly fell out of his chair in a fit of laughter. The moment lightened the mood of the entire gathering, and some players would later swear that it relaxed the team and, three hours after, helped them play at their best. Now, nearly two decades and umpteen Tide victories later, she was still the consummate fan.

Like so many people throughout Alabama, Loryn had awakened early in the morning of April 27 to crackling thunder. The power in the house had flickered on and off. She'd called her mother, Ashley Mims, now remarried and living in Wetumpka, Ala., a town about two hours to the southeast. Loryn always phoned her mom when storms threatened. Even as a small child she had a deep-seated fear of severe weather; it scared her even more than the dark.

Less than two weeks earlier Loryn had downloaded a Weather Channel app onto her mother's phone, setting the two main cities of interest as Wetumpka and Tuscaloosa. "Mama, can you pull up the weather on your phone?" Loryn asked. "We're having a bad storm. What's going on?"

Ashley Mims looked at her phone. There was a triangle-shaped storm over Tuscaloosa, but it appeared small. "Oh, baby, you'll be fine," she said. "It will blow over in a minute." She was right.

But a few hours later she read another weather report on her phone. This one suggested that conditions would be favorable for tornadoes later in the afternoon in Tuscaloosa. Ashley called her daughter and asked if she should come pick Loryn up. "No, Mama," Loryn said. "I don't want you to get stuck somewhere. I don't want you on the road. I'll be fine."

For the rest of the afternoon, Loryn stayed in her bedroom, cramming for her exam, wearing an oversized T-shirt from Big Daddy's Fireworks, where she worked in the summer in Wetumpka to earn money for school. At just before five o'clock, with the skies darkening over Tuscaloosa, one of Loryn's roommates, Kelli Rumanek, left the house to drive to the library on the Alabama campus to take an on-line test. Kelli had planned to stay at home to take the exam, but, fatefully as it happened, the Internet connection in the house had failed.

Minutes after Kelli drove away, Loryn heard the emergency sirens wail. With her other roommate, Danielle Downs, Loryn called Will Stevens, a close friend, and asked him to come over; the girls were nervous and their anxiety spiked with every passing minute. At approximately 5:07, Stevens parked his car in front of 51 Beverly Heights. Several Alabama baseball players living across the street saw Stevens rush into the house to comfort his friends.

From her living room in Wetumpka, Loryn's mother flipped back and forth between news stations, which had cameras mounted in downtown Tuscaloosa. At 5:12, her heart jackhammering with fear, Ashley Mims called her daughter. "Baby, it's coming right at you!" Ashley said in a panicked voice. "Get your head down."

"Mama, I'm scared," Loryn said.

Loryn and her friends moved to a center hallway on the first floor of the house, with her mother still on the phone. Ashley could hear Stevens telling Loryn and Danielle that everything would be fine, that they had to have faith, that they needed to be strong.

"It's going to be O.K., baby," Ashley told her daughter over the phone. "It's going to be O.K."

"I'm scared, Mama," Loryn said, clutching a pillow over her head. "It's just black outside. It's just *black*."

Then the line went dead. It was 5:13 p.m.

Overwhelmed with fright, her body shaking uncontrollably, Ashley Mims ran out of her house. On the front lawn, frantic, she dropped to her knees, raised her face to the heavens and called out with all the strength she could summon, "Oh, God, no! Please be with her, God. Please. Please, God, please don't take her. Not my baby girl."

CHAPTER 2

The Short Wait

HIS CELLPHONE rang at 4:30 in the morning on April 27, jarring Mayor Walt Maddox awake in his home in north Tuscaloosa. Maddox, a fresh-faced 38-year-old who'd graduated from Tuscaloosa's Central High in 1991, answered quickly. An official from the local Emergency Management Agency (EMA) informed him that a tornado warning had been issued for his city. Rising from his bed, Maddox moved to his den and punched into the remote the numbers for a local TV station, looking for a weather report.

Maddox wasn't overly concerned. Logic told him not to be. Just 12 days earlier, on April 15, a dangerous tornado with winds of 140 miles per hour (an EF3-level storm in the official nomenclature) had hopscotched through the southern part of Tuscaloosa, damaging about a hundred houses, snapping off trees and downing power lines. No one was killed, but it was the most significant natural disaster in Maddox's nearly six years as mayor. How likely was it, really, that such a short time later a second tornado would strike Tuscaloosa? No way, he told himself. No way in the world.

His wife, Stephanie, joined him in their den, and at 5:00 Maddox received another call from the EMA informing him that the warning had been lifted. Just as he'd figured. By 6:00 the mayor was at the YMCA preparing to head outside for a jog. Several locals who were there at the Y asked Maddox if more dangerous weather was forecast to blow toward Tuscaloosa. Outside the rain had passed and the temperature was rising. "We'll see, but I'm hoping that our weather event was April 15, not today," Maddox said. "I mean, what are the odds of another tornado coming again this soon?"

When Maddox reached City Hall around 7:30, the building was dark. The morning storm had caused much of the city to lose power; it had also knocked out the backup generator at City Hall, but it was fixed in short order. At 11:00, as Maddox was sitting in his expansive, second-floor downtown office overlooking University Boulevard, his EMA director called again. The news was ominous: According to the National Weather Service (NWS), there was a 45% probability of tornado activity in Tuscaloosa and the surrounding area before nightfall. This time the call was disturbing to Maddox. "We've got to start preparing right now," Maddox said to the director. "The National Weather Service has *never* attached a percentage to us getting hit by a tornado before."

Maddox called all of his key staff members into what is named the Daugherty Room, a meeting room down the hall from his office that, he said, would have to serve as the team's makeshift command center. The city's usual command center was located in the City Hall basement, but that was presently under renovation. By four in the afternoon, Maddox and 10 of his close advisers had clustered in the small room with their laptops and iPads open, monitoring the weather, making sure that key emergency responders in the city— police, firemen, the hospital staff, the National Guard—were alerted to the approaching danger. With concern on his face but a soothing calm in his voice, Maddox asked everyone on his staff if they were ready; each nodded yes. Shortly before 4:00 Maddox's wife texted him: *Do I have time to make a run to Target before the storm arrives?* Maddox texted, *Yes.* He did not know then, of course, that most of the structures at a bustling intersection that she would drive through—at 15th Street and McFarland Boulevard—would be torn off the ground barely an hour later.

TUSCALOOSA, KNOWN commonly and affectionately by the locals as T-Town, is Alabama's fifth-largest city, a hub of several local, state and federal government agencies, as well as various manufacturing, transportation and service companies. It covers 60 square miles and has a population of around 93,000. More than anything else, it is known as the home of the University of Alabama. It is also, however, known to be sitting in the heart of a rich spawning ground for tornadoes.

By the time Mayor Maddox and his staff had gathered elbow-to-elbow in their cramped command post, Wednesday, April 27 had already been a deadly day in Alabama. To the northeast of Tuscaloosa, some 57 miles away, several tornadoes had descended at 5:30 that morning across central Alabama. The first death was reported in the town of Odenville, where 56-year-old Gayle McCrory, the manager of a Chevron station, had been sleeping in her mobile home on McCrory Drive when three trees fell on it, one of them landing directly on her bed. She died instantly. Later that morning in the Cahaba Heights neighborhood, 68-year-old Milton Baker Sr. was watching his son help a neighbor remove a downed limb from his car when part of a large tree fell on Baker. He died within minutes.

Now in Tuscaloosa, as Maddox continued to monitor the National Weather Service, he again reminded all of the city's emergency personnel to remain vigilant—conditions were ideal for increasingly severe weather. The temperature had risen well into the 80s, unseasonably warm for mid-spring. The air was thick with moisture from the Gulf of Mexico; dew points in the area measured in the low 70s. On the ground the wind gusts were 10 to 15 mph out of the southeast, but at 40,000 feet above the ground, a crosswind out of the southwest blew at 80 to 100 mph. Meteorologists around the state were uniform in what they believed they were seeing: a stirring of ingredients that could produce massive tornado activity, perhaps on a record scale.

At 3 p.m. the NWS issued warnings that the worst of the conditions, potentially, had yet to arrive. Then, just five minutes later, a tornado touched down in northwest Alabama a few miles from the Mississippi border in Marion County along Highway 78. It remained on the ground for 90 miles and killed 70 people. The tornado was so powerful that even when radar was unable to detect hail or rain in the system, it did register an airborne debris field—trees, cars and houses being carried along by the 210-mph winds. Maddox and his staff closely followed that twister; though its path was not one that threatened Tuscaloosa, they were fearful that a similar storm could churn its lethal way in their direction—even though the sun continued to shine brightly outside City Hall, sending warm shafts of light streaming through the windows of the Daugherty Room.

At around 4:00 another intense group of super cells began to organize over Mississippi and western Alabama. At 4:30 Maddox and his team in City Hall were convinced that the swirling skies above them were poised to spawn a tornado. Suddenly the emergency sirens blared. At 5:00 Maddox ordered everyone in City Hall to move to a safe area in the building's basement.

But Maddox didn't follow his team; instead he moved back to his office with Chad Palmer, a police sergeant assigned to the mayor on this day. The two settled in front of a large flat-screen television on which they could view every one of the more than 50 cameras mounted at various intersections throughout the city. When Maddox called up the traffic camera located at the crossing of Interstate 20/59 and Interstate 359—about three miles southeast of his office—the image before him was terrifying: a massive tornado charging hard, aimed at his city and, he believed, directly at the

Alabama campus and Bryant-Denny Stadium. His heart dropped. He knew that horror was coming, that holy hell was about to be unleashed on his city, and, like the first rumbles of sliding snow in an avalanche, that it couldn't be stopped.

"Mayor, we're moving you to the basement right now," Palmer said. "Right now, sir."

Maddox hustled down two flights of stairs. When he reached his staff they were huddled around a single television, watching the twister charge toward their city. For a moment the mayor had the strange sense that *this must be happening someplace else*. Then reality: *This is going to be a nightmare*. At that instant, the TV lost its feed. Cell service was down. In silence, the mayor and his staff sat—didn't move, didn't speak.

It was 5:13 p.m.

JAVIER ARENAS was watching the local news in his Tuscaloosa house shortly after 5:00; outside the emergency sirens wailed. Arenas had been a celebrated punt returner and defensive back as a senior on Alabama's national title team in 2009—he set an SEC record for punt return touchdowns (seven) that season—and had now completed his rookie season for the Kansas City Chiefs as a second-round draft pick. Like so many former Crimson Tide players, he lived in T-Town in the off-season because it was the place he'd experienced the best moments of his life. That was about to change.

Early that morning Arenas had seen pellets of hail, an inch in diameter, pounding the ground, but the skies had cleared, and he spent the early part of the day on campus lifting weights at the Mal M. Moore Athletic Facility. Afterward Arenas went for his usual postworkout smoothie at the Smoothie King at the intersection of 15th Street and McFarland Boulevard. Arenas was a regular at the place, where the owner, a devoted Alabama fan named Lee Henderson, always greeted him warmly.

Dozens of current and former Crimson Tide players were steady customers at the Smoothie King. Henderson was like most fans in Tuscaloosa: He wouldn't pester the players with questions; he'd simply ask how they were doing, then take their orders.

Arenas was in a buoyant mood, happy to be home in T-Town. His big smile revealed a row of white teeth gleaming like piano keys, and that grin, to the staff, seemed to light up the place as Arenas chatted and joked with them.

A bit later Arenas returned to his house on Gardenia Avenue, less than half a mile from the Smoothie King, to wait for a friend on the track team to finish practice. The two had planned to enjoy the evening out on The Strip—the cluster of bars and restaurants on University Boulevard, which slices through the Alabama campus. Arenas had his TV on but with no volume; when he saw a weather reporter interrupt the show, he turned up the sound. The reporter was saying that a tornado was blowing close to downtown, four miles from Arenas's house. Minutes later, looking out his window, what he saw left him cold with fear: There was the twister, barreling straight toward his house and straight toward 15th and McFarland, the corner where he'd just been—a location that Tuscaloosa residents would soon refer to as ground zero.

LEE HENDERSON was fretting. The owner of three Smoothie King stores in Tuscaloosa—he had opened his third just three months earlier, this one on The Strip in the heart of the campus— Henderson worried about how he was going to staff his stores over the summer months. So he spent the morning of April 27 examining his employee roster; he had 24 people working for him in all, most of whom were students who would be leaving the next week once the semester ended. Performing this head count was an annual rite of spring for Henderson, now more complicated with the addition of the third store. Still, the 38-year-old Henderson was delighted with the new location. He loved being on campus with the kids. It made him feel young.

Henderson had a home on Lake Tuscaloosa where he lived with his wife, Leigh (yes, Lee and Leigh), and their two children, six-year-old Blake and four-year-old Riley. That morning Leigh couldn't take her eyes off the television screen and James Spann, the chief meteorologist for the ABC affiliate in Birmingham. Spann, a tall, slender man with a receding hairline, is the state's most respected weatherman; whenever a storm approaches, he rolls up his shirt-sleeves and delivers his rapid-fire coverage, issuing warnings to the affected communities in the authoritative, urgent voice of a pastor advising his congregation.

Spann's words today were alarming to Leigh. She called her husband. "James Spann is saying that it's not *if* bad weather is going to come, it's *when*," Leigh said. "This could be bad."

Because of the day's treacherous forecast, school had been canceled at Rock Quarry Elementary, where Blake was in kindergarten. Around noon Leigh drove her two kids to the Chick-fil-A on McFarland. Inside the Chick-fil-A she bumped into two friends, Cissy Cochran and Mary Beth Smart. Cissy, the wife of Alabama strength coach Scott Cochran, and Mary Beth, married to Crimson Tide defensive coordinator Kirby Smart, had brought their kids in for lunch too. The three women discussed the day's only vital topic of conversation: the weather. "I don't like what I'm hearing from James Spann," Leigh told them.

At the same time, Lee Henderson was driving his SUV to his new store on The Strip when he got a phone call from Ryan Holland, the manager of the Smoothie King at 15th and McFarland. "The power keeps going in and out," Holland told his boss, "and we have cars wrapped around the building in line."

Henderson turned around and went to help Holland. As he approached the store, he noticed that the clear sky seemed to be glowing, as if lit by some strange unseen source. Entering the store, he could hear the smoothie blenders sputter, fail, then suddenly start up again. The lights flickered. He looked out at the sky again; it remained cloudless. "Something in the atmosphere is just not right," Henderson told Holland. Then, seemingly without reason, power was fully restored and business resumed as normal.

At 3:00, still listening to Spann, Leigh was convinced there was impending danger, and she called her husband. "Lee, you need to close the stores," she said. He was hesitant, but the tone in his wife's voice bothered him. She wasn't suggesting that he shutter his businesses—she was *demanding* it. "This is either going to be the biggest false alarm of all time," Lee told her, "or this is going to be really bad."

Henderson called each store and firmly instructed his three managers: "I want everyone out of there by 4 p.m. This isn't our normal protocol"—in the past he would have told his employees to take refuge in the old walk-in coolers if a tornado was approaching—"but I've got to go with my gut. So let's shut everything down and everyone get home and get to a safe place."

At 4:45 Henderson joined his wife and kids at his parents' house about two miles north of the Alabama campus. They had a basement full of toys to occupy the children while the adults nervously waited out the storm. Minutes ticked by slowly. With Lee's father listening to a handheld radio and with the basement television tuned to ABC and Spann, the Henderson clan grew increasingly worried. A tornado appeared to be tracking directly toward Tuscaloosa. At 5:03 Henderson told his wife and kids to get in the bathroom and climb into the tub. Henderson stood outside the bathroom with his father, their eyes fixated on the television and the frightening images of the approaching tornado. "Oh, my gosh," Henderson said, "this is going to wipe out the University of Alabama."

On TV, Spann continued to urge every man, woman and child in Tuscaloosa to seek cover immediately. Another realization hit Henderson: "It's going to take out the Smoothie King," he said softly to his father. Seconds later, the power went out. It was 5:13 p.m.

BOB DOWLING opened the front door of his mobile home in eastern Tuscaloosa county. It was a few minutes past 5:00. He gazed into the dark sky. Moments earlier he'd been watching TV with his wife, Dana, and their two teenage children, Marilyn and Drew, when a local weatherman instructed everyone in the area to find a safe place. A tornado was on the ground, just south of Bryant-Denny Stadium, meaning it was only three miles from the Dowlings and their three-bedroom trailer in the Chalet Ridge Mobile Home Park, which had about 75 trailers. But Dowling wasn't fazed; Chalet Ridge was situated in a small valley and surely, he believed, a tornado would fly harmlessly right over them.

Not that he wasn't wary. Dowling had seen firsthand the devastating power of wind. He'd lived in Florida when Hurricane Andrew struck in 1992, destroying entire neighborhoods and leaving 65 dead. That hurricane had an emotional impact on Dowling, and he would remember it later in his life when he started working on disaster relief crews. He logged five months on the Louisiana shoreline in 2010 after the oil spill in the Gulf of Mexico. He frequently told his children of the gut-level gratification he felt when helping others, especially after a tragedy such as Andrew. The lesson he had learned was that possessions can be replaced; lives cannot.

Dowling and his family continued to look up into the churning clouds, scanning the skyline for danger. Around them now were dozens of their neighbors running in a panic to an underground storm shelter, located in the middle of the trailer park. The entry to the shelter was slathered in mud, and one frantic resident lost his balance as he ran to the concrete opening, slipping and breaking his ankle.

At that moment, Marilyn, Dowling's 13-year-old daughter, raised her right hand to the sky. Dowling looked up and froze in astonishment: A van was spinning in the air 300 yards above them—a van!—soaring past like some Hollywood special effect. Then, lowering his eyes, Dowling saw, for the first time, the twister. It was only a quarter of a mile away. Worse, it was hugging the ground, charging directly into the valley where Dowling stood. He now wanted to move his family into the shelter, but it was already overflowing with frightened people. There was no more room for them.

"We're in big trouble!" Dowling yelled. "Let's move to the laundry room, now!"

IN THE backyard of his town house on Veterans Memorial Parkway, Josh Chapman fired up his grill. It was 5:05 and, as he did on so many evenings, Chapman was rustling up a barbecue dinner for some of his teammates. The senior noseguard had been one of the first players Saban had recruited upon his arrival in Tuscaloosa in 2007, and now Chapman saw himself as the big brother to everyone on the team. If any player had a problem, he went to Chapman. And if any player was ever hungry, he went to Chapman's backyard, where Josh could be found standing at his grill, which sizzled with chicken or ribs or steaks.

This evening, as wide receiver Marquis Maze and a half-dozen other players milled around the grill with Chapman, a female voice from inside the town house yelled for everyone to immediately come inside. They ran in and she pointed at the television in Chapman's living room: There on the flat screen was a massive tornado. "It's downtown and heading right at us," a young woman yelled.

Everyone scattered throughout the house, some to a hallway, some to a laundry room. Chapman headed for an interior, windowless, first-floor bathroom. He tried to stay calm and controlled, masking the fact that he was suddenly as scared as he'd ever been.

Just down the road, Barrett Jones had slumped on his living room couch in his third-floor off-campus apartment. Jones, a junior offensive lineman, had spent the afternoon working out at Mal Moore, the athletic center. Exhausted, he'd been relaxing quietly until he heard emergency sirens blare.

The blond-haired, blue-eyed Jones stepped out onto his balcony. In the distance he saw, outlined against the graying sky, a tornado so incomprehensibly vast it seemed supernatural, a thing miles wide, stretching from the ground to the ceiling of the world. And it was spinning straight toward Bryant-Denny Stadium. "Oh, my Lord," Jones muttered in awe as he watched the monster moving before him.

NICK SABAN sat alone in his office on the second floor of Mal Moore, deep in concentration and oblivious to the increasingly dire weather reports. Spring practice had recently concluded, and now Saban was preparing for a videoconference. It was almost 4:30, and he needed to change clothes, so he headed home in his black Mercedes, driving to his ivy-covered, French-chateau-style house just outside of Northport, on the other side of the Black Warrior River from the university, a few miles northeast of campus.

After he'd crossed over the river on the Paul Bryant Bridge and neared his home, bursts of lightning flashed in the sky and thunder rumbled through the clouds. The warning sirens were in full song across Tuscaloosa now, but Saban, like so many in the city, had become desensitized to the piercing sound. The sirens had gone off a few times every week over the previous month or so, and except for the tornado 12 days earlier that had caused relatively minor damage, each time had been a false alarm. Now his cellphone bleated. His 24-year-old son, Nicholas, was calling from his house in town, near 15th and McFarland, to say that the winds were picking up there. Saban noted a tone of fear in his son's voice. He suggested that Nicholas get into his bathtub as a precaution.

Saban pulled into his driveway and walked into his house. He went to his bedroom and changed clothes.

It was now 5:13. Saban, like everyone else in Tuscaloosa, had no way of knowing that the tornado now on the southwest outskirts of town would become one of the deadliest in the history of the South. The next six minutes would change everything.

CHAPTER 3

After
The Bear

ON A sun-soaked afternoon
just 11 days before the storm,
a black drape covered a yet-to-
be revealed statue. A crowd of
thousands stood waiting.

Bryant-Denny Stadium sits on the southern edge of the University
of Alabama campus. On the stadium's north side is its main entrance
gate, and there, tucked between the looming structure and nearby University Boulevard, lies a brick-and-grass plaza that is called the Walk
of Champions. On football Saturdays, two hours before kickoff, three
buses carrying the Alabama team park here in the shadow of the stadium. The doors slide open, and the Crimson Tide players and coaches
walk through a crush of adoring fans, a pregame tradition that began
with a few hundred fans in 2006 and now draws a throng of 15,000.

As the players approach the entrance that leads to the locker room,
they pass beneath a line of larger-than-life bronze statues of all the
Alabama coaching legends who have led their Crimson Tide teams to
national championships: Wallace Wade, Frank Thomas, Gene Stallings and, of course, Bear Bryant.

On Saturday, April 16, 2011, A-Day in Tuscaloosa, a new statue was ready to join them, a nine-foot-tall bronze of Nick Saban. Standing in front of dozens of TV cameras and the horde of crimson-clad fans, the flesh-and-blood Saban looked up at the draped figure and flashed a disbelieving smile as he prepared to speak. He briefly reflected on his 2009 championship team, then, with his wife, Terry, pulled the covering away. The bronze Saban gleamed in the bright spring sunlight, the posed figure clapping his hands, leaning slightly forward, urging on his team from the sideline. It is a pose familiar to any Alabama fan, and the crowd burst into a roar of approval. With the fans still cheering, Saban moved away and strode into the stadium for the annual spring game.

Only four years into his coaching tenure at Alabama, Saban had been immortalized, his likeness forever grounded alongside the others. But unlike the other statues, all created by professionals, the figure of Saban was crafted by an Alabama student. Jeremy Davis, a fine arts major, was asked by two of his professors to produce a model for a statue of Saban. Less than 24 hours after being given the assignment, Davis was in Saban's office meeting with the coach and his wife to review his sketches. The Sabans liked what they saw. After a 15-minute photo shoot with the coach dressed first in a business suit and then in his sideline attire, Davis left to begin his work. He would spend some 250 hours sculpting from a design of the hand-clapping Saban. Davis consulted with Terry, no less a perfectionist than her husband, and she tweaked small details— the shape of an earlobe or the tip of her husband's nose. Working between classes and late into many nights, Davis produced a three-foot mold, which was then shipped to MTM Recognition in Oklahoma City, where the form was tripled in size to create the final figure. It is now the most photographed structure—man-made or natural—in the state of Alabama.

If giving a coach his own statue after a mere four seasons on the job seemed to be a bit of a rush to judgment, one needs to be reminded of how long the loyal fans of the Crimson Tide had waited for this man to come and how grateful they were to have him.

For more than a generation Alabama had been looking for an heir to Paul Bryant—the Bear. Except for Stallings, who won a national title in 1992 and spent seven years in Tuscaloosa, no coach had lasted more than four years at Alabama since Bryant retired in 1982 as the winningest coach in college football history (an overall record of 323-85-17). Successive coaches passed through the Alabama football program almost as fast as Tide fans push through the gates at Bryant-Denny. The Bear had made the job sacred, and his shadow haunted those who followed him: Ray Perkins, Bill Curry, Mike DuBose, Dennis Franchione, Mike Price (briefly) and Mike Shula. Indeed, the shadow was almost literal: It was, after all, Paul Bryant's name on the stadium that towered over them.

Could anyone ever replace Bryant in the hearts of Alabama fans? Oh, how they loved the Bear. His final game was a 21–15 victory over Illinois in the 1982 Liberty Bowl in Memphis. Bryant had announced two weeks before that he would be stepping aside at season's end. And though it was a lower-tier bowl game played between two middling teams (the Crimson Tide had finished the regular season 7–4), a huge viewing audience on 110 stations around the nation tuned in to see Bryant patrol the sideline one final time. Days before his final game *Sports Illustrated* writer John Underwood had phoned the 69-year-old Bryant (their conversation is recounted in Allen Barra's book *The Last Coach*) to ask him why he was hanging up his famous houndstooth hat.

"Because four damn losses is too damn many," Bryant said. "I'm up to my ass in alligators, John. These new young coaches just have too much energy for me. We need someone younger."

"So you really are tired?" Underwood asked.

"Naw," said Bryant. "To tell you the truth, I feel great. I got so many things I've been wantin' to do for so long, and now I'm gonna get to 'em."

"Like what?" Underwood said.

"I'm not sure just yet," Bryant replied.

But the Bear *was* tired. Twenty-seven days after he stalked the Alabama bench for the last time, he experienced severe chest pains and was driven to Druid City Hospital (now DCH) in Tuscaloosa. By the next morning, though, he was feeling better and his family expected him to be released. Around noon he was sitting upright in his bed with a yellow notepad in his hands, writing down reminders of things he wanted to do and things he wanted to say to those who mattered most to him. Ray Perkins, his replacement, stopped by to check in with his mentor; Bryant upbraided him for not being out on the recruiting trail. Then, while in his bed eating lunch, at 12:24 on Jan. 26, 1983, Bryant suffered a massive heart attack. Doctors frantically tried to revive him, but at 1:30 p.m. the pronouncement was made: The Bear was dead. In past years Bryant had often joked that if he ever stopped coaching he would "croak within a week." It actually took 28 days.

The news spread quickly from Tuscaloosa, as if carried across the state by the cool winter breeze that blew on this gray southern day. Grown men openly wept, as if they'd just lost a beloved family member. From the cotton fields to the steel plants, from the offices to the schoolrooms, the people of Alabama came to an abrupt halt. It was as if the realization that Bryant was gone took away the collective breath of the entire state in one seismic gut punch.

Bryant's passing was a lead story on all the national networks. "The Bear is dead," said Tom Brokaw on NBC. Local broadcasters labored to gather composure so as not to break down on camera; some were more successful than others. Schoolteachers across the state, many teary-eyed, stopped their classes to break the news to their students. That night President Ronald Reagan called Bryant's widow, Mary Harmon, to offer condolences and told her that the nation was mourning with her.

Oh, how they loved the Bear. He was the only coach in America, it was often said in the Heart of Dixie, that "can take his'n and beat your'n, and take your'n and beat his'n." On the rare occasions when Bryant did lose a game, he'd appear on his weekly television show looking grim. One time the host told him, "The Lord just wasn't with us, Coach." Bryant, without missing a beat, growled back, "The Lord expects you to block and tackle."

The day after he died, nearly 7,000 students and friends attended a service on campus at Memorial Coliseum. Later, thousands more visited Hayes Funeral Home to touch the casket. Many were overcome with emotion as soon as they spotted the closed casket covered in crimson and white carnations. Two days after his death, Bryant's funeral was held at the First United Methodist Church in Tuscaloosa, but the 400-seat chapel couldn't come close to accommodating the surge of well-wishers who had flown in from around the country to say goodbye to Bryant.

Every head coach from the SEC was present, as were former coaches Bob Devaney of Nebraska and Woody Hayes of Ohio State. Hundreds of former players arrived in town along with reporters from as far away as New York and Chicago. To enable everyone to see the short service, closed-circuit television cameras carried the funeral to monitors in two nearby churches. After the closing prayer was delivered, eight players from the '82 Alabama team carried Bryant's casket down the steps of the church. As his body was placed in a white hearse, more than 200 photographers frantically clicked away, their flashes popping like lightning through the gray afternoon.

The funeral procession stretched three miles and consisted of close to 400 vehicles, including six buses filled with former and present-day players and coaches. As the cavalcade rolled down 10th Street in Tuscaloosa, thousands of locals stood four, five, six deep to see the Bear one last time, waving at the hearse in respectful silence. The procession slowed as it passed Bryant-Denny Stadium, as if to give the coach a final look at the grand cathedral where he made so many dreams come true. Then the hearse pulled onto Interstate 20/59 and headed east for Birmingham.

Oh, how they loved the Bear. All along the interstate, cars and trucks and 18-wheelers pulled to the side. The drivers and passengers stood next to their vehicles in silence as Bryant rolled toward his final resting spot. Overpasses were clogged with onlookers—men placed their fedoras over their chests, women wept, children in Crimson Tide jackets gazed in wide-eyed wonder at the spectacle. For the 55 mournful miles from Tuscaloosa to Elmwood Cemetery in Birmingham, the interstate was lined with people, young and old, Yankees and Southerners, all compelled by history to stand in the chill of the winter afternoon and cry and grieve and tell stories about Paul William Bryant. For Alabamians, this was a state funeral, every bit as significant as a president being laid to rest in Arlington National Cemetery. *The Birmingham News* estimated that 250,000 people had witnessed the procession, which meant that one of every 12 residents of Alabama had bade farewell to Bryant in person.

Oh, how they loved the Bear.

And now, almost 30 years after Bryant was buried, the Alabama faithful, at long last, had their worthy successor. Saban, wasting no time, had raised Crimson Tide football out of irrelevance and back into the realm of the elite. It wasn't only the 2009 championship, it was the whole feel of the program: the prized recruits year after year, the consistency of performance and, most of all, the assurance of winning that Saban seemed to embody. There was no doubt in the mind of any good Tide fan that the statue of Nick Saban belonged on the Walk of Champions.

It would be less than two weeks after the statue's celebratory unveiling that the huge and frightening tornado would swirl into sight, seeming to take dead aim at Bryant-Denny Stadium and threatening to obliterate the Walk of Champions and the legends who stood there. Like any twister, it had no heart.

A TORNADO is not like a hurricane, which typically forms several days before it makes landfall. Or a flood, which is created gradually by extended downpours. Or a wildfire, which is at least somewhat predictable as to which direction it will move and how fast. And a tornado is not even like an earthquake, which erupts so suddenly and without warning that there is no time to fear it.

Each of these natural disasters carries its own elements of terror, but a tornado may be the scariest of them all. There is time for warning, yet even with the chilling warning sirens, not enough time to run from it. Once the twister is on the ground, it can have a will of its own, capable of altering its track and punishing anything and anyone standing helplessly in its path. It can move at 70 mph in a straight line or dawdle at 15 mph and then, in an eye-blink, change course. It can zigzag along the ground or hopscotch up and down, killing or sparing with frightening randomness. And unlike most natural disasters, which are spread out and diffuse, a tornado presents a singular and sinister image; anyone who has ever watched a tornado approach knows the feeling of being stalked by an evil beast.

There is little you can do to combat a twister. The common defense is to head for a basement or cellar if available, or, if not, to cower in a bathtub and cover yourself with a mattress. And then wait. Wait for the noise, that horrifying sound that's been described as a jet engine or an onrushing train or a thundering waterfall or a cloud of a zillion buzzing bees. Wait for the whirling winds so strong that they can lift 5,000-pound objects and hurl them for miles, yet so unpredictable they've been known to pluck feathers off chickens without moving them but a few feet.

When a tornado is chewing up the earth and hurtling in your direction, the wait for its arrival—say those who have lived through the experience—is hide-your-head-under-the-pillow terrifying, a feeling of utter powerlessness and galloping fear. Those who have waited say there is an urgent need to assure one another that the odds of being hit by a tornado are infinitesimally small, all while trembling as if death is at the doorstep. Then, as quick as this heart-thumping panic seizes you, the tornado passes by or slinks back into the sky. Or not.

Tornado survivors can suffer from post-traumatic stress. The symptoms don't typically manifest themselves until weeks afterward; then survivors often cry uncontrollably and for no apparent reason. They have trouble concentrating, become irritable and can feel generally adrift. Insomnia is prevalent among these survivors; when they finally sleep, their dreams are haunted by dark funnels or a sense of entrapment. Depression can follow. Tornado victims can be left visibly shaky for weeks and often have the feeling of reliving the disaster—a feeling that can last for months or even years. According to counselors, a sense of guilt can grip survivors for the rest of their lives. Some ask unanswerable questions: *Why did I survive and my friend next to me didn't?*

Every year in the U.S. there are more than 100,000 thunderstorms; only one out of 1,000 may spawn a tornado. Typically between one-tenth of a mile to one mile wide, the average twister stays on the ground for about 10 minutes and covers three to four miles before retreating back into the sky or simply fading away. Tornadoes can happen at any time almost anywhere on earth and produce the strongest winds on the planet. (Tornadoes are categorized according to wind strength on what is known as the Enhanced Fujita scale, from the lowest, EF0, to the highest, EF5, which can produce wind speeds on the ground of more than 230 mph.)

The most historically infamous place on earth for tornados is the south-central United States in the spring and summer. The so-called Tornado Alley in the U.S. runs from the foothills of the Rockies to the western portion of the Mississippi Valley, encompassing the states of Texas, Oklahoma, Kansas, Nebraska and Missouri. Some meteorologists, however, are beginning to revise that definition, suggesting that the hotbed should also include Arkansas, Louisiana, Mississippi and Alabama, and that this stretch be called Dixie Alley. At present, Alabama ranks 11th among states in the number of recorded tornado strikes since 1953 but first in deaths—largely because of the state's population density relative to most midwestern states, as well as a preponderance of mobile home parks (which are especially vulnerable to powerful winds) and a scarcity of homes and other structures with cellars or basements. The peak time of day for a tornado in Alabama, where warm, moist air from the Gulf often mixes with dry, cooler air blowing in from the north—the basic ingredients for Mother Nature to bake a tornado—is between 4 p.m. and 9 p.m. Every spring in the Yellowhammer State, these are the witching hours.

METEOROLOGIST JAMES SPANN was standing in the ABC 33/40 studio in Birmingham, 60 miles from Tuscaloosa. It was just before 5 p.m. when a live feed from a video camera mounted on top of the Tuscaloosa County Courthouse captured an image of a tornado. Immediately his blood pressure spiked at the sight of the swirling black funnel on the feed, at the sheer size of it. He turned to the camera, with an unmistakable look of grave concern. "This is a large, violent tornado coming up on downtown Tuscaloosa. Be in a safe place right now," Spann ordered his viewers, his voice still even and steady. "That is something you pray that you never, ever, ever see. . . . This thing looks like it might be over one-half-mile wide, maybe up to three-quarters-of-a-mile wide. . . . Get into a safe place."

Jason Simpson, another meteorologist at the station, was also watching the video feed. When he spoke on the air he sounded like he'd just seen the devil himself walking across the landscape: "That is something significantly wicked on the horizon of Tuscaloosa that is just about to move into the city."

CHAPTER 4

Stalked By A Monster

CARSON TINKER had, quite literally, a lifelong history with tornadoes. Just a few hours after Carson's birth, on Nov. 15, 1989, his mother, Debbie, had looked out the window of her room at Decatur General Hospital in Decatur, Ala., and watched as the afternoon sky suddenly darkened. Even before the emergency sirens began to wail—weather radar had failed to pick up the funnel cloud—a tornado coursed through the town, only miles from the hospital, with winds topping 200 mph. Vehicles were tossed 200 yards into the air like they were matchbox cars. Commercial buildings that had stood nearly a hundred years were vacuumed from their foundations. In a matter of a few heartbeats, homes were consumed by the swirling funnel, then spit out in bits of chimney brick, siding and shingles. Everything, including kitchen sinks, covered the landscape.

Inside the hospital, the staff, hearing the rumble of the storm, wheeled Debbie out of her recovery room and into a hallway, away from the windows. A nurse grabbed baby Carson from the nursery, cradled him in her arms and hurried into a windowless room. She cooed in his ear and rocked him in her arms, keeping the infant boy calm. The tornado—which would kill 21 people and injure near-ly 500 and destroy 80 businesses and a thousand cars—narrowly missed the hospital, but the sights and sounds of it were seared into Debbie Tinker's memory like a near-death experience. From that day forward, whenever she heard the emergency sirens blare, her pulse began to race and her eyes frantically scanned the sky, always with a terrible dread that she and Carson wouldn't be as lucky as they had been on the day that he first opened his eyes. "I had always hoped," she would say, "that would be the last time I'd have to worry about a tornado."

TWO DECADES later the tornado now on the ground in Tusca-loosa was moving with frightening directness toward Carson's house on 25th Street. Cowering in the closet, crouched on the floor, Carson held Ashley Harrison tight. As the winds roared—"It sounded like there was an F-18 in the front yard" is how roommate Estis would later describe it—they could hear the walls creak. "I'm scared, Car-son," Ashley said, trembling.

"It's going to be O.K.," Tinker shouted above the noise as the house began to disintegrate. He wrapped his arms around Ashley like she was the most precious thing on earth, and in that moment she was. "It's going to be O.K., Ashley," he shouted again.

But it wasn't. Seconds later Tinker was sucked out of the closet, catapulted into the air like a stone from a slingshot and thrown 65 yards into the field across the street, the field he loved so much. He blacked out, concussed. When he opened his eyes moments later he didn't recognize anything. The bordering oak and pine trees had vanished. His house had utterly disappeared; there was now just a big pile of indistinguishable rubble on the other side of the road. And Ashley was gone.

In the suddenly perfect silence characteristic of the aftermath of a tornado, Tinker stood and wandered around the field, looking for Ashley. He had a broken right wrist, gashes in his head and a severe cut on his right ankle. Blood covered his face. His body moved in slow motion, as in a desperate dream. "Ashley, where are you?" he screamed. "Ashley!"

For at least 10 agonizing minutes, Tinker roamed in zigs and zags, in a haze, searching for the girl who had become the center of his life. "Ashley," he yelled, "where are you? Where *are* you?"

ONE MINUTE after pulverizing Carson Tinker's house, the tornado spun directly toward Javier Arenas. As the former Tide defensive back looked out his window, he was in denial. Surely, he thought, this twister won't hit me. So convinced was he that he took out his phone and began to shoot video of the tornado. After 20 seconds he felt the wind dramatically intensify and, lifting his eyes from his phone, realized the funnel was closing on him rapidly. In a panic, he called a childhood friend, Stephen Adkins, who was traveling on his baseball team's bus in Georgia. "I can see it!" Arenas yelled.

Adkins, who lived in Rome, Ga., had been awakened in his apartment there that morning by tornado sirens. A friend had told him to get into the bathtub. The twister had missed his neighborhood and now he shared the advice he'd gotten only hours earlier: "Stay calm, Javier," Adkins said. "Go to your bathroom and get in the tub. Do it *now.*"

As Arenas rushed to his bathroom, Adkins stayed on the phone; he could hear the howl of wind, then the sound of breaking glass. A moment later, as Arenas clutched the side of the bathtub with all his strength, Arenas told his friend, "I think my car just blew into my living room." Then the phone cut out. Arenas was shaking with a mind-numbing fear unlike any he had ever known.

He lay in the bathtub; he wanted to grab a mattress from his bedroom, something to pull over his body, but there was no time. He had shut the bathroom door. Outside it sounded to him like gunshots were peppering the front of his house. Rocks and debris were shot into his living room like shrapnel. Then the lights went out and the bathroom door burst open. He thought the roof was about to crash down on him. He prayed. *Please, God, let it be over. Please let it be over.* . . . And suddenly it was. The tornado had passed, the heart of the funnel missing his house by little more than the length of a football field. Arenas, his heart hammering, walked outside. Several houses in his neighborhood were flattened. A couple of women ran down his street screaming. Arenas, as if in a fog, vaguely in search of some sort of comfort, wandered toward his favorite place on 15th Street, the Smoothie King.

From a short distance away the building looked to Arenas as if a fist from the sky had reached down and punched it into the ground. As he moved closer to where the Smoothie King had stood not 10 minutes earlier, he heard the pleading voices of women buried in the rubble, begging for rescue. Quickly Arenas approached to help, but he was overcome by the noxious smell of gas. He ran to a fireman close by, and within minutes two women were pulled to safety, bruised but alive; they were passersby who had been caught in the maelstrom.

Bewildered as to where to go or what to do, Arenas walked to a nearby mall, which seemed to be untouched. He sat on a curb for nearly an hour, trying to process what he had just lived through. Eventually his cell service returned, and the first call he made was to his mother in Tampa. "I just got hit by a tornado," Arenas said, "but I'm fine, I'm fine." Then his phone went dead again.

When service returned minutes later, he reached his friend Adkins. "I made it," Arenas told him. "It's the scariest thing I've ever been through, but I made it." He paused. "I think a lot of people aren't going to be as lucky as me."

That night Arenas stayed at a friend's house, but he struggled to sleep. And whenever he did, his dreams were tormented by images of the black tornado. He awoke feeling haunted.

KAYLA HOFFMAN may have been the happiest student on the Alabama campus on the afternoon of April 27. Eleven days earlier in Cleveland, Kayla, a 5' 1", 120-pound senior, had led the Crimson Tide to the NCAA women's gymnastics title. On the final day of competition, she performed the routine of her life, earning a 9.95 on the floor exercise—the highest score in the team competition at nationals—as Alabama edged UCLA for the championship. Then, on the morning of the 27th, Hoffman was named winner of the Honda Award, given to the top female gymnast in Division I.

That afternoon she received dozens of congratulatory texts, voice mails and tweets. At around 4:00 she jogged around campus with her boyfriend of three years, Michael Hughes, a decathlete on the Alabama track team. Michael then drove to his apartment in Northport, while Kayla went to her second-floor off-campus apartment at 1509 6th Avenue, which sits a couple of blocks west of McFarland.

Moments after she'd showered, Kayla's apartment lost power. She heard the now-familiar warning sirens but thought little of it. As she dressed, though, she got a text from a teammate who lived in a ground-floor apartment just 200 yards away: *Hurry, come here. It's coming. It's huge.*

She grabbed a hairbrush and stuffed nail-polish remover and cotton balls in her purse—she had hoped to do her nails while waiting out the storm—and rushed down her stairs. She walked into the suddenly cool afternoon and began to run toward her teammate's apartment. She took three steps, maybe four, then looked up: The tornado was directly in front of her. Cars were flying through the air not more than 30 feet away.

She turned to run back to her apartment, but she was battered by flying debris: glass shards, rocks, clumps of mud. She was out of time. Seized with fear, Kayla pounded on the door of a first-floor apartment in her complex, screaming for help. No one answered. Still being slammed by debris, she crouched in the door frame, put her purse over her head and scrunched herself into the smallest ball she could manage. Still, she was pummeled by pieces of glass, insulation, even furniture as the tornado slashed through her building. The ferocious wind sucked the stones out of Kayla's stud earrings.

Three miles away in Northport, Michael Hughes was shaken to his core when he heard news reports that 15th and McFarland had been hit hard. He had to be sure Kayla was alive. He left his apartment but quickly got stuck in traffic. A mile and a half from his girlfriend's apartment, he hopped out of his car and began sprinting. "It was easily the fastest I've ever run," the decathlete said later. When he arrived, the facade of the apartment complex was virtually gone and Kayla was nowhere to be found. In the midst of his desperate search, Michael stepped on a nail, puncturing the bottom of his right foot. When he heard from a friend that another tornado was coming, he took off running once again, covering the mile to Coleman Coliseum, where he sought shelter in the basement's track and field locker room. His foot was a bloody mess, his sock soaked red.

Gasping and frightened, Hughes had a trainer bandage his foot. Minutes later the all-clear signal was broadcast, and Michael sprinted back to Kayla's apartment, his foot throbbing with every stride. He pounded on doors. No one answered any of them. He ran to another complex. "Is Kayla Hoffman here?" he yelled into apartment after apartment. Finally, after long panicky minutes, he found her in the apartment of another gymnast. Kayla was bloodied—she had suffered a six-inch cut on her right calf and a four-by-two-inch piece of glass had lodged in her sports bra. But she was alive. The couple embraced, a flood of tears washing their faces. "I just can't let go of you," Kayla sobbed to her boyfriend. "I thought I was going to die. I was almost sure of it."

The two then walked out onto 15th Street and looked toward campus. The sun was setting now, the western sky painted pink. Tranquility had fallen over Tuscaloosa. In the distance Kayla and Michael saw the silhouettes of mangled metal, twisted trees, splintered structures. Everywhere were mounds of indescribable rubble, and debris was strewn as far as they could see. With their arms around each other, Michael said softly, "It's gone. It's just all gone."

IT WAS shortly after 5:00 when Josh Rosecrans, a catcher and relief pitcher on the Alabama baseball team, peered out a window of his house on 17th Street East, near a small lake less than two miles from Bryant-Denny Stadium. His eyes grew wide at what he saw: The tornado was on the other side of the water, ripping up power lines, throwing flashes of red and blue bolts into the black sky.

Rosecrans and his roommate, pitcher Nate Kennedy, hurried to the bathroom in the center of the house and jumped into the tub, pulling a mattress over them. Taped on the bathroom mirror was a piece of paper with a Biblical passage from Psalm 121:7. THE LORD WILL PROTECT YOU FROM ALL HARM; HE WILL PROTECT YOUR LIFE.

The storm hit, the shrieking wind a jet engine. Their ears popped. "Nate, there went the roof," Rosecrans yelled, holding on to the mattress with all his might as Kennedy, curled in a fetal position, lay atop him, also gripping the mattress. "Hang on, man, just hang on."

For 30 terrifying seconds, they were pounded by debris, burying the two of them in the bathtub. "This could be it for us," Rosecrans yelled above the din. "If we go out, we go out together."

Then, a few seconds later . . . silence. Ominous, deathly silence. Rosecrans poked his head out of their virtual grave: Their house had crumbled—the only walls left were those of the bathroom they were in—and Josh could see the sky. "Oh, my God," he said. "Everything is gone."

They lifted themselves from the tub and looked around. The bathroom mirror was intact, unbroken; still taped to it was the Biblical passage.

The two roommates went out into their neighborhood to search for other survivors.

IT WAS Dana Dowling's mother, Lynn Matthews, who had passed down to her daughter a love of Alabama football, like some kind of family heirloom. Matthews had worked at the Hotel Capstone in Tuscaloosa, where the Crimson Tide players and coaches have stayed overnight before home games since 1990. She'd always loved seeing the players come and go from the hotel, and all her life she never missed watching Alabama football games on television. Seated in a reclining chair in her living room in the glow of the TV, Matthews would talk to the players during the games as if she were the coach, telling them to block better, run faster. She pleaded with them to understand the importance of what was happening. The opponent was a thief, there to steal not only from the team but also the entire town of Tuscaloosa. Lynn Matthews had been on the waiting list for season tickets for more than a decade.

Now, as Dana huddled with her family on the floor of their mobile home, bracing for the twister, she thought of her mother and of how she might never see her again.

Bob Dowling had guided his wife and two teens to the center of the trailer and into the small utility space, the only windowless room. The Dowlings had lived in Chalet Ridge for just over a year and were unaware that the house just behind them—outside the trailer park—had an underground storm shelter. Two boys from the house were now outside screaming for the Dowlings to come to their shelter, but the roar of the wind drowned out their cries.

The moment of reckoning arrived. Trailers on their street started blowing apart, as if a bomb had detonated inside. Other mobile homes were lifted into the air and shredded in the violent winds. Sixty-foot trees that had lined the street leading into Chalet Ridge for a century were ripped from the ground and hurled into the air, neither their heft nor their thick roots a match for this tornado.

The Dowlings prayed together that this would not be their last moment on earth. The front wall on their mobile home caved into the kitchen. The entire bathroom was sucked outside. Then a refrigerator in the laundry room slid across the floor and pinned Bob against the wall. He looked up at the trailer's ceiling and could see that the roof was coming apart. It lifted several inches off the structure, allowing Bob to peer outside and stare directly into the eye of the monster. The light inside the tornado was brilliant, awesome in its brightness. At once, the sight calmed Dowling; he felt as if he were looking into the face of his Maker, and now the Almighty was going to decide the fate of the entire family. It was out of the hands of mortals.

Outside a power pole was uprooted and thrown like a spear through the center of the mobile home next door to the Dowlings. The pole served to pin that trailer to the ground and created a wind shear for the Dowlings' trailer, just enough protection, perhaps, to have saved their lives.

Then it was over. The Dowlings were uninjured. Bob walked outside and into what looked like a postapocalyptic landscape. He didn't recognize his world. Everything on their street had vanished: the trees, the homes, the cars that minutes earlier had filled Chalet Ridge. But, to the southeast, several miles away, he could see the outline of Bryant-Denny Stadium. It was still standing. To this diehard Crimson Tide family, it was almost a sign of some kind, of survival or even redemption. But between the Dowlings' door and the stadium stretched a long swath, a mile wide, of sheer devastation, creating what looked like a gigantic fairway, now void of all standing vegetation and solid structures.

Within minutes, residents of Chalet Ridge emerged from the storm shelter, unharmed. But now they milled around in stunned silence, glassy-eyed, unable to make sense of the scene around them. Dowling and his 18-year-old son Drew ran from one mound of rubble to the next, listening for cries of help, searching for anyone who might be trapped. All they found was debris. All they heard was silence.

LEE HENDERSON was in his father's basement when he learned from James Spann on his father's radio that the tornado had passed through Tuscaloosa. Lee heard Spann say that there were reports that DCH—the town's main hospital, the same one in which Bear

Bryant had died—had been hit by the twister (a report that proved erroneous) and that several businesses near 15th and McFarland, including a Krispy Kreme and a Taco Casa, had also been severely damaged. After taking a deep breath to process this news, Henderson ran up the stairs, out the door and jumped into his SUV. He wanted to drive into the heart of the destruction to see if he could help any victims. And, of course, to see if his own business, the Smoothie King, was still standing.

But the streets were impossibly clogged with cars, so Henderson swung through campus and parked near the Alabama football practice field, less than two miles from 15th and McFarland. He walked to 15th Street, a section that hadn't been touched by the tornado but already was cordoned off by police. Henderson spotted one of his most loyal customers, a Tuscaloosa police officer. "It's not good," the officer told him, grim-faced, "but I'll let you come through."

Henderson moved as fast as he could. When he was a mile away from his store, he could see, for the first time, what the storm had wrought. Snapped trees, downed power lines and so much debris it looked to him as if a city's worth of stuff had been collected in a giant laundry bag and dumped from high in the sky. The closer he moved to 15th and McFarland, the worse it got. Then, breathing hard, he saw it for the first time. Or rather, he didn't see it. His Smoothie King was gone, reduced to a pile of bricks and drywall.

A friend of his, Richard Ellis Jr., stood near the store. They embraced, hard and long, grabbing each other by the neck. "Oh, my gosh," Henderson said, tears filling his eyes. He looked around at the devastated neighborhood. "How many people must have died? Oh, my gosh. How many?"

Henderson stumbled around the rubble of his store, hands on his head, wondering insanely to himself, *Did this really happen?* He eventually sat on the curb in front of the remains. An AP photographer at the scene snapped a photo of Henderson there, an image that within hours would appear on websites and in newspapers across the globe. The photograph captured Henderson at his lowest moment, his face a harrowing portrait of abject uncomprehending despair.

For several minutes he sat there in the twilight, struggling even to think. He felt so alone, so helpless and overwhelmed. Everything he'd poured into this place—the borrowed money, the sweat equity, the years of emotional investment—now reduced in a matter of seconds to an unrecognizable heap. More than anything, he just wanted to cry.

He tried to call his wife, but there was no cell service. He walked back to his car in silence and drove a few miles. When his phone came to life, he dialed Leigh. "It's just all gone" was all he could say to her before he was overcome and began to sob.

CHAPTER 5

Tinker's Tale

NO COLLEGE coach of his generation has proved to be more skilled in the homes of high school players than Nick Saban. Rather than smooth like an Urban Meyer or folksy like a Steve Spurrier or enticingly eccentric like a Les Miles, Saban is distinctly paternal and authoritative. His pitch is that he knows how he's going to make each young player perform better on the field and in the classroom and how he's going to help each player grow into a man of substance. Why do Alabama players remove their hats when they shake the hand of the mother of a prospective recruit? Because Saban teaches proper manners as much as proper football techniques.

Saban is direct, he is persuasive and, most of all, he is prepared. If Saban is considering offering a scholarship to a recruit, he'll watch film of every snap of that player's high school career, assessing his talent, his technique and his competitive spirit. Even before Saban steps into the home of a prospect or invites a recruit to his office, the Alabama staffers have done what they call a "seven deep" dive into the player's life, meaning they've contacted his friends, family, teachers, coaches—almost anyone who has had an interaction with that player and shaped his development.

When Saban talks to a high school coach about a prospect, he doesn't ask about his athletic skills—he has plenty of game tape for that. Instead he grills them with questions like these: Is the player a team leader? Is he a good teammate? Can he digest and understand complex concepts? How does he practice? Does he listen? Does he show up on time for meetings and appointments? Does he attend all of his classes? Is he dependable? Is he active in the community? Can he play through pain? How does he react to adversity? Saban pokes and prods like a doctor with a new patient, looking for every possible detail that could prove important.

Jim McElwain was the Crimson Tide's offensive coordinator from 2008 to '11. "We didn't even want to know about a guy's physical ability until we had gone more than a few layers deep into his life to find all the answers about him and see if he had the character to fit at Alabama," McElwain says. "We wanted to know if he had the drive to succeed and the character to handle all that we were going to demand of him. It's hard at Alabama. It's not for everybody. You can't be an ego guy at Alabama. Nick won't tolerate it, no matter how much talent you have. But that's why he goes so many layers deep into a player's life before really getting serious about recruiting him."

Upon his arrival at Alabama, Saban promptly put his recruiting skills to work. By late 2007, as he garnered verbal commitments from some of the most sought-after players in the nation, the coaching staff was also receiving truckloads of packages from high school players who sent their highlight DVDs to Alabama in the hope of attracting interest. Most of the tapes came from under-the-radar players who had no shot at playing at any Division I school, much less in the SEC. But the Tide recruiting staff was always search-ing for that diamond in these lumps of video coal, looking for a player who may not warrant a scholarship but who showed enough potential to merit an invitation to walk on. They were looking for players like Carson Tinker.

Carlton Tinker, Carson's father, is a lifelong Crimson Tide fan, and his ardor for Alabama football was passed to his son. Little Carson, from his stroller, liked to shout "Roll Tide" to people passing by. But the teenage Carson was unsure of where he wanted to go to college. Carson played on the offensive line and as a long snapper at Riverdale High in Murfreesboro, Tenn. Though he didn't have the SEC-caliber size for a lineman—he was 5' 11", 190 pounds as a junior—or the speed to make it in the secondary, he clearly possessed a never-quit attitude and had an internal motor that redlined in every practice and every game. He was a classic overachiever.

On Oct. 14, 2006, Carlton and Carson, who was then a high school junior, traveled to Tuscaloosa to watch Alabama play Ole Miss. Before the game father and son strolled around the leafy campus. Young Carson's eyes lit up at what he saw: thousands upon thousands of fans tailgating on the Quad, excitement on every face; the ultrafestive atmosphere that felt to him like a gigantic Fourth of July picnic. His dad bought him an Alabama jersey. Even before they found their seats at Bryant-Denny Stadium, Carson told his father, "Daddy, I want to play at a school like this. This is where I want to be."

Tinker was just a backup offensive guard at Riverdale High, though he did play significant minutes in that role as a senior. He excelled, however, in short and long snapping. Long after the final whistle at practice, Tinker would remain on the field perfecting his craft, firing one long snap after another between his legs as the sunlight faded from the Tennessee sky. "Carson's desire and his dream was to be a short and long snapper at a major Division I school," says Ron Aydelott, Tinker's high school coach. "No one worked harder than him. After a weight room session, if he had a spare few minutes, he was always snapping. He never got tired of doing it. And by the time he was finished here at Riverdale, he was the best long snapper I'd had in almost 30 years of coaching."

And that wasn't all. "Everybody loved Carson," Aydelott says. "He's a pleaser, always smiling, always wanting to do right. He almost seemed too genuine to be true. He never had an angle with people or some hidden agenda. His teammates and his coaches had deep respect for him. We had a feeling that if a college staff gave him a chance, they wouldn't regret it."

As a junior Carson had sent his recruiting tape to the Alabama coaches and to other Division I schools. No full scholarship came his way, but that really wasn't a shock to Tinker. He elicited interest from Washington State—and the Cougars offered only a partial scholarship. When Tinker determined that it was about a 32-hour drive from Murfreesboro to Pullman, Wash., it didn't take long for him to decide he wouldn't become a Cougar.

When Tinker told his friends in Murfreesboro that he was considering walking on at Alabama, they looked at him like he had three eyes. How in the world would the undersized Tinker survive in practice, let alone make the team? But Tinker had attended football camps and clinics in the South and had made an impression on coaches as a long snapper; he even earned a spot on the All-Saban team at Alabama's special teams camp.

Tinker eventually long snapped a second time in front of the Alabama coaches, who were looking for a long-term solution at the position. Saban was impressed with what he saw. Tinker had the arm speed, the technique and the relentlessness that he was searching for in a long snapper. If Tinker could gain 15 pounds of muscle, he had the potential to fit Saban's physical prototype for the position. While Saban rarely offered scholarships to long snappers coming out of high school, he viewed the position as vital. After watching Tinker on tape and in person, and noting the glowing reports on the drive and character of this young man, the Alabama staff kept Tinker's name on its recruiting board; Saban believed there could be a spot for him in the 2008 class of recruits if he was willing to walk on. He liked this kid.

ON THE second-story balcony outside of Saban's office at the Mal Moore facility, just off Paul W. Bryant Drive, several staffers had gathered shortly after 5:00 on the afternoon of the April 27 storm to see what was happening outside—and now they saw the twister. One staffer flipped on a video camera. It captured a huge, whirling funnel on the ground less than three miles in the distance, lifting chunks of earth into the air. Despite the dire scene, nervous laughter can be heard in the background of the video. But after less than 25 seconds of filming, the staffers hurriedly fled the balcony and headed for the basement.

Christopher England, a producer for Tide TV, had been watching the Weather Channel in his office at Coleman Coliseum, which sits next to the Mal Moore building. When England learned that a tornado had descended, he grabbed his camera and sprinted up three flights of stairs to the top floor of Coleman. He looked out a window and there it was; the sight of the huge twister caused his heart to thump. England flipped on his camera and recorded a few minutes of video that would soon be seen around the world. He zoomed his lens to full range but still couldn't fit the entire tornado in the frame. "I stood there as long as I could and then it felt like the top of the coliseum was creaking," England said later. "That was when it was time to run as fast as I could to the basement."

Meanwhile out in Northport, Saban was still unaware of the whereabouts of the tornado or the gravity of what was happening on the south side of town. He left his house at around 5:25 and drove back to his office where he phoned Nicholas, checking to see that he was safe. His son told him that his house was intact, but that a few blocks away several homes and structures had been destroyed.

Saban quickly got back into his car to drive to Nicholas's house, and with each passing block he became more terribly aware of the destruction that had befallen his town. It was growing dark; as Saban peered out the window, he could barely make out the tattered landscape. "You could see it a little," he recalled later, "but more than anything, you could feel it." What he was feeling was that his life, and everyone's in Tuscaloosa, had just radically changed.

Saban was able to reach Nicholas's place, after having to walk the last few blocks, and eventually drove his son, four of his son's friends and his son's dogs back to the family home in Northport, where power never went out. Saban opened the garage doors; immediately his two dogs bolted out and raced into the dark.

Inside the house Saban's daughter, Kristen, a sophomore at Alabama, was in the living room with several of her sorority sisters; they had gathered there soon after the first reports of threatening weather. In the same room later that night, they would learn from a post on Facebook that Ashley Harrison, one of their Phi Mu sorority sisters, was missing. Terry Saban, also a Phi Mu, had come to know Ashley well and was something of a mentor to her. The young women spent the entire night texting Ashley, calling friends and scouring Facebook in a frantic search for information. At 5:30 a.m. they were joined by Saban, who took a seat in a reclining chair. When the girls told Saban that Ashley was unaccounted for, his heart dropped. Saban knew that Ashley was Carson Tinker's girlfriend.

MINUTES BEFORE the tornado had hit, Ashley had called her parents, Darlene and David Harrison, who live in Dallas. She often phoned home when a storm was approaching. She told her mother that she was at Carson's house. "Well, honey, are you O.K.?" Darlene asked.

"We are getting ready to get in the closet," Ashley told her. "We're O.K."

"Are you sure?" her mother asked.

Ashley giggled. It was 5:11. Yes, she said, they were fine.

"I love you, Mom."

"I love you," Darlene said.

When threatening weather had arrived during the past few weeks, Ashley always called home as a storm approached; these phone calls came from basements of academic buildings, from the sorority house and from her off-campus apartment. After the all-clear was given, she would phone again to assure her parents that she was safe. This time, as the minutes ticked by, there was no follow-up phone call from Ashley.

News of the severity of the storm in Alabama was the lead story on the 6:00 news in Texas. A friend of Darlene's was watching the horrifying footage and had a bad feeling. She immediately called Darlene and asked, "Where's Ashley?"

Unable to reach their daughter, Darlene, nearing panic, phoned another friend, a former executive with Southwest Airlines. Darlene told him they had to get to Tuscaloosa immediately and had no plane reservations or tickets. "Can you help?" she asked. Within minutes the friend called back and told Darlene it appeared they'd missed the last flight of the day so they should begin to drive toward Tuscaloosa; he'd help them find an airport with an available flight somewhere along the way. David and Darlene jumped in their car and set off. When they were just 30 minutes out of town, the friend called back: It turned out there was one flight still at Love Field in Dallas that could take them to Birmingham. But hurry, he said, it would be leaving shortly. David turned around and mashed down on the gas pedal.

All the while, Darlene tried Carson's cellphone; no answer. She called Ashley's roommates in Tuscaloosa and her friends in Dallas—all she got anywhere was the cold reply of a voice mail message. Finally she reached Payton Holley, one of Tinker's roommates, who was at that moment in a police cruiser with Carson on the way to the hospital. Miraculously, Tinker's roommates were mostly unharmed and had found him wandering in the field searching for Ashley. Now Holley handed Carson the phone. Darlene asked if he knew where Ashley was. "I don't know," he said in despair. "We can't find her."

Darlene and David arrived at the airport and rushed to the gate. The plane had been held and an airline employee was waiting; the two desperate parents in search of their child were the last to board, and the cabin door shut behind them. After what felt like the longest plane ride of their lives, they landed in Birmingham, rented a car and drove southeast through the darkness, an agonizing 55 miles on Interstate 20/59 to Tuscaloosa. They reached town at 11 p.m., a little less than six hours after the tornado had struck. Darlene's father, Marion Perret, and her brother, Marion II, were driving an SUV up from New Orleans to join them in the quest to find Ashley.

The Harrisons hurried to DCH hospital to see Tinker and search for Ashley, but the National Guard blocked them at the entrance; no visitors were allowed inside. When Marion II, a police officer in Gretna, La., arrived at the hospital parking lot, he grabbed his police vest out of the backseat; he breezed past the guardsmen at the hospital doors and went room to room looking for Ashley, his niece. Failing to find her, he returned to the front of DCH to retrieve the other family members. Together they eventually tracked down Carson, lying in a hospital bed recovering from the concussion and other injuries. He didn't have any news about Ashley and begged them to keep looking for her.

Not sure where to start, Marion II decided to drive to the police station close to Tinker's house, only to discover that it had been destroyed by the storm. At this point he reasoned that Ashley must still be at Tinker's house—the house that was no longer standing.

BEFORE BEING taken to the hospital, Tinker had called his mother in Hoover, Ala. Though his mind was clouded by the concussion, he told Debbie that he was O.K. but that he was looking for Ashley.

Later that night Brandon Gibson, a senior wide receiver and one of Tinker's closest friends on the team, learned from a text message from Scott Cochran, the strength coach, that all team members had been accounted for; however, he informed Gibson, Tinker was in the hospital, and Ashley had yet to be located.

Gibson and Tinker maintained a special bond that had been created on the Alabama practice fields, one hit at a time. It was Gibson's responsibility to block against Tinker in practice on punt returns. From snap to whistle, with a wild-eyed look behind his face mask, Tinker would fight through Gibson's block and charge down the field at the punt returner. He played with the determined desperation common to so many walk-on players at big-time programs like Alabama's. "Carson may not be that big, but man, he is a damn tough kid," Gibson says. "Stronger than you think and as driven as anyone you'll ever meet."

Gibson had spent many carefree, contented hours with Carson and Ashley, hanging out on The Strip and joining them at gymnastic meets and basketball games. Ashley had been an athlete herself. As a high school honors student in Dallas, she had played four years of lacrosse. She also loved the theatre and the arts, but it was her affection for sports that deepened her connection with Carson. Even if she had freshly manicured nails, she'd grab a dusty mitt and throw a baseball with Carson in the field across the street.

"Everywhere you saw Carson, you saw Ashley," Gibson says. "They were inseparable. And they were in love." Now, in the chaotic hours after the tornado, he prayed that Ashley was as lucky as Carson had been.

DARLENE AND David continued to look for Ashley, visiting the VA Medical Center and its makeshift morgue, where workers told them that their daughter was not there. Meanwhile, Ashley's uncle and grandfather drove their SUV to Tinker's house. They approached through a wasteland of fallen power lines and mounds of rubble 20 feet high. Reaching Tinker's address on 25th Street, they were horrified: The house had been plucked from the earth. It was as if it had never existed. Two firemen were across the street in a field using infrared lights to search for survivors and bodies, but all they had found were the remains of two dogs. The firemen concluded that Ashley likely was trapped in rubble somewhere in the area, so for the rest of the night, Marion and Marion II frantically dug through the remnants of other houses. Their voices, calling her name, seemed to echo each other's.

Throughout the night, in the field where Carson and Ashley used to play catch, family and friends searched in the quiet darkness.

Several of Carson's teammates joined them and, with Darlene and David, spent hours crisscrossing the debris-strewn field, calling out for Ashley. Just as the sun started to rise, sending red-orange streaks into the clear Alabama sky, a police officer arrived on the scene and approached Marion II. Speaking officer to officer, he explained to Ashley's uncle that the body of a young female had been found in the field minutes after the tornado had struck, about 65 yards from Tinker's house and just a few feet from where Carson had awakened. This female body had been nestled in high grass between the branches of a downed pine and had indeed been taken to an emergency morgue in the VA Medical Center. The officer said he had a picture of the girl on a digital camera.

Marion II braced for the worst. From the time he and his family had first received word that Ashley was missing, this was the moment they'd dreaded. They had held out hope that they would find Ashley trapped under a sheet of plywood or maybe under the limb of a tree. There were thousands of places the wind could have taken her, and they'd vowed to stay as long as it took. But now an unfamiliar police officer was saying he had a picture of a dead young woman. Of course Marion II had to look at it.

Yes, said the uncle. Yes, that was Ashley, precious Ashley, in the photo. He turned to Darlene and David. "She's gone," he said. In the stillness of the morning, the family hugged each other tight. Their search was over. It was all they could do to keep from completely falling apart.

Gathering his emotions, Marion II took charge. As a police officer he had been hardened by witnessing gruesome things. He drove with the family to the morgue but went inside ahead of the others in order to inspect the condition of Ashley's body. He wanted to prepare the rest of the family for what they would see. He worried that some of the bodies of the deceased would be grotesquely mangled, and he wanted to be sure that Ashley would be presentable. Then he saw her: Even after being ripped from Carson's arms and thrown 65 yards by 190-mph winds, she had barely suffered a scratch. She had died from a broken neck. He reached down and closed the lids of her brown eyes.

When Ashley's parents entered, Darlene stepped toward the metal table. To her, Ashley looked so beautiful, at perfect peace. She stared at her for five, 10, 15 minutes, unable to pull her eyes away. "Wake up," she told her daughter. "I love you. I'm sorry. I wish I could have helped you."

AT AROUND 7 a.m., Carson, still in his blood-stained clothes and with tiny fragments of glass in his hair, awoke in a private hospital room, chaos still filling the halls outside. His mom, in tears, was at his bedside. He immediatcly asked if they'd found Ashley. She told him that Ashley was gone.

"No, she can't be," Carson responded. "You're wrong. You're wrong." His mother gently explained that Ashley's body had been found, her neck broken. Carson cried until he had no tears left.

The next day Carson demanded to attend a memorial service for Ashley at Tuscaloosa Memorial Park and Chapel. But the doctors, citing his head trauma and the potential for infection in his ankle wound, refused to release him from the hospital. Tinker would not relent. He kept begging and badgering until the medical staff finally agreed. With his family at his side, Tinker was strapped onto a rolling bed and wheeled into the back of an ambulance, which carried him to where Ashley lay in her casket. His bed was tilted up so that he could see her and, looking at her through watery eyes, Carson softly offered his everlasting goodbye to the girl he'd been certain he would marry one day. It was a moment so profoundly painful that Tinker would never want to speak of it—or think of it—again.

CHAPTER 6

Dark
Curly Hair

JUST PAST 6:00 on the day of the storm, Shannon Brown called his ex-wife. Shannon was at his home outside of Huntsville in Madison, Ala., 150 miles to the northeast of Tuscaloosa; he was now a high school football coach at Ardmore High, remarried and father of two children with his new wife. His ex, Ashley Mims, was in Wetumpka. "Have you heard from Loryn?" Shannon asked her.

"I was on the phone with her, and it cut off," Ashley replied, shaken.

"Ashley, I'm sure she's O.K.," Shannon said.

"Shannon, if she was O.K., she'd crawl out of the rubble to let her mama know that she was fine," Ashley said. "She'd call me."

After hanging up, Shannon phoned Diane Rumanek, the mother of Loryn's roommate Kelli and the owner of the house they rented. "Can you go to the house and call me back?" Shannon asked. "We're getting worried."

Rumanek called back later that evening with bad news. "I'm sorry, Shannon," she said. "I can't get there. The streets are blocked with trees and power lines. I thought everyone was fine. I had no idea. It looks like a bomb went off."

Shannon's father, Jerry Brown, lives 40 miles south of Tuscaloosa in Greensboro and owns a company called Blackbelt Tree Service. Having learned that no one could reach Loryn, Jerry hitched up his tree-cutting equipment; if necessary, he would carve a path to reach his granddaughter's house. It was now around 10 p.m. Before long, Jerry and his grandson Chad Richey were driving through the night to Tuscaloosa to find Shannon's little girl.

Shannon was a mess of jangled nerves. He believed his daughter was alive and that the only reason she hadn't called was because cell service was out. Still, deep down in a place he didn't want to explore, he knew there was the possibility of a parent's worst nightmare. His hands trembled and his legs shook as he prepared to leave home for Tuscaloosa.

Shannon's thoughts drifted back to the last phone conversation he'd had with Loryn. She had recently informed him that she wanted to become a sports broadcaster and planned on majoring in journalism at Alabama. Shannon had made a deal with Loryn: If she made good grades, he would take care of her financial needs. "I am so proud of you," Shannon had told her. "I love you so much."

"You have no idea how much that means to me," Loryn had replied. "I love you too, Daddy."

Loryn's mother was also now en route to Tuscaloosa to find her daughter. A friend from church drove Ashley; Ashley's husband, Dewayne Mims; and Ashley's mother, Carol Denham. They sped north on I-65. Ashley had read Facebook posts from a few of Loryn's friends saying they thought that Loryn had been taken to DCH, but Ashley deemed the information unreliable. No one had actually seen Loryn at the hospital, they'd only heard a rumor that she was there.

Ashley looked out the window as the car cut through the darkness. The power was out in this region of the state, and it seemed to her as black outside as she'd ever seen it. *This isn't happening,* she thought.

I'm not driving to Tuscaloosa to look for my child. She felt as if she were floating, having an out-of-body experience. *This isn't happening.* She saw a rescue vehicle buzzing past in the opposite direction. *Why aren't they looking for Loryn?* she wondered.

Something didn't feel right. It was a twisting, gut-deep sensation, a feeling she'd never experienced before. She didn't know if this feeling meant her daughter was injured or if she was dead, but she knew—*she just knew*—that something was horribly, horribly wrong.

IN JANUARY 2009, Shannon had called another former Alabama football player, Bob Baumhower, and asked a favor: Could he help Loryn land a job at Baumhower's, his sports-themed restaurant in Tuscaloosa? Within days Loryn was working as a waitress at the restaurant on McFarland Boulevard.

It was so fitting, Loryn spending 20 hours a week at a place where she was surrounded by hundreds of photos of former Alabama football players hanging on the walls, including one of her dad. Crimson Tide football had consumed her early life, after all.

From 1991 to '95, when Shannon was on the Alabama football team, little Loryn lived with her parents in the Wood Village mobile home park, lot 42. On the night before a game, Shannon would hold his baby girl in his big arms as Ashley would pack a bag for the next afternoon. "Is tomorrow game day, Mama, is it?" Loryn would ask. Then she would pack her little pink bag with pom-poms, an extra cheerleader outfit and a few juice boxes. The next day at the game she would become captivated by the real pom-poms the cheerleaders waved and by Big Al, the team's elephant mascot. Even then, to Loryn, Bryant-Denny Stadium was the most wonderful place in the world. It was a feeling that would never change.

Shannon was named a team captain in his senior season. This meant he would be able to leave a permanent mark on Tuscaloosa by putting his handprint and footprint in cement at the base of Denny Chimes—a 118-foot bell tower built in 1929 on the south side of the Quad, the vast green lawn in the heart of campus. His prints would join those of all the other Crimson Tide team captains. On the day of the ceremony, Shannon carried his daughter, resplendent in her blue dress with yellow sunflowers and her dark curls, to the Chimes. He set her down and placed his left hand in the soft wet cement. Loryn crawled next to her daddy and helped him press his fingers down. Afterward, holding Loryn, Shannon spoke to a crowd of several thousand. "I just want to thank Coach Stallings for taking a chance on me," Shannon said. "I was married and I had this little girl, and that didn't stop Coach from asking me to come here. I'll forever be grateful."

Loryn, as she grew older, typically started her personal countdown to Alabama's opening game of the season in April. From Tuscaloosa she would tell Ashley over the phone, "Mama, it's only 127 days until game day!" On fall Saturdays Loryn would always stop by the Chimes and, surrounded by thousands of Alabama fans, place her hand in her father's handprint. Nothing made her happier.

JERRY BROWN and Chad Richey arrived in Tuscaloosa at dusk; downed trees and power lines blocked many of the roads into town. Using the heavy tree-cutting equipment when needed, the men hacked their way toward Loryn's house on Beverly Heights. Power in the area was out, leaving the neighborhood dark and unrecognizable. Even the police were barricaded by the tangled debris; seeing Jerry and his equipment, the officers encouraged him to continue his work. Jerry was determined to reach his granddaughter.

By the time Shannon arrived in the area, a police blockade prevented him from getting near Loryn's house. Shannon demanded that the police let him through. "My daughter is in there," he pleaded, "my daughter is in there."

"Sir," an officer replied curtly, "you're only prolonging the discovery process."

Shannon, desperate, was finally able to reach his father on the phone; by now Jerry had made his way to Loryn's house, where more police were at the scene. Eventually one of the officers walked down the street to meet Shannon at the blockade, then escorted the distraught father back to his daughter's house.

There, in the back of an ambulance, Shannon saw two bodies carefully wrapped in blankets. (He would soon learn that they were the bodies of Loryn's roommate Danielle Downs and her friend Will Stevens.) Just then an officer, driving a small utility tractor, emerged from the house. Another casualty was wrapped in a green comforter in the back of the vehicle. An officer approached Shannon with photos on a digital camera, photos of the three victims from the house, and asked Shannon if would look at them to see if one was his daughter.

Shannon took the camera in his quaking hands and as soon as he saw the dark curly hair, the devastating reality came crashing down on him. Yes, oh, dear Lord, it was Loryn. He realized then that the wrapped body on the back of the tractor was that of his daughter.

Shannon stumbled backward. He screamed and screamed and screamed, producing a wail so loud, it may well have carried all the way to Bryant-Denny. He swung his fists through the air, wanting to hit something, anything. His father grabbed him and hugged his son tighter than he ever had before. In that instant, something deep inside Shannon Brown left him, escaping into the nighttime air, never to return.

THE CAR carrying Ashley Mims to Tuscaloosa had reached the outskirts of town when Dewayne's phone rang. He answered; it was Shannon. "She's gone" was all Shannon could say.

All Ashley's feeling, all sensation, simply evaporated, as if in an instant she had turned to stone. All she could mutter to her husband was that she wasn't leaving Tuscaloosa until she saw her daughter. "We need to get a hotel room," Dewayne said quietly. They did, but Ashley didn't lie down. She sat in a chair and stared at the ceiling for several hours. Even as the sky lightened with the morning sun, Ashley stared at that hotel ceiling, not thinking, not moving, not feeling. Nothing.

At 8 a.m. Dewayne and Ashley drove to the morgue set up in the basement of the VA Medical Center, where Loryn's body was being kept. When Ashley saw her daughter, she ran her fingers through Loryn's hair—just like she had on Easter Sunday four days earlier when they were at church together in Wetumpka. There was a speck of blood on Loryn's cheek, and her mother delicately removed it. Loryn's face was untouched, as beautiful as ever, as if she would soon awake.

Ashley rubbed her daughter's hands, her arms, her face. She didn't want to stop. Loryn's fingernails were broken off; Ashley rubbed her daughter's fingers too.

At last Ashley kissed her little girl goodbye—kissed her hands, kissed her cheeks and, finally, kissed her forehead. It was the worst moment of her life.

CHAPTER 7

A Coach
And More

IT WAS just after daybreak
on April 28, the Day After.
Nick Saban had spent the
dark early hours in his home
with his daughter and her
sorority sisters, who were still desperately trying to contact Ashley
Harrison. At first light Saban drove to the football offices to meet
with Thad Turnipseed, director of external affairs. Standing in his
office at 7:00, he told Turnipseed, "We've got to do something. I'm
going to change clothes and get a chain saw, and then we're going out
there to do whatever we can."

The two men filled the back of Turnipseed's white pickup truck
with 20 cases of Gatorade and bottled water that had been left
over from the spring game. With Saban riding shotgun, Turnipseed first drove to the Ferguson Center, located in the center of
campus and the hub of student activity. More than 300 students
had gathered outside the brick building, scared, confused, wondering what to do. Upon seeing their anxious faces, Saban stepped
out of the truck and climbed to the top of a small brick wall. The

students fell silent, stunned by the sudden appearance of their famous—and beloved—coach.

"Your time will come," Saban began, "when you will be able to help and volunteer. We're going to need everybody's effort for a long time to get our city back on its feet. Life is all about challenges, and now we're facing a really big one. But working together, we will get through this. Remember, we have to do this together as one team."

For nearly eight minutes Saban continued what felt like the most important pep talk of his life. For the students, his words were nourishment, and when he concluded, the crowd was clearly energized. As Saban hopped off the wall and stepped back into Turnipseed's truck, the students applauded and yelled his name, ready to begin the business of cleaning up what the storm had left behind.

Saban instructed Turnipseed to head to 15th Street, where the tornado had so narrowly missed campus, and Saban's office, by no more than a mile. Viewing the storm damage in daylight for the first time, Saban had yet to see the worst devastation from the storm. "This might affect you," Turnipseed warned. "It's awful."

"Let's go," Saban replied.

As they approached the town's hardest-hit area, an Alabama National Guard soldier carrying an M-16 rifle raised his arm, signaling the truck to stop. "This road is closed," the guardsman barked. Then he saw Saban in the passenger's seat and quickly waved the truck through the checkpoint.

Turnipseed slowly navigated east on 15th Street, weaving through debris. The coach was silent. Not even his most vivid imaginings were anywhere close to the catastrophic ruin that lay before him: houses shredded as if they'd been put through a blender; cars ripped into jagged sheets of metal; tree trunks shot into the skeletal remains of homes like giant wooden arrows. And the smell: Already the stench of dead animals polluted the air. When Turnipseed reached a Wendy's on 15th that had somehow been spared by the twister, Saban opened the door, jumped out, rushed to the back of the truck, grabbed an armful of Gatorade bottles and handed them to first responders, who were now sadly and methodically searching for survivors and for bodies.

As Turnipseed drove slowly forward, Saban followed behind the truck on foot, passing out bottles; a steady flow of people—a mixture of locals who lived in the area and emergency workers—surrounded Saban. Worried for the coach's safety, Turnipseed asked Saban if he wanted to get back in the truck. Saban shook his head no.

Instead he listened to stories, asked questions and shook every hand thrust at him. Crimson Tide football had long inspired this college and this town, and Saban's presence was somehow settling to all those around him. If the coach looked like he was strong, if *he* was O.K., well, then, maybe . . . maybe things weren't as hopeless as they seemed.

Turnipseed slowly continued to drive through the wasteland that was 15th Street, Saban handing out the Gatorade and water as he walked, with dozens following close behind him, as if they had found the savior who could lead them to sanctuary.

Further along the street, Saban encountered a command center of sorts, where an assembly of some 60 male and female National Guard soldiers, police officers and EMS workers were gathered. "Let me know what I can do," Saban told them. "We're here for you, and we're going to do everything in our power to help you do your job."

He eventually returned to the truck, rejoining Turnipseed. Nearing 15th and McFarland, the truck rolled close to the home of Saban's son. He could see now, in the daylight, that it remained intact; just one short block away, however, every structure on the street had been obliterated. Saban didn't utter a word as he gazed down the street at Nicholas's still-standing house and had the chilling realization that death had blown past here, just around the corner from his son. His son's house could so easily have been a graveyard. For some 20 seconds Saban simply stared at the place where Nicholas had ridden out the storm. It was then—on this soft, blue-sky morning—that Saban fully comprehended the terrible capriciousness of the Tuscaloosa tornado.

IT WAS not the first time in his life that Saban had felt the overwhelming impact of a community tragedy on a college town. As a freshman at Ohio's Kent State University in the spring of 1970, the young Saban had been fully absorbed in his classes and playing football, focused as always, largely insulated from the real world outside of campus. It was a chaotic time for the nation, torn by violent disagreement over the war in Vietnam, but it all seemed a distant distraction to Saban. That changed during the first four days of May, when the Kent State campus was roiled by fierce anti-Vietnam war rallies. The ROTC building was burned to the ground, and hundreds of Ohio National Guard soldiers arrived on May 3 to quell another protest and to protect against further school disruption during a scheduled rally at noon the next day, a Monday.

That morning Saban had attended his 11:00 English class; afterward he met up with his friend and teammate Phil Witherspoon, and the two went to lunch in the cafeteria. After eating, Saban and his friend decided to check out the rally. Moments after they'd stepped outside, a frantic and frightened student ran past them, screaming that shots had been fired at the protesters.

Saban and Witherspoon ran quickly to the Commons—the rally site—but were prevented by the guardsmen from getting too close. The grassy lawn looked like a battlefield. The air was filled with plumes of smoke and the howl of ambulance sirens. Saban could see students on the ground, some covered in blood, some who appeared to be gasping for air. He had no idea what to do; he stood and stared as emergency personnel attended to the wounded. It was unreal, this kind of carnage in the middle of campus. Saban later found out that four students had been killed, including a girl named Allison Krause, who was in his English class.

The feeling he'd had that day, the shock of sudden, inexplicable tragedy, returned to him now as he stood near the wreckage of 15th Street. He remembered, too, the aftermath of that day in Ohio, the slow and painful healing of a traumatized town. He knew better than most what the next days and weeks would bring and what would need to be done to help the people of Tuscaloosa. Pressing ahead was the only way to put the past behind. Advance, never retreat.

LEIGH HENDERSON had been told by her husband that the Smoothie King had vanished, but she had to see for herself. The store at 415 15th Street East was so much more than a structure of brick and concrete, more even than a business. It was part of their love story.

The best part of that story had happened in April 2001, when Lee Henderson ran into an old friend, Prince Wimbley, at a restaurant in Birmingham. Wimbley had been a flanker and a team captain on the 1992 Alabama national championship team, and now invited Henderson to a party at the Hotel Capstone in Tuscaloosa to celebrate that '92 team. Dozens of former players were scheduled to attend—Antonio Langham, George Teague and Chris Anderson were going to be there—and Wimbley told Henderson, "You should come to this thing."

Lee was thrilled; the party would fit perfectly into the plan he'd been hatching. Henderson asked his girlfriend, Leigh Hudson, to go with him to the party. (Leigh had been a freshman at the university during that '92 season.) As the young couple traveled down McFarland Boulevard, in the direction of Lee's recently opened Smoothie King, his heart was aflutter. When the store came into view, Henderson told his girlfriend to look at the big sign above the Smoothie King. She lifted her eyes, then put her hand over her mouth. The sign read, LEIGH WILL YOU MARRY ME?

"Of course I will," Leigh told him immediately, spilling happy tears. They went on to the football party at the hotel and were congratulated on their engagement by dozens of former players, each proudly wearing a national championship ring. The couple hugged one player after the next; it was one of the best nights of their lives. A few days later Lee put a new message on the Smoothie King sign: SHE SAID YES.

It wasn't the last time Henderson would use the sign as his personal loudspeaker. When the Hendersons had their first child, Blake, in 2004, the sign announced, THE PRINCE HAS ARRIVED. And after their second child, Riley, was born two years later: PRINCESS RILEY HAS ARRIVED. "That sign became our way of communicating with the community," Lee says, "and people all around town would ask us what the different messages meant. It was special."

But today, the Day After, there was no message to share. The sign, like the store, lay in waste. Leigh, though, still wanted to view the remains, as if seeing would allow her to begin grieving. She had so many memories now entombed in that rubble. "I need to see it," Leigh told her husband.

"I'll take you," Lee said, "but it's not pretty. Be prepared to see some horrible things."

Lee parked about a mile from the store, and then husband and wife, hand in hand, began walking, past downed power lines and crumpled buildings. As they neared the store, a white pickup stopped next to them. It was Lee's close friend Thad Turnipseed—and beside him was Coach Saban. "I'm so sorry to hear about your store," Saban said. "I'll be thinking of you."

For Lee and Leigh Henderson—ardent Alabama fans—the timing could not have been better. Their spirits momentarily soared. Saban was the last person they'd expected to see out here near ground zero.

But after walking another quarter of a mile, Leigh Henderson saw the pile of debris, all that remained of the store. The sign was gone, and their delivery car had been thrown two blocks away. Leigh cried and couldn't stop.

SABAN AND Turnipseed traveled to a church where 1,500 volunteers had gathered outside to help. Saban worked the line, shaking hands, encouraging them, emphasizing again and again that Tuscaloosa was now one team. He entered the church and asked a church official if there was anything he could do. "Go to the

American Red Cross shelter at the Belk Activity Center," the man told Saban. "Fourteen hours ago those people lost everything. They are the ones who need you."

When Saban stepped through the doors at Belk, he was confronted with one of the harsh new realities of life in Tuscaloosa—hundreds of people left instantly homeless. Most were lying or sitting on canvas military-style cots, but everyone seemed to still be numb with shock. No one noticed that the state's most famous person had just entered the building. Saban could see the fright on their faces; he asked a Red Cross member what he could do. "We've got a thousand people in this shelter, and they need food," he was told. The coach now had his mission. He told Turnipseed, "I'll pay for it. And let's rob the football facility of every hat and shirt we've got. I'll write the check for everything."

A few hours later Saban returned to the activity center with his wife, Terry. Some of the victims' shock may have subsided because people now recognized the coach and his wife, and soon the Sabans were surrounded. The coach offered hugs and handshakes and signed hundreds of autographs. He and Terry handed out Alabama T-shirts, caps, long-sleeved shirts and gift cards to Walmart. They helped serve plates of hot food. But more than anything, the Sabans listened. "Everyone has a story, and everyone needs to share their story," Saban said later. "No one who was affected by this will ever be the same. Tuscaloosa will never be the same."

For the rest of the day he would listen, story after story. The details were different each time, but the pain and confusion were always the same. He allowed victims to vent their anger or cry their despair. He met with business owners who had been picking through what was left of their livelihoods and with homeowners who had begun sorting through the crushed remnants of their lives. Some moved in silence, their eyes speaking for them with a look that screamed, *What in heaven's name will I do?* Others openly sobbed, often uncontrollably. A local man with only one leg explained to Saban that he had worked for three years to purchase a specially designed truck that allowed him to drive. Now, the man said, the truck had been cartwheeled away by the storm. Saban heard these grieving tales nonstop, and all he could do was grab those in pain, pull them close and tell them that he would do everything in his power to help.

For hours Saban comforted and consoled; he embraced more people in a four-hour stretch than he had in his whole life—and this did not come easily to him. While Saban can stand in front of a crowd of 10,000 and deliver an off-the-cuff speech that enthralls even non–football fans, he's often achingly ill at ease in smaller groups. "Nick is a shy person," says Phil Savage, who coached with Saban in Cleveland in the early 1990s and remains a friend. "He's uncomfortable standing in a group of two or three people. He doesn't make small talk because he usually just doesn't have time for it." Yet here he was, out in the shattered city, trying to comfort one victim after the next.

Saban eventually called Mayor Maddox. "Walt, anything you need from me, consider it done," Saban said. "Whatever you ask." It was a brief conversation, but Maddox was struck by the tone. He sensed that already this tornado, this tragedy, had touched something deep in Saban, perhaps even changed him.

Perhaps it had. In just a matter of hours Saban had certainly come to understand that he was more than a football coach. He was the person in this town who others looked to for assurance. He was the one these people wanted to tell their story to. It *did* impact Saban; facing these survivors was breaking down at least a few of the walls that he had so carefully built around himself, walls that had stood strong for decades. A changed man? His wife said that the hours and days after the tornado were the first time in his professional life that he stopped thinking about football.

Yes, he was changed—his friends attest to that. "Absolutely," says Turnipseed. "From April 27 forward, he no longer spoke in coach-speak to the team or the town. His whole speech from that day onward became about, What does it mean to be alive? He started talking about how life is all about the relationships you build, and he himself started building new relationships. Before the tornado he only had a couple of close friends; a year later he had 10 or 12 close friends. No, it's not a lot, but he really widened his inner circle. Before he had always been so isolated from what everyone would consider a normal life, but after the storm he began getting out into the community and really making Tuscaloosa his home. And make no mistake," Turnipseed continues, "he told his players every day from April 27 forward that they were no longer playing for themselves; they were now playing for Tuscaloosa. That was a constant theme, and that was powerful."

CHAPTER 8

Dressed
In White

SHE HAD already touched her lips to her daughter's forehead, kissing her goodbye at the morgue, but Ashley Mims wasn't ready to leave Tuscaloosa. Not yet. She desperately needed to do one more thing.

Four days before the tornado Ashley and Loryn had spent Easter Sunday together. They attended a service at New Home Baptist Church in Wetumpka—they sat in the same pew they'd occupied since Loryn was a little girl—and, as she always did during the sermon, Ashley gently ran her fingers through her daughter's long curly hair. Afterward they visited Loryn's grandparents, Ashley's parents, and extended family who lived nearby. Later, mother and daughter rode two of their horses on Ashley's 27-acre property. Loryn hopped on her beloved Prissy, a sorrel quarter horse, and galloped around the grassy pasture beside their house; she was a picture of joy riding her horse, her long tresses flowing behind her, in the same white dress she had worn to church.

Just days later, on the morning after the storm, Ashley felt an overwhelming need to find that white dress. She had bought it in Birmingham six months earlier for her daughter, who had looked absolutely angelic in it on that Easter Sunday. Ashley wanted to bury Loryn in that dress. To find it, she and her husband drove back to Loryn's house on Beverly Heights.

They parked at the bottom of a hill. To reach the house, they had to walk over the crest of a knoll. When Ashley reached the top of the hill and looked down the road at the house, she fell to her knees, short of breath. "Oh, my God," she cried. More than 20 trees—all so thick you couldn't wrap your arms around them—had been ripped out by the roots, lifted into the air and dropped on top of the house.

One month earlier Ashley had stood at the front door of that house. Her daughter was heading to New Orleans later that day to celebrate her 21st birthday. Every year to commemorate Loryn's special day, Ashley had decorated her daughter's front door with balloons and posters. So early on a March morning, Ashley had left Wetumpka at 5:45, driven to Tuscaloosa and placed streamers and balloons on Loryn's door. Ashley then waited in her car until her daughter stepped outside at 8:15 and saw the decorations. Ashley ran to Loryn, and mother and daughter happily embraced.

Now the house was flattened. Inside, furniture and kitchen appliances had been sucked up and rearranged as if they were miniatures in a dollhouse. Loryn had been found underneath a tipped-over refrigerator. Despite facing the mangled house and feeling inside her a searing pain, Ashley was determined: She didn't know how, but she was going to find that white dress.

AFTER SURVIVING the tornado pinned together in the bathtub of their house, baseball players Josh Rosecrans and Nate Kennedy had spent hours moving from house to house, pulling survivors from the rubble. The next morning, after spending the night at a friend's apartment, they walked to the house of a teammate, Jon Kelton, who lived across the street from Loryn Brown.

Several massive fallen oaks were strewn about Kelton's yard, but the house stood defiantly intact. Kelton, who had been in his basement during the storm, was terribly shaken when he learned that three people had died across the street, not 50 yards from where he'd hidden from the tornado. By mid-morning nearly the entire Alabama baseball team had gathered in Kelton's yard to help cut up the huge trees now littering the property. As the players worked, Ashley Mims and her husband arrived across the street.

Ashley was the spitting image of her daughter, so Kelton knew immediately that she was Loryn's mother. He crossed the street and offered condolences, telling Ashley what a sweet and engaging girl her daughter was. "Is there anything we can help you find in the house?" Kelton asked Ashley.

"Yes, there is," Ashley said, choking back tears. "There is a white dress we'd like to have. We'd like to bury her in it. Could you help us find it?"

The 15 baseball players formed a line that stretched from the remains of the house to the street, picking up anything salvageable and passing the items along the line until they reached Ashley's grateful arms. Everything was covered in mud; it was difficult to discern a dress from a towel. They picked up so many pieces of Loryn's garments that at one point, trying to cut the tension, one of the players said to Ashley, "Ma'am, your daughter sure had a lot of clothes."

Ashley smiled, if only for a moment. The players pulled out several of Loryn's dresses, some of them white, but they couldn't find the one that Ashley was seeking. She was about to give up and return home when, from down the human assembly line, came a white dress covered in muddy red clay. *This could be it*, Ashley thought. With her arms shaking, she laid it on the ground and reverently spread it out. As she inspected it, her legs were trembling so violently that she dropped to her knees. *Yes, this is it.* She began to sob. She pressed the dress to her face, still able to smell the perfumed scent, faint as it was, of her daughter. The red clay smeared her face like war paint, but Ashley kept rubbing the dress on her cheeks. It almost felt as if she were holding her beautiful girl once again. At that moment, she never wanted to leave this spot. If she did, it seemed, the distance between her and Loryn would somehow grow and grow.

Her husband gently lifted her to her feet. She hugged Nathan Kilcrease, the player who had found the white dress. "Thank you so much," she said to the team, tears running down her mud-stained cheeks. Then she climbed back into her car.

The players were visibly upset. "I wish I could have gone my entire life without having to do something like that," Kilcrease told his teammates. They stood in silence and waved goodbye to a mother whose life would never be the same. For the entire 130-mile car ride home to Wetumpka, Ashley held the dress in her lap, clinging to it like a lifeline. When she walked into her house, a friend was waiting for her. Ashley handed her the dress. It took a few days, but eventually every stain was removed, every smudge and smear and tiny speck of evidence of that terrible day had been lifted away. The lovely white dress would be ready for Loryn to wear one final time.

SHANNON BROWN had just finished making final arrangements for his daughter at the funeral home in Wetumpka when his cell-phone rang. He was standing in the parking lot about to get into his truck as he pulled his phone from his pocket. The caller ID revealed that the number was private, and Brown briefly considered not answering. No one in the world could say anything to him now that would really matter. How could they? There was no meaningful relief from the mind-numbing pain he was feeling. He had trouble remembering things he'd done five minutes earlier and felt as if he were merely drifting about in the world, emotionless and empty.

But for some reason he lifted the phone to his ear and said, "Hello?"

"Shannon, this is Nick Saban," said the voice on the other end of the line. "I'm so, so sorry for your loss. There's nothing I can say that will make you feel any better, but just know that the entire Alabama family is here for you. You're a great ambassador for us. If there is anything that I can ever do for you, please call me. I'll do it. I'm here for you, Shannon. You call me, you hear?"

Brown was moved. Here was Saban, whom he barely knew, reminding him that he wasn't alone, that the arms of his football family were extended. The call was like a shot of adrenaline—Saban's voice did make him feel momentarily better, but the pain quickly returned, still crippling in intensity.

There were others from the Alabama family who reached out to Shannon. Gene Stallings called, his former coach who used to smile at the sight of little Loryn running about. "You have to stay strong," Stallings said. "It's not easy, and it's a long hard road you're about to go down, but you need to stay strong." Mal Moore, the school's athletic director, delivered a similar message.

One of Brown's former teammates, running back Siran Stacy, contacted him. Stacy's life had been torn by tragedy in a moment as sudden and brutal as the tornado. In November 2007, outside of Dothan, Ala., Stacy was driving a van on Alabama Highway 123 late on a Monday night when a pickup truck, on the wrong side of the road, struck Stacy's vehicle. The crash killed his wife and four of their children, as well as the driver of the pickup.

"The pain you are going through is unimaginable, the worst kind of pain," Stacy told Brown. "But lean on the Alabama family. We're here for you. All of us. I understand what you're going through. I've been there. You have to have faith and believe that your daughter is now in a better place. If you ever need to talk, call me."

The phone calls were heartfelt, and appreciated. Still, Shannon felt a darkness closing in around him. His girl was gone, and no words could change that. He didn't want to go out. He didn't want to see people who would try to console him. He just wanted to be alone.

CHAPTER 9

Diamond In The Rough

SABAN STOOD in front of his team in the large Alabama recruiting room at Bryant-Denny, the only space with electricity where the coaches and players could meet. It was two days after the storm and the first time the team had been together since the tornado. As the players ate a catered meal, Saban's voice was emphatic: "I know you all have seen a lot of things in the last few days, and if you have any issues, come see us. I've found through the years that professional help can get you through major things. But we've also got a community to support. We can't just be a team for them on Saturdays. The fans are with us in the best times, and we have to be with them in the worst of times. Just by your presence and being with them, you can help people."

Saban had been introduced very early in his life to the nature of tragedy and loss, having grown up near the tiny mining town of Monongah, W.Va., in a hardscrabble region where tales of disaster are not uncommon. Back in 1907 the nearby Monongah mine was the site of the worst coal mining accident in American history; 362 miners were killed. Years later, in 1968, when Saban was 17, his grandfather Conway had barely escaped being entombed in the Consol No. 9 mine just outside of Farmington, W.Va. He'd already left the mine on a shift change; 78 of his fellow miners didn't survive.

Saban had come to learn that in times of heartbreaking loss, people needed diversion to help them reclaim normalcy as quickly as possible. So now, to his players and to his town, he preached a gospel of resiliency, of focusing on what lay directly ahead and going out and getting things done. Freud had once labeled grieving as "work," and to Saban, grief did not have to be incapacitating. Fighting back was the best medicine.

Progress was, essentially, a matter of determination. And nobody is more determined than Nick Saban. His father had made sure of that.

ON ROUTE 19 in northern West Virginia, at a speck on the map called Helens Run, Nick Saban Sr. operated Saban's Service Station. A young and growing family, the Sabans lived behind the station in a three-bedroom house, across the street from a Dairy Queen, which they also owned. Helens Run, tucked into the rugged, undulating terrain, was the place where locals from the area gathered to share news, fill up on gas and talk sports with Nick Sr.

In 1962, when Nick Jr. was 10, his dad formed the Idamay Black Diamonds, a Pop Warner team for kids in four nearby small towns. Big Nick, as the locals called him, acquired a few dozen pairs of black-and-orange hand-me-down uniforms from a team that had long since disbanded, and he recruited two college-age boys to serve as coaches. Big Nick hoped to be a sort of commissioner for the team, but on the first day of practice the college kids didn't show up; so even though he'd never done it before, Big Nick became the head coach. He bought every book on football coaching he could find and studied the game as though pursuing an advanced degree. But in his first season leading the Black Diamonds (named for the coal mining towns in the area), his team won only one game. What he needed was a couple of talented kids or at least one special player, a game-breaker. He didn't have to look far to find him. He tapped his son.

When Big Nick's wife, Mary, had been pregnant with their second child, Big Nick told his daughter, Dianna, who was almost two at the time, that she soon would have a brother. From that day forward Dianna called the baby Brother. In truth, Big Nick had no idea what gender the baby would be, but he'd guessed right. Nicholas Lou Saban Jr. was born on Halloween in 1951; Brother was the nickname that would stick to him as he grew up.

As soon as he could walk, Brother had a ball of some kind in his hands. He and his sister liked to shoot baskets at the hoop in their yard. Their mother, who worked at the family's Dairy Queen, often joined them. And when Big Nick could break away from work—he ran the service station from 7 a.m. to midnight and sometimes made extra money working the coal mines—he'd become the fourth player in games of two-on-two. By the time Brother was in grade school, the Sabans' yard had become the local playground; his mother bemoaned the fact that the grass wouldn't grow given all the feet that were trampling about.

Brother began working at the gas station at age 11, weeks after his dad had started coaching the Pop Warner team. Father and son would throw a football to each other in front of the gas pumps until a car pulled in. One of them would then grab the nozzle and pump the gas while the other would check the engine oil and clean the windshield. Brother did a little bit of everything at the station: He checked tire pressure, washed cars, did grease jobs, changed filters, replaced oil. One time young Nick was cleaning out a drain in the floor of the station. A perfectionist even then, by the time he finished, the drain was as shiny clean as the counters at the Dairy Queen across the street. "The biggest thing I started to learn at 11 years old was how important it was to do things correctly," Saban said years later. "There was a standard of excellence, a perfection. If we washed a car—I hated the navy-blue and black cars because when you wiped them off, the streaks were hard to get out—and if there were any streaks when [my father] came, you had to do it over."

That standard of excellence extended to the football field, where Brother became the starting quarterback for the Idamay Black Diamonds at 11. Though the team practiced on a field littered with rocks—every player had to pick up 10 rocks at the end of practice and remove them from the field—that didn't stop Big Nick from holding marathon practice sessions. He always announced the starting time for practice but never the ending time, in keeping with one of his favorite mottoes: Practice makes players. On countless occasions, as darkness descended, Big Nick would simply crank up his car, flip on the headlights and run his boys through additional drills in the high beams.

He pushed them hard, but Big Nick cared deeply about his boys. With what little extra income he had, he purchased a used bus, painted it orange to match the team's colors and used it to drive his players to and from practice. His wife plastered inspiring quotations on the inside of the bus—WHEN THE GOING GETS TOUGH, THE TOUGH GET GOING—for the boys to read as Big Nick drove 40 miles daily along the narrow, winding roads, traveling up and down the hills and hollows to the four towns where his players lived. The boys, in return, not wanting to disappoint the man who had given them so much, played their hearts out for their coach. Nick Jr. took note of it all.

To build the fittest team in the league, Big Nick ordered his players to run up the hill behind one of the end zones after practices. The top of the hill was not visible to Big Nick standing at the bottom when evening approached, but trees stood atop the incline. Big Nick told his players to each bring back a leaf to prove they had run all the way to the top.

Even if his team won, Big Nick wasn't satisfied. One season the Black Diamonds beat an inferior team, but the defense committed the sin of giving up a score. At the next practice Big Nick had his players form a circle and run in place for nearly an hour. If he thought a player's knees weren't pumping high enough, Big Nick sent him to climb the dreaded hill.

He was as tough on his son as any other player. If young Nick threw a touchdown pass, Big Nick always had a critique: The ball didn't travel in a tight enough spiral or he didn't look off the safety before unleashing the pass. Big Nick was a natural-born perfectionist, and his chief concern was that his players perform to their maximum potential, something he reminded them of at every practice. Brother soaked it in. Many of the phrases his father repeatedly counseled—*Invest your time, don't spend it*—remain in Saban's repertoire today.

Big Nick could not tolerate insubordination or disrespectful behavior—from his team or his son. One day after the Black Diamonds lost a game, Brother was working at the gas station when an elderly homeless man approached. The man had been to the station many times before and had been given free coffee and snacks, but now Brother was in a bad mood; he was still disgusted by the recent defeat, and he'd just struggled to repair a flat tire. Frustrated, Nick Jr. teased the old vagabond. His father overheard and slipped off his belt. He quietly approached his son and smacked him across the butt. He looked piercingly at young Nick and said, "I don't ever want to hear you talk to someone older than you like that ever again." The son apologized, lesson promptly learned.

On another day Big Nick didn't like the way his son was dealing with customers. Brother had just broken up with his girlfriend, and now he was failing to say thank you to people when they paid. His father confronted him.

"Your mom told me you broke up with your girlfriend. You're a little upset about that?" he asked.

"Yeah, I'm a little upset about that," young Nick replied.

"Let me just tell you this," Big Nick said. "When you let one bad thing that happens to you affect other things, sometimes you create more negative consequences than you like. You're about ready to cause a couple more. You don't have a girlfriend right now. Pretty soon, you're not going to have a job because I'm going to fire you. And if I fire you, I'm going to whip your ass." The boy would never forget that one.

The father had great expectations for his son, including making sure he went to college. When young Nick was in eighth grade, he was earning a D in music, primarily because he was so shy he wouldn't stand in front of the class to sing; his parents were called in to school. Big Nick told his son to turn in his basketball uniform—he wouldn't be allowed to play until his grades improved—and then the two drove to a nearby coal mine. The father took his son to the shaft elevator, pushed a button, and they descended 550 feet deep into the earth. Standing in the cold, damp darkness, Big Nick said, "Is this what you want? You want to work down here for the rest of your life?" Nicholas Lou Saban Jr. has not been in a coal mine since.

ON THE football field Brother had no peer in his Pop Warner league; he was an elusive, athletic quarterback who called his own plays. Over the years the Idamay Black Diamonds strung together winning streaks of 26 and 33 games. After each win the owner of a local store would allow the boys to play pinball free for a week. In one memorable victory, the Diamonds toppled a Pop Warner squad that featured a young quarterback named Joe Montana. Though Big Nick's team wasn't always the most talented, his players had more than their share of desire and toughness. "He took these country kids that didn't have an opportunity to play, taught them how to be successful, how to compete," Saban would later say of his father. "That certainly is something that stuck with me as a person and as a player.... It made me better. The work ethic he taught, the standard of excellence, the integrity that you do things with, the attitude that you carry with you and the character that you carry with you, what you do every day. Those kinds of values affected me."

The Black Diamonds even had cheerleaders. Terry Constable, dressed in a cheerleading skirt that fell halfway down her shin, always smiled at young Nick, the seventh-grade quarterback. She tried hard to catch his eye; once when Nick walked by, she did a dramatic twirl in her skirt. He didn't notice. But that would change by the time Nick was in eighth grade and Terry in seventh.

They attended a 4-H science camp over the summer. Nick had little desire to go to a science camp—he would rather have been playing sports from sunup to sundown. But his interest shifted when Terry, a dimple-cheeked brunette with the sweetest of smiles, showed up at the 4-H camp. A member of the junior Audubon Society, Terry suggested they go bird-watching one morning at 5. Nick agreed but later realized he had a softball game at 8 that morning and never showed up for their first date. It was not a promising start to their relationship, but Nick would eventually be forgiven.

Nick became the starting quarterback at Monongah High early in his sophomore season. Many evenings he and his father would watch eight-millimeter film of his high school games, the father critiquing and instructing as the son listened intently, the X's and O's flowing from Big Nick's mind. These one-on-one tutorials, which often lasted deep into the night as the two sat in front of the flickering black-and-white images, would help transform Nick into one of the top high school players in the state. He was nowhere near the most athletic, the strongest or the quickest, but his football IQ was unmatched.

Late that fall Monongah traveled to Masontown for a critical game: The winner would advance to the state playoffs, the loser's season would be over. As the team bus ferried the Monongah players 35 miles to Masontown Valley High, nearly every resident of the town motored behind. Seeing this river of cars, young Nick felt the weight of a town pressing hard upon him. Adding to his unease, the players had to walk through a cemetery to reach the Masontown football field from their locker room. Once on the field, Nick squinted in frustration at what he thought was a poorly lit facility.

The first half was a calamity for Monongah. With Big Nick and family watching from the stands, the 15-year-old quarterback called the team's offensive plays, but nothing worked. At halftime Monongah trailed 18–0. As he walked back across the cemetery to the locker room, Nick could almost hear his dad telling him, *No matter what the circumstances, never stop fighting.*

In the second half Nick and Monongah fought. The score was 18–12 when they got the ball for the final time with just 1:30 left in the game. Nick quickly moved his team down the field but faced a fourth-and-12 on the 20-yard line with less than 30 seconds remaining. Monongah coach Earl Keener called a timeout. Saban ran to the sideline with relief, happy that now Keener would tell him the crucial play to call on what would be the final snap of the game.

"Coach, what do you want to run here?" he asked.

"I tell you what," Keener replied. "You have a three-time all-state split end, and the left halfback is the fastest guy in the state. I don't care what play you call, just make sure one of those two guys gets the ball."

The decision, and the game, had been placed in Nick's young hands. In the huddle he confidently called out 26 crossfire pass. He took the snap, faked a handoff to his left halfback, then rifled the ball to his split end in the corner of the end zone for a touchdown and a 19–18 Monongah victory.

Afterward Keener told his quarterback, "It really doesn't make any difference what play you call sometimes. It's what players you have doing it." Those words stuck with Saban and would one day serve as the first commandment in his coaching bible.

Nick guided the Monongah Lions to the Class A state football championship in his senior year, 1968. Earlier that autumn Nick and Terry, who was a majorette at rival Fairmont High, had renewed their junior high friendship after bumping into each other at a game. Nick was so taken with this stylish, classy girl that on weekends he would often hitchhike the eight miles from his house in Helens Run to her home in Fairmont to spend time with her. Their first date was over Thanksgiving weekend, when Saban took her to the Lee movie theater to see *Gone with the Wind*. Then, on many weekend nights, they'd go to the dances at the Pleasant Valley Fire Department. Nick would be leaving soon for college, with Terry a year behind, but that wouldn't end the romance.

Before graduating from Monongah—where Nick was also a two-time all-state baseball player, a one-time all-state basketball player and sports editor of the yearbook—he had planned to attend the Naval Academy. He had been nominated for an appointment to Annapolis by West Virginia senator Robert Byrd, but he withdrew his application. The Vietnam War was raging, and Saban knew he'd likely serve multiple tours overseas during the five-year military commitment required of graduates. When he told his father he was no longer interested in Annapolis, Big Nick replied, "I want you to leave the state of West Virginia. You need to see what it's like some-place else. And if you choose to come back, then come back."

Nick chose Kent State because it was only a 186-mile drive from Helens Run and, thus, not too far from Terry. He spent his fresh-man year learning the college game, learning how to play corner-back and learning about heartache. He missed Terry badly; the two wrote letters every day and talked on the phone whenever they could, confirming what they both already knew: They were going to spend their lives together. Even though at the time, as Saban would say later, "she didn't know what a first down was."

Three years later, in the fall of 1972—a year and a half after the traumatizing shooting on the Kent State campus—Saban was a 21-year-old senior and a team leader. Together with future NFL Hall of Fame linebacker Jack Lambert, he helped the Kent State Golden Flashes win five of their last six games and earn a berth in the Tangerine Bowl. It was the high point in the program's his-tory. The Kent State community was still deeply scarred by the shootings, still mourning that gruesome day and trying to come to grips with it, but the students and locals all rallied around the team that fall with such exuberance that it surprised even Kent State coach Don James.

The football team had clearly become a unifying force in rebuilding the morale of the student body. "I think everybody felt like something really good had to happen at Kent State," James has said of that season. "The school needed positive publicity, and the community wrapped its arms around the sport." Saban had felt it as powerfully as anyone.

SPEAKING TO his team in the recruiting room at Bryant-Denny Stadium, some 44 hours after the tornado, Saban's mind was churning. He knew that some of his players were emotionally wounded. More than a dozen of the young men on his roster had pulled the injured and the bleeding from the rubble left by the storm. Saban was concerned that many of his players might suffer post-traumatic shock; he informed them of a treatment center set up by the athletic department where they could meet with psychologists to help them understand and process what they had just experienced. (Saban himself would meet with a counselor—to "give me direction," he said.) The university had canceled classes for the semester, and Saban informed all his players that they were welcome to leave town and go home the following day. "It might be for the best for some of you to leave," he said. "That's up to you, and it's a personal decision."

Saban didn't yet know precisely what other actions he would take in the coming days, but he was fully aware of one critical fact: The school and the community needed not only help but hope. These people were in desperate need of a reason to feel good about life again, and Saban knew well that he held in his hands the perfect tool to help this town heal its collective psyche. He had the Alabama football team.

He looked hard at his players and said, "Once we all get back here and really start preparing for the season, we're going to have a chance to do something very special for our community. These people are hurting, and we're going to be able to show them that we've got their backs. We're going to win for Tuscaloosa."

AFTER THE team meeting, Saban went to the hospital, DCH, to visit Carson Tinker. Lying in his bed, Tinker could only remember being in the closet with Ashley in the terrifying moments before the tornado hit. Everything after was a blur. But he knew the worst, and he was unbearably sad.

Saban tried to comfort his player. Sitting at Tinker's bedside, he had no magic words—they simply didn't exist—but he emphasized to Tinker that he wasn't alone. "You have to have gratitude for being alive," the coach said, gathering Tinker's hand in his. "We are here for you, all of us, everyone on the team and the entire university." More than 50 of Tinker's teammates and coaches would visit him at the hospital.

A few days after the tornado, in the field across from where Tinker's house once stood, where he used to hit golf balls on lazy springtime afternoons, three small wooden crosses now marked where the storm had left the three victims of 611 25th Street—one for Carson's dog, one for Ashley's dog and one for Ashley.

About 100 yards from the crosses, someone had nailed a crimson-and-white University of Alabama flag to the trunk of a tree that had been split in half. Carson's friend Brandon Gibson stood close to that flag as it fluttered in the warm breeze. Surveying what was left of Tinker's house—scores of bricks, a few books, a lawn chair cast on the ground—he spoke in a voice thick with emotion.

"Ashley was such a wonderful girl, beautiful, always smiling, the kind of girl you wanted to be around," he said. "Now you look at Carson's place and you wonder how he's still alive. I look up to Carson. He's such a positive guy, and he's so strong. He's just damn tough. But all of us athletes are going to have to be tough in the next few months. We can help carry this community. We can give them something to be proud of, give them something that can bring us together as one. We are going to be there for them, and we are going to work our butts off for the people of Tuscaloosa. We're going to help bring this place back."

CARSON'S MOTHER, Debbie, pushed her son in a wheelchair down a hall in the DCH medical center. It had been three days since the storm, and Carson wanted to escape the confines of his room, if only for a few minutes, and get a snack from a vending machine. The loss of Ashley was tearing at him constantly, and he was suffering from nightmares, but his identity as an Alabama football player was intact. He was wearing a crimson-colored Alabama T-shirt. Before Tinker and his mother reached the snack machine, a female hospital employee approached.

"Roll Tide," she said.

"Roll Tide," Tinker replied.

"We've got a lot to look forward to this fall," the woman told Tinker. "A whole lot."

And just then, in the hallway of the hospital where nearly a thousand people were treated for injuries in the wake of the storm, Carson Tinker did something he hadn't done since the winds had ripped apart his life. He smiled.

CHAPTER 10

The Pull Of The Tide

THE GRAINY images flickered on a concrete wall of the cavernous Alabama National Guard armory in Northport, four miles northwest of Bryant-Denny Stadium. Row after row of canvas cots filled the floor, arrayed in what the military calls "squared away" fashion. This had been home for hundreds of National Guardsmen and Guardswomen—mostly from Alabama—since the tornado had descended on Tuscaloosa days earlier.

A unit from Mobile was relaxing—sleeping, reading, listening to music on their iPods or watching the highlights of Crimson Tide football projected on the wall. In one clip Bama was scoring a touchdown against hated cross-state rival Auburn; in another Bear Bryant was prowling the sideline, his steely eyes fixed firmly on the field. In yet another clip the Tide was beating Texas in the Rose Bowl to claim the 2009 national title. *Sweet Home Alabama* wafted out of large speakers in an endless loop of reassuring sound. One guardswoman held a crying baby, rocking the child in her arms. "If you're not nice," she said, "they'll send you to Auburn."

Staff Sgt. Greg Stocks, 54, a native of Fayette, Ala., spoke to a visitor. "The troops here are tired," he said. "We put in long hours, 12-hour shifts. I went through hurricanes Katrina and Rita, and this is as bad as it gets. Horrendous tragedy. But hearing that music and seeing those highlights lifts us up. This is Roll Tide country. Like most of the people in here, I've been an Alabama fan since even before I was born."

As Stocks spoke he glanced into a far corner of the drill hall, and what he saw prompted a smile on his sunburned face. A former Alabama football player had just entered, and his sudden presence created a jolt of activity as he shook hands with soldiers, posed for pictures and signed their tan-colored patrol caps. Then a hush settled on the scene as the 150 troops leaned in close to hear Javier Arenas tell his story.

He recounted how he had survived the tornado crouched in the bathtub in his house and told them of the horror show that had played out before his eyes as he stared out his window, watching in disbelief as the tornado churned toward him. The troops had heard similar tales before, but this one was different. Here was a local legend, a football star, telling them he'd never been so frightened in his life. It was another reminder that the tornado didn't discriminate.

IN THE state of Alabama, the passion for Crimson Tide football runs so deep that fans name their newborns after star players and then lovingly wrap those babies in houndstooth diapers. They plan their weddings around—or rather, away from—game dates, recognizing that they might otherwise find themselves saying "I do" in a near-empty chapel. They tattoo their bodies with elephants and ROLL TIDE. They build personal shrines to Bear Bryant in their living rooms, replete with houndstooth fedoras, Alabama candles and framed photographs of the Bear. They have been known to sink more money into a motor home to follow the Tide to away games than they paid for their actual home. They spend thousands of dollars on oil paintings by local artist Daniel Moore—Alabama's version of Michelangelo, who re-creates special moments from special games—then they gaze into these paintings and experience all over again how good it felt when the Tide won that '92 championship or how they'd been filled with pride when Alabama stopped Penn State on the goal line in the '79 Sugar Bowl.

Throughout much of Alabama, and certainly in Tuscaloosa, the collective mood of the populace is determined by one thing more than any other: whether the Crimson Tide is winning or losing. There are rabid college football constituencies across the nation—Baton Rouge, Ann Arbor, Lincoln, Austin, Columbus—but none are as hyperobsessed with their team as those in Alabama, where funeral homes keep custom-made caskets in stock featuring the Crimson Tide logo.

"Our fans are a powerful recruiting tool," Saban said one afternoon in his office. "I've been to a lot of places in my life and seen a lot of football, and I can honestly tell you that there is no fan base that is as devoted to their team as Alabama. Our fans are the backbone of our program. You come here, man, and nearly everyone in this state will be behind you. That's powerful."

There's a joke told in the Yellowhammer State. A man is talking football with his preacher.

"Aren't you upset," the man asks, "about all this money that people are giving to the athletic department at Alabama?"

"Upset?" the preacher replies. "I'm encouraged by it."

"Why?"

"Because," the preacher says, "it's good for people to give to their religion."

Raw numbers testify to the fervor of that religion. For 13 consecutive years Birmingham has been ESPN's No. 1 market for college football games. For four straight years Alabama has led the SEC in average attendance—101,505 in 2013—and for 15 consecutive years the SEC has been the top-drawing conference in the nation. (Its stadiums were filled, overall, to 99% capacity in 2013.) And Alabama fans put their money where their faith is: According to Alabama author Warren St. John, in his book *Rammer Jammer Yellow Hammer*, the state is second only to Nevada in the amount of money its citizens bet on sports (college football being, of course, the most popular), never mind the fact that in Alabama, unlike Nevada, gambling on sports is illegal.

If this deeply rooted passion had a formative moment, it is commonly identified by Crimson Tide historians as Jan. 1, 1926, when Alabama traveled to the Rose Bowl to play Washington, at the time a rare trip to the West Coast for a Southern team. After falling behind 12–0 at halftime, Tide coach Wallace Wade snarled in the locker room, "And they told me Southern boys could fight." Alabama stormed back in the second half. When the Tide's Johnny Mack Brown caught a 59-yard touchdown pass from Grant Gillis in the third quarter, Alabama seized a 14–12 lead. The teams then traded touchdowns. With a few minutes remaining and Washington trailing 20–19, the Huskies had driven deep into Alabama territory when Herschel Caldwell intercepted a pass thrown by UW's George (Wildcat) Wilson. The Crimson Tide had won their first national title.

"Alabama Wins" zipped through the wires and blared from radios, setting off a wild celebration in Dixie; it was then that football first became fundamental to Alabama culture. Football was something Alabamians could point to and proudly say they did better than anyone else in America, even as the rest of the country mocked the state for wrongheaded racial relations and Civil War–era backward thinking.

The 1926 Rose Bowl is incorporated into the school's fight song ("Fight on, fight on, fight on, men! Remember the Rose Bowl, we'll win then"), and stories of that game have been passed down with reverence through the generations in Alabama: how great-granddaddy sat next to his radio in his farmhouse outside

Horseshoe Bend and listened the day the Crimson Tide punched the rest of the country squarely in the nose. Many Southerners still clung to the notion that one Confederate soldier was worth three Union soldiers on the battlefield. This game confirmed in the minds of many Alabamians that their state still produced the toughest, roughest young boys in the land.

Young Paul Bryant had never listened to a radio broadcast of a college football game before that New Year's Day in 1926, but he wasn't about to miss this one. The 12-year-old sat excitedly in front of a radio in Fordyce, Ark., awaiting the Rose Bowl kickoff. Bryant was still learning to play the game of football, and now he wanted to know how a Southern team would hold up against the West in a big game like the Rose Bowl. Like millions across the South, Bear leaned into the radio speaker and strained to hear the calls of the action through the rise and fall of the crowd noise. The announcers' words transfixed young Bryant: images of hard hits, dashing runs and crowd-pleasing touchdowns played across his mind. And after the game, of course, he dreamed of playing for Alabama.

That Rose Bowl inspired an affection among Tide fans that would only intensify over time. Alabamians could, can and always will find comfort in their Crimson Tide, in how their boys can achieve great things and make an entire state feel superior, even if only in football. And those players, and their coaches, became larger than life, each triumph a validation of each fan, heroes not just admired but loved.

AS MUCH as any person in America, Mike Slive has witnessed and analyzed the devotion to college football in Alabama and the South. With an unlit cigar dangling from his lips, Slive sat in his spacious second-floor office in the SEC headquarters in downtown Birmingham (the tornado had missed the building by less than five miles); he was recalling for a visitor the beginnings of his job. Before being hired as SEC commissioner in July 2002, Slive had been the commissioner of Conference USA. While considering the SEC position, he phoned another commissioner who had roots in the South and asked him about the job. "The difference between being the commissioner of the SEC and what the rest of us do," the fellow said, "is that in the SEC it's a 24/7, 365-days-a-year job. The rest of us can take a break at times. You can't. The fans there are just different than anywhere else."

This was new territory for Slive, who had spent time as a judge in New Hampshire (where college sports barely registered) and as a partner in a law firm in Chicago (where professional sports ruled). Still, the silver-haired, professorial Slive loved a challenge, so he accepted the offer. Now he spends many autumn Saturdays watching every SEC game from a command center in the conference headquarters: a windowless room with five flat-screen televisions and several laptop computers. Slive's Saturdays typically begin at 6 a.m. with breakfast at a small diner in nearby Homewood. Then he'll be in the office by 7:00 and in his command center seat in time for the 11:00 kickoff of the day's first SEC game.

Like so many others in Alabama, Slive traces the South's deep and abiding love for football back to Jan. 1, 1926, crediting the Crimson Tide's Rose Bowl victory as the Big Bang moment when college football became ingrained in Southern life. "That game was really a statement by the South that it could compete nationally and generated a tremendous amount of pride," said Slive, sitting at a coffee table topped with a biography of Winston Churchill and the *Encyclopedia of Southern Culture*. "In the South our youngsters learn early on that competition in sports is important to family, to towns, to regions. It becomes inculcated in the children.

"Early on in my tenure I was walking on a concourse at a stadium. I saw a mom, dad and two children. I knew that in 20 years, after those children had their own children, the same parade would continue. It's generational and so woven into the fabric of Southern culture. The DNA has been passed down from generation to generation."

JAVIER ARENAS had originally wanted to get out of Tuscaloosa soon after the storm. He had nowhere to live and seeing the massive damage everywhere he looked was only more distressing. Some of the places he liked most in T-Town—the Smoothie King, for one—had been wiped away. The city he knew seemed to have been snatched away from him. So the day after the tornado Arenas headed west, driving 11 hours to his home in Kansas City and leaving the ugliness behind. But as soon as he reached his K.C. apartment, he was overwhelmed by survivor's guilt, the feeling that he had abandoned his neighbors, his friends, his teammates, his town. Within hours he steered his black SUV to a Sam's Club, where he purchased $1,600 worth of necessities—bottled water, baby food, soap. He maxed out one credit card and put the remainder of the tab on another. The following day he returned to Tuscaloosa, and as he neared the outskirts of town, he tweeted that he would be giving away supplies outside of a mall on McFarland Boulevard. As soon as he parked, hundreds of victims, now homeless, surrounded the vehicle.

For the next few hours Arenas embraced everyone within arm's reach; he handed out supplies until his SUV was empty. There were no cameramen, no p.r. reps, no agents, just Arenas. And when he had no more food or water to give them, the people stayed to talk to him. They had no notion of what to do or where to go, so for these few minutes, being close to an Alabama football player—a player who, 16 months earlier, had helped the Tide win a national title—was a welcome distraction. They just wanted to talk football, and Arenas happily complied. He told them about the punts he returned for touchdowns, about playing for Saban and even about the lows of the 2007 season, his sophomore year, when the Tide lost to Louisiana-Monroe and finished the season 7–6. The wide eyes and smiles that Arenas saw around him told him that these stories were helping everyone escape briefly into memory, to a time when what mattered most was Crimson Tide football.

After he finally left the mall parking lot, Arenas drove around town. He spotted a man searching the debris of his house, and Arenas stopped to check on him. The man was looking for photo albums with pictures of his wife and daughter; both had been killed. Arenas talked with people whose crumpled cars were now parked in their kitchens. He asked people what they needed, then went to stores and returned with the requested supplies.

Arenas visited National Guard security positions throughout the city. "I never realized that as a former Alabama football player, I can bring a smile to someone's face just by hugging them," Arenas said as he signed an Alabama T-shirt at the armory in Northport. "That's why I've been going to see the National Guard guys. I'm just trying to brighten their days."

"I can't emphasize enough how much seeing Javier boosts the morale of everyone here," said Sergeant Stocks. "I guess you could say that's the power of Alabama football. It's going to take a ton of hard work to get this town back in championship form."

Upon leaving the armory, Arenas donned a Kevlar helmet and climbed into a tan military Humvee. It was nearly nightfall now, and he was riding into one of the hardest-hit sections of town, which essentially was under martial law. A curfew was in effect for the area known as Brookwood, and only military and police vehicles were allowed to enter.

Looking out the window of the Humvee, Arenas saw emptiness where bustling neighborhoods had once stood. In the emerging darkness he could make out the plaintive messages that had been spray-painted on pieces of plywood: PLEASE SEND HELP! And he could faintly see items randomly littered on the ground: a child's shoe, a cracked family portrait, the real evidence of shattered lives. Arenas rode in silence, unable to utter a word.

"This group that we're going to see has been out in the woods and in the rubble looking for bodies all day," said an Army lieutenant in the vehicle with Arenas. "They're tired but dedicated. We'll get the job done."

They pulled into the parking lot at Tuscaloosa County High School. Hundreds of National Guard troops were bedded down in the gymnasium, their lives reduced to three activities: eat, sleep, search. At least six people were still missing in the nearby area. As a recording of the Bama fight song blared over the P.A. system, Arenas walked through the door of the gym wearing his number 28 Alabama jersey. The troops pushed aside their dinner—or rather, their military-issued MREs (Meals Ready To Eat)—and swarmed to greet him.

A female guardsman, severely fatigued and emotionally drained, nearly collapsed into Arenas's arms. "We almost feel guilty sleeping," she said, "knowing that there are people out there that need us right now. But seeing you just makes me feel so much better. I just love you, and I love Alabama football."

The unit chaplain grabbed a microphone. "Javier, thank you so much for taking the time to visit and encourage our National Guard troops," he said. "Together, Tuscaloosa will overcome the devastation of this tornado. May God bless and lead you."

When Arenas eventually waved goodbye, the troops whistled and cheered, like fans at a game. He stepped back into the Humvee and continued to tour Brookwood, hoping and praying to find one of the missing. But no such luck. *Maybe tomorrow*, he thought. *We'll continue the search tomorrow.* But tomorrow came and went, and with it his hope of finding a survivor.

CHAPTER 11

The Mantra

NICK SABAN'S first season at Alabama in 2007 had fallen off a cliff when the Tide dropped four of their last five games. Saban and his staff feared that the losses on the field would translate into losses on the recruiting trail. One of the players whom Saban and his staff were targeting especially aggressively that year was a kid named Barrett Jones, an offensive lineman in Germantown, Tenn. He was unlike any 17-year-old Saban had ever come across.

Growing up in Germantown, a suburb of Memphis, Jones was a natural—with the violin. He'd started playing at age three; two years later little Barrett was toting his violin to nursing homes, where he'd make music with members of his church. Barrett liked sports too, but his parents wouldn't let him play football until sixth grade; so he continued to perform in front of crowds at hospitals and weddings, wowing them with his violin. If you hummed a tune to Barrett, he could play it just a few minutes later. His parents and instructors believed he could one day be a professional if he stuck with it.

"The violin taught Barrett discipline because he practiced one hour a day and it taught him how to perform in front of people," says his father, Rex, who played basketball at Alabama under Wimp Sanderson. "He was never fazed by crowds, and he still isn't."

In the classroom Jones was an intensely inquisitive student, repeatedly asking questions from his front-row desk. His third-grade teacher once joked to his parents that she needed to hire an assistant whose full-time job would simply be to answer Barrett's queries. "Barrett always wanted to know how things worked and why," says his father. "For Barrett, the more you throw at him, the better."

In sixth grade Jones put on a football uniform for the first time to play for his middle school team. Bighearted and smiling off the football field, he relished the physical contact between the lines and was as ruthless as anyone on his squad. When he blocked an extra point in his first season of action, he broke his arm. "Dad, I'm not going to miss any games because of a broken bone," Barrett said. And he didn't: The next week, with his arm in a cast wrapped in a bulky protective pad, Barrett was back on the field.

In seventh grade he grew eight inches and wore size-15 shoes. By eighth grade he stood 6' 3" and weighed 200 pounds. He could explode vertically to dunk a basketball and move laterally with agility and power to dominate football games as an offensive tackle and defensive end. He loved the game, and by the time he reached Evangelical Christian School, he stopped playing the violin to concentrate on football. ("I don't even like to tell my teammates that I ever played," he would later admit, "because of the grief they give me.") As a senior Jones was ranked by SuperPrep as the 20th best offensive lineman in the nation and No. 1 overall player in Tennessee.

Nearly every school in the SEC offered Jones a scholarship. He was still considering a number of options when he first walked into Saban's office in the fall of 2007. Saban knew all the finer points of Jones's biography, as if a private investigator had handed him a dossier on everything Jones had ever done in his life. Saban had all the details: from Jones's violin-playing to the mission trips he'd taken with his family to placing 15th in a national Scrabble competition as an eighth-grader. The coach laid out his detailed vision of how he planned to build the Tide into a power. Jones was mesmerized.

"Coach Saban was very determined and very adamant that he was going to turn this program around," Jones would say later. "I wanted to be a part of that. It took some faith to come to Alabama back then. I remember watching them go 7–6 and thinking, 'Whoa, is that where I want to be?' But after meeting with Coach Saban, I knew."

JONES WAS out on the streets of Tuscaloosa at the first blush of sunlight, some 36 hours after the tornado had struck. He was riding shotgun in a souped up golf cart known as a Gator, with a chain saw lying across his big thighs. Joined by his younger brother Harrison, they drove block to block; wherever they found a downed tree that had barricaded a street or cleaved a house, the 6' 5", 305-pound Barrett would yank the chain saw to life and go to work, slicing the trunks and branches into movable pieces.

As the Jones brothers moved through the destruction, amid a steady flow of ambulances carrying the dead and wounded away, Barrett could not help but be reminded of Haiti a year earlier, in the spring of 2010, when he'd traveled on a mission trip during spring break to the earthquake-ravaged island. What he'd seen in that far-away country was now happening, unbelievably, in his own town.

Five days after shaking the hand of President Barack Obama at a White House ceremony to honor Alabama's 2009 title team—the President even said, "Roll Tide"—Jones had flown to Haiti. The January earthquake had left more than 230,000 dead and 1.5 million homeless.

As a boy Barrett had gone with his family to Honduras for missionary work. There he saw horrendous poverty: homes that were nothing more than boards, people wearing mere scraps for clothing, children too weak to crawl out of makeshift beds. That experience, helping those people in even the smallest ways, was powerful for Jones. When the chance came, he felt compelled to go to Haiti.

Jones and six friends boarded a plane in Memphis and flew into the Dominican Republic. From there they rode in taxis for three hours to the Haitian border, then climbed into the back of an old landscaping truck. As the truck banged over muddy, rutted roads, Jones and his buddies bounced up and down, all the while trying to keep their bags and themselves from flying around. After eight bumpy hours, in 100° heat, their Alabama T-shirts soaked in sweat, they reached their destination: Pignon, Haiti, which had been transformed into a refugee camp for children who had lost their families in the earthquake.

Jones, wearing his crimson-colored "A" baseball cap pulled down tight on his head, went to work. On the first day he and his friends built showers, dug ditches for plumbing and laid pipes. In the evening Jones served meals of goat meat, which he ate every night as well. But what he most enjoyed was sitting with the children—sometimes as many as six at once would crawl aboard his ample lap—and listening to their stories. Jones was a giant to these orphaned boys and girls, but they quickly grew comfortable with him; he taught them the card game Uno and brought smiles to their faces. Sometimes he could give them a silly look and watch the sadness magically melt from their eyes.

Midway through the trip Jones and his buddies had traveled to Port-au-Prince, the Haitian capital and center of destruction. They passed mountains of rubble—under which, he knew, were hundreds of lifeless bodies. Arriving at what had once been a large open field, Jones saw a city of more than 10,000 tents. "That's when a very hard reality hit me," Jones would later recall. "They lived in those tents because their houses were destroyed. It was heartbreaking."

Now Jones was again looking at whole neighborhoods in ruin, but right here in T-Town. With his brother—Harrison was also a teammate, a 241-pound tight end, not quite as big as Barrett—they moved with their chain saws from one yard to the next, the buzz of their work echoing for blocks in the otherwise eerie quiet.

Expanding his own rescue operation, Jones organized a group of other football players to take chain saws around town and cut trees. For three straight 12-hour days Jones and his teammates were fixtures in the hardest-hit areas, attacking the downed trees like a pack of Paul Bunyans. Jones cut and cut and cut some more, until he could barely lift his arms.

"It was not the textbook, safest thing to do with the chain saws, but we really felt like we had to do something meaningful to help," Jones said a few days later. "And just being seen and visible in the community was important. Alabama football is just so big here. Next season we're not going to play for ourselves, I promise you; we're going to play for Tuscaloosa. That will be the biggest motivation we've ever had, to do something special on the field for this town."

Saban's mandate had become a mantra.

IN HIS apartment at the University Downs complex on 15th Street, Courtney Upshaw, a Bama linebacker, had been hanging out with a friend on April 27 when he heard the emergency sirens wail. He walked over to his window and casually looked outside—right into the face of a monster. The tornado was directly in front of him, bearing down on the apartment. Upshaw wanted to run, but he knew he didn't have time. He and his friend jumped into the bathtub just as the twister traveled down the other side of 15th Street.

They were uninjured—the tornado had skirted their complex—but Upshaw stumbled outside into a surreal scene. People were screaming; others staggered about in a daze. The windows of his Buick LeSabre had been sucked away. Upshaw stared in disbelief down the path the tornado had cut. He couldn't recognize anything. *This is not real*, he told himself. *This can't have just happened.* He sprinted from one pile of rubble to the next, pulling victims out from under trees or the remains of their homes. At nightfall he began calling teammates, every call freighted with the fear that someone would be missing. He soon learned that every Alabama football player was accounted for—and alive. But he also found out that several people who lived near him had been killed.

During the next few days, Upshaw moved up and down the streets of his neighborhood, using his 6' 2", 265-pound bulk to push aside downed trees, lift chunks of concrete and toss aside the clods of drywall that had been the buckshot of the twister's winds. But it wasn't enough. How, he wondered, could he help in some larger way?

Upshaw had an idea. He would hold autograph sessions, and in return for his signature, he would ask for a donation, of any type or size, food, building supplies, whatever—including money. He took his idea to his hometown of Eufaula, Ala., where he had grown up in public housing, his family often struggling to get by. Eufaula is located on a lake on the Alabama-Georgia border, right in the heart of Auburn Tigers country. Upshaw set up his autograph operation at a Walmart, and a thousand people, many wearing Auburn hats, stood in line in scorching heat to get the Alabama linebacker's autograph. For more than five hours Upshaw continued to scribble his name. After the final signature he was able to fill three trucks with the donations he'd collected and send the supplies into afflicted areas.

Over the next few weeks—in places like Alexander City, Birmingham and Tuscaloosa—Upshaw signed more than 20,000 autographs. He went on local radio stations and appeared on television to ask for donations. He distributed fliers. He wound up raising more than $25,000. Near the end of the signing in Alexander City, two state troopers arrived. They informed Upshaw that once the event was over, they had been instructed to escort him to a nearby town, where Alabama governor Robert Bentley was waiting to shake the hand of the young man who had given so much to the relief effort and to T-Town.

A few weeks after the storm, Upshaw sat in a lounge in the Crimson Tide football offices. "Everyone in Tuscaloosa looks up to Alabama football players and coaches," he said. "And we know that because we live it and see it every day. So I'm using that power to help. And once the season starts, man, we are going to have an edge to us that you've never seen before. This isn't about just our team anymore."

BRANDON GIBSON had pushed himself hard. He was starting his last set of sit-ups in the Alabama weight room at Mal Moore when the sirens started to roar. Gibson continued his workout—until "it sounded like a freight train was coming right at us." Still dripping sweat, Gibson, along with several other players, had run to the front of the complex, confused and unsure what to do. They heard the howling wind and felt its battering force. For a few heartbeats, Gibson feared that the concrete walls wouldn't hold. Then, suddenly, the winds died; the tornado had missed them by less than a mile.

Gibson rushed outside; debris was falling from the sky, battering the building. He drove to his apartment, checked in with a few friends and then headed for 10th Avenue. Houses on both sides were in ruin. Gibson jumped out of his car and moved from house to house, asking if anyone needed help. A man with blood-soaked rags wrapped around his head stumbled down the street in hysterics. Gibson guided him to an ambulance.

For the next week Gibson handed out food and water to relief workers. "We as athletes need to carry a big load for this community," Gibson said several days after the twister had hit. "We have to stay strong, stay visible and let everyone know that we're here for them. This is going to take a long time to come back from, but we will. And I've already talked to a bunch of the players, and we're promising to make this a special season for the people of Tuscaloosa. We're going to make it a season that no one here will ever forget." The mantra.

In the two weeks after the storm, the Alabama athletic department had donated more than $1 million to the relief efforts. And nearly everywhere you looked throughout T-Town, there was a Crimson Tide athlete aiding in the recovery. In many ways the effort was much like Saban's coaching philosophy: Tackle one task at a time—remove a tree, console a broken survivor, bring food to a victim—and then take one step forward and confront the next job. And the next. And the next. Saban encouraged his players who stayed in Tuscaloosa to be active and to maintain a high profile.

"So many people in this town and this state identify with the football team and all of Alabama athletics," Saban said. "It's a point of pride. When we finally get to play another game, hopefully we can create a psychological escape for them, even if it only lasts a few hours. People who lost everything in the storm have repeatedly told me how much they are looking forward to our season. And that's great because it's always good to be looking ahead, especially when the immediate past has been so traumatizing."

ON THE morning of April 29, Barack Obama issued the most important military order of the first term of his presidency: He instructed his commanders to go forward with the mission to take out Osama bin Laden. A few hours later the President was aboard Air Force One on his way to Alabama. As the flight approached Tuscaloosa, Obama and his staff, looking down from the plane's windows, could see the huge swath of destruction.

After meeting with Mayor Maddox, Obama and his motorcade toured the city for two hours. When the White House had first contacted Maddox, his inclination was to continue working and forgo escorting the President during his visit. "At the time it just didn't seem important," Maddox said later. "We were so tired and focused on finding survivors, it was almost like him coming was a secondary concern. But then I saw the anguish on the President's face and how excited people who had lost everything were to see him. He genuinely made a difference that day. It was hard to believe that basically his whole presidency was hanging in the balance on what would happen with the raid on Osama bin Laden some 45 hours later."

During his afternoon tour of Tuscaloosa, the President said, "I've never seen devastation like this. We were just talking to some residents here who were lucky enough to escape alive but have lost everything. They mentioned that their neighbors had lost two of their grandchildren in the process." He went on. "The mayor said something very profound as we were driving over here. He said, 'What's amazing is when something like this happens, folks forget all their petty differences. Politics, differences of religions or race, all that fades away when we are confronted with the awesome power of nature. And we're reminded that all we have is each other.' "

The President asked Maddox to join him in the motorcade as it ferried him back to Air Force One. Inside the bulletproof SUV, Obama spoke to Maddox about the Alabama football team, noting the fact that four Tide players had just the day before been selected in the first round of the NFL draft. Maddox confessed that he didn't know that; he'd been so busy he hadn't followed that news. The President then named the four Alabama first-rounders: Marcell Dareus, Julio Jones, James Carpenter and Mark Ingram. Later, when Maddox's Blackberry rang, the President asked to see what model it was. Here, for a few minutes, Obama and Maddox were just two guys talking football and gadgets. It was the first time since he'd spotted the tornado on the traffic camera that Maddox wasn't solely focused on healing his wounded city. For the three weeks after the storm the mayor would average two hours of sleep a night.

Later that evening, CNN asked Maddox for a live interview at 9:00. He was sitting outside in the blown-away neighborhood of Cedar Crest, waiting for the cameras to roll, when something caught his attention in the distance. He looked to the southwest and saw that three homes had caught fire. The smell hovering in the air was already atrocious, a nauseating mix of spoiled food and dead animals. Maddox knew that several undiscovered bodies were likely nearby. He sat and stared, tired and alone, struck by one thought: *This must be what hell looks like.* He secured his earpiece and fingered the small microphone attached to his shirt, waiting for a faraway anchor to start asking him questions.

CHAPTER 12

A House Where None Stood

DANA DOWLING and her mother drove west in her mom's white Camry from Anniston, Ala., on Interstate 20 toward Tuscaloosa. It was late May now, and once again the Alabama sky looked sinister—dark and thick with swirling clouds. Dana felt a surge of anxiety when she saw, in her rearview mirror, a funnel drop down and kiss the earth a few hundred yards behind them, like a snake sprung suddenly from the black, churning cloud. "Please. Not again," Dana whispered.

It was only a month earlier that Dana and her family had been huddled in the laundry room of their mobile home; since then they had lived in a 28-foot RV parked in the front yard of Dana's mother's house, which the tornado had narrowly missed. Now she tried to keep the awful memories from rushing back as she raced down the interstate. Just then a commercial crackled over the radio and caught her ear. Habitat for Humanity, the voice was saying, was accepting applications from those who had lost their homes in the tornado and wanted to rebuild in Tuscaloosa. Even as the dark clouds behind seemed to stalk her, Dana felt a flutter of hope, something missing from her life for the past month. When she and her mother safely arrived in T-Town, Dana called Habitat and asked for an application.

After sending in the form, she didn't expect to hear back. How many others must be doing the same thing? But days later she felt like she'd won the lottery: A worker from the organization called and told her that Habitat—together with several other nonprofit groups, including Saban's Nick's Kids Fund—would build a new home for the Dowlings down the road from where their trailer had once stood. Hers would be the first of dozens of houses that Habitat and other organizations would ultimately erect in the area. The call was life-changing. As she said joyfully to her husband, "We won't have to live in my mother's front yard for the rest of our lives!"

Ground was broken at 4214 5th Street NE in July, less than three months after the tornado hit their trailer. Two weeks after the first shovels dug into the dirt, a group of burly young men walked onto the site. As Dana greeted these fresh-faced college kids, her eyes were drawn to the biggest in the group, a hulking fellow who had to weigh well over 300 pounds. He looked as if he could single-handedly lift a small house and set it down here on the site. He introduced himself as D.J., and Dana knew she was looking at an Alabama football player. D.J. Fluker was a lineman for the Tide and, as it turned out, seven other Alabama players were with him, including AJ McCarron and Barrett Jones. Also in the group were a half-dozen players from Kent State—Nick Saban's alma mater and the team Alabama was scheduled to play in less than two months in the 2011 season opener. The Kent State boys had driven 12 hours from Ohio to assist in the rebuilding of T-Town.

Dressed in an Alabama warmup suit, Fluker lumbered forward with the smile of a friendly giant and gently hugged Dana, telling her they were here to help. Dana hugged him tighter, filled with gratitude.

Fluker understood better than many the despair the Dowlings

had been feeling since April 27. He might not have even been in Tuscaloosa if it hadn't been for another natural disaster.

In 2005, Fluker lived in the Lower Ninth Ward of New Orleans. A 14-year-old, D.J. was a big LSU fan and daydreamed of playing in Baton Rouge, running into Tiger Stadium on Saturday nights in front of 92,000 screaming fans in the Bayou. In late August he was preparing for his freshman season of high school football in New Orleans, but on the 27th a hurricane that had been named Katrina was bearing down on the Gulf Coast. D.J. and his family drove to Mobile to stay with family members. Fluker expected to be back in the Lower Ninth within a week; instead, two days later, Katrina demolished his family's house. "We lost everything, absolutely everything," Fluker says. "We tried to go back home, but there was five feet of water in it. I basically was displaced until I came to Tuscaloosa for school, and that was a long time. My mom and I lived in a little trailer for a while and then an apartment. It was really hard, but it made me understand what it feels like to lose your home and all of your belongings. It just, just . . . *destroys* you, basically."

D.J. spent his senior year of high school at Foley (Ala.) High, where he developed into one of the most sought-after recruits in the nation. Rivals.com named him the country's top offensive tackle prospect. Landing Fluker was one of Saban's top priorities for his 2009 recruiting class, and Saban and members of his staff frequently flew to Mobile to spend time with the five-star player. But Fluker didn't need to be sold on the virtues of Alabama. He canceled a recruiting trip to Baton Rouge—his dream of playing for the Tigers died at the same time Katrina blew up his life. He signed with the Crimson Tide, eager to start a new life in a new town.

In the summer of 2010, D.J. traveled to New Orleans to see where his old house in the Lower Ninth Ward had once stood. He was greeted by a vacant lot. As he walked around the bald patch of land, he remembered his boyhood—especially the stories his grandparents would tell about how things used to be in the Big Easy—and he felt a rising anger that Katrina had stolen precious years from his youth. The hurricane had forced him to grow up too soon: living homeless, sleeping some nights in a car with his mother, not knowing where they would be a night later. As he looked around the empty lot, he was calmed by one thought: He'd survived the worst, and Mother Nature would never take such a vicious swing at his life again. It couldn't happen twice.

AS THE dangerous weather approached Tuscaloosa on April 27, D.J. left his apartment. He'd been dozing on his couch when he got an urgent text message from his friend and teammate Chance Warmack: *Come to the academic center now. It's safer here.* He joined several teammates in the basement of Paul W. Bryant Hall, the athletic department's academic center and one of the most secure buildings on campus.

After the twister spun violently through the city, D.J. and his teammates left the academic center and immediately headed toward Fluker's apartment, which they calculated had been in the direct path of the tornado. As they hurried along, they frequently stopped to check mounds of rubble for signs of life.

He couldn't get to his apartment that evening; police had cordoned off the area. Two days later he finally inspected what was left of the place he called home. There was nothing there; the skeletal remains of the building were five blocks away. Fluker searched for his possessions, looking for clothes, photos, anything. He only found one item: his pair of size-22 penny loafers. "I've learned twice that everything can be taken away from you at any time," Fluker would say. "The only way to get through it, I've found, is to help others. That's it."

On the sunbaked July afternoon less than three months later, D.J. wrapped his arms around Dana Dowling, who at that moment surely must have been the happiest Alabama fan on the planet. Fluker and the other players, none with much experience in construction, went to work. With the midday temperature pushing into triple digits, it took only minutes for all of them to be soaked in sweat. They steadily moved lumber, pounded nails, poured concrete, installed insulation. Over the next six weeks the players would return again and again to the construction site. So would members of the gymnastics team—whom Bob Dowling swore were the strongest at the task of house building—along with rowers, soccer players and scores of other Crimson Tide athletes. The Alabama cheerleaders pitched in as well; the female cheerleaders would stand on the shoulders of the male cheerleaders to paint the higher reaches of the single-story structure.

Dana called herself the Water Nazi because she constantly reminded the athletes to drink. The three-bedroom, two-bath house was rising in a wide-open, treeless field, so there was no shade—the tornado had done its work on the site. During the storm, a life-less body had been thrown into the field nearby; when the corpse was later identified, it was someone who didn't even live in the area. Down the way a brick home more than a century old now sat alone in the middle of the block. On the few days that rain fell, the construction site turned into a massive mud pit of red clay. On those wet afternoons Dana laughed at the sight of Fluker, always covered in so much red clay that he looked like Bigfoot after a mud bath.

On a sizzler of a morning in mid-July, a rumor circulated among the four to five dozen volunteers—some of them football players, many of them not—that Coach Saban was going to stop by. No one knew for certain if it was true, but the mere prospect was refreshing, like being promised a glass of cold sweet tea. For the rest of the day the workers glanced occasionally over their shoulders to see if the coach would appear.

The hours ticked by. Saban and his wife had pledged to build 13 new houses in the Tuscaloosa area—one for each of the national titles the Crimson Tide had won. But now the coach was running late. He'd spent the afternoon in Hoover, near Birmingham, at the annual SEC Media Days event. Saban was the star attraction on Day 3. He'd arrived early, slipped through a private entrance, walked through a restaurant kitchen in the hotel, trying everything he could to avoid the dozens of television cameras that had staked the place out. With a state trooper by his side, he strolled past a crush of iPhone-wielding Alabama fans—one wearing a T-shirt that read I HATE AUBURN— then rode up an escalator and walked into a second-floor ballroom. He stepped to the dais and addressed more than a thousand reporters. They asked Saban about the state of his team, which had just been picked by the media as the favorite to win the SEC. His reply was typically bland, an answer without answering. "It's always a challenge to have the right kind of team chemistry, for your team to have the right stuff," Saban responded. "I feel like this team has the ingredients for that, but that's always the challenge because the consistency and performance is what helps you have successful seasons, especially in a league that is as challenging as ours in terms of the number of good teams."

Reporters pressed Saban about who would be his starting quarterback—AJ McCarron or Phillip Sims—and whether his team had gotten over the 28–27 loss to Auburn in the Iron Bowl the previous fall. Saban's answers were clipped; he was in a hurry to leave the press conference. There were workers and a family back home he wanted to visit.

SABAN HADN'T said so to the media, but he had a very good feeling about the chemistry that was developing among his players, many of whom had spent their summer working side by side in the relief efforts. As Barrett Jones put it to a reporter a few weeks later, "You form a bond and brotherhood that has nothing to do with sports when you're out working your tail off and helping other people for 12 hours a day. That level of camaraderie just doesn't exist if you don't go through what we as players went through and what this whole town went through. There's no question it's brought us closer and made us even more determined."

After driving the 50 miles from Hoover through the fading twilight, Saban arrived at 4214 5th Street NE, still dressed in the tan jacket, white shirt and red tie he'd worn at his press event. For the volunteers, this was a moment worth waiting for; having been assured Saban was on the way, two dozen members of the construction team had stayed an hour and a half past the normal quitting time in order to see Saban. Dana Dowling was thrilled to get 90 minutes of extra work from her crew.

Saban stepped from his car and waved to the volunteers; he hugged Dana and shook the hand of everyone there, each time holding his vice-like grip an extra beat and looking each worker squarely in the eye. He offered a few words about teamwork, about overcoming adversity, then inspected the frame of the house. Saban had stopped by the house several weeks earlier, when some of the Alabama players were helping clear debris in order for the foundation to be poured. He would stop by again and again, sometimes just driving by on his way to work—Dana knew what his car looked like—to check on the progress. When he did visit, often unannounced, he usually said very little. But his presence always made a deep impression on 13-year-old Marilyn Dowling, who enjoyed organizing the players into task teams during the building of her house. Marilyn loved to joke to her friends that she regularly had Coach Saban over to her new house.

Today, Saban posed for pictures, then slid back into his car. The visit was brief, but for the Dowlings and everyone else there, it felt as if the coach were on the front lines rebuilding with them.

THE CEREMONY was finally held on a steamy Saturday morning, Aug. 6, at Coleman Coliseum. Originally scheduled to take place in May, graduation exercises at the University of Alabama had been delayed in the wake of the storm as school administrators had canceled final exams and encouraged students to either help clean up Tuscaloosa or return to their hometowns. Now, in the gymnasium

that hosts basketball games and gymnastics meets, university president Robert Witt presided over the handing out of more than 3,000
undergraduate diplomas to young men and women draped in black
gowns adorned with red script A's.

The president also awarded undergraduate degrees post-
humously to the six students who had died in the storm: Scott
Atterton, Danielle Downs, Ashley Harrison, Melanie Nicole Mixon,
Morgan Sigler and Marcus Smith. For each of the six, Witt called
out the names of the parents, who stood to applause. Darlene and
David Harrison, wearing badges with a photo of Ashley, eventually
stepped onto the stage to accept the diploma for their daughter;
Darlene cradled it to her chest.

Before the tornado, Ashley had been studying for the LSAT, with
designs on going to law school. At the time of the storm she was
only days away from leaving Tuscaloosa to go to Washington, D.C.,
for an internship with an international bank; her future was brim-
ming with possibility. After the graduation ceremony, Darlene tried
to explain what the diploma meant. "This erases the horrible receipt
of the death certificate, which is the worse certificate a parent could
ever receive," she said. "We're just very fortunate that she touched
our lives, that God gave her to us. We didn't know that the best she
could be was an angel."

LATE THE next day, on a Sunday afternoon, a crowd formed outside
the wrought-iron gate 46 at Bryant-Denny Stadium. When it swung
open at about 4:30, thousands—young and old, fit and flabby, true
believers all—stormed inside the portal, through the concrete under-
belly passage of the stadium and rushed onto the field. Underneath a
tar-bubbling August sun, they hurried across the lush grass to the opposite end of the stadium. Most were carrying something: footballs,
helmets, T-shirts, posters, anything that could be written on. Several
carried babies. They came from the Gulf Coast, the Black Belt and
Sand Mountain, from big cities like Birmingham and dots on the map

like Bear Creek, from mansions in Mountain Brook and from trailers in Mulga. They knew that at the end of their 100-yard dash awaited their prize: Nick Saban.

It was the annual Fan Day at Alabama, and the first, of course, since the tornado barely 90 days earlier. This was an afternoon to focus on the future, on the excitement and promise of a new season. And so they ran to Saban. The coach, wearing a white shirt with an Alabama logo, sat behind a table in the far end zone, a black Sharpie in his hand, ready to sign autographs. Within minutes hundreds crowded around him. Many of those nearest to him looked awe-struck, wide-eyed. Saban's players sat at tables along the sideline. Both the coach and his team signed their names on every conceivable sort of Alabama memorabilia and posed for photos, hundreds and hundreds of them.

ON THE first day of September, two days before Alabama's home opener against Kent State, a dedication ceremony was held at the Dowlings' new house. Saban and his wife were given a personal tour by the Dowlings, who showed them every inch of every room, including a "safe room" in the interior of the house that was built to withstand a tornado. "Isn't this a wonderful idea," Saban said, so impressed with the safe room that he'd called Terry in from the kitchen to admire it.

Then, with Saban and several of his players standing in the front yard, Pastor Kelvin Croom of College Hill Baptist Church spoke to the gathering. "I anticipate the Alabama nation coming together," he said, "and remembering how good God was to bring us through such a powerful storm. We, of course, will remember those who lost their lives. They will always be a part of us. Healing has to occur. What is a better way to heal than with Alabama football?"

CHAPTER 13

Encouraging Words

THE LIMP, the bandage on his right ankle, the cut above his left eye, the gash on his right thigh—they were all gone. The physical wounds from his day of terror had healed. But what was most striking about Carson Tinker, four months after the tornado, was that the sadness in his eyes, embedded there in the weeks after the storm, had vanished. When he walked through the school's football offices just days before the season opener, his face was aglow and his smile was back.

"I don't allow myself to have bad days anymore," Tinker said. "When people hear my story and see what I've been through, maybe they think I should be moping around and have this poor-me attitude. But I'm the complete opposite. When I see the huge banners around town that say WE'RE COMING BACK, it fires me up. Because we are."

With the 2011 season about to start, Tinker was like Tuscaloosa itself: recovering from injury and looking ahead. The twister's final toll, in the Tuscaloosa area alone, had been monstrous. Categorized as a massive EF4 storm, it had killed 53 (including the six students), destroyed or damaged close to 6,000 homes and businesses, and left 7,000 without jobs.

"Those few minutes that the tornado was on the ground changed the city forever," said Mayor Maddox as he stood in the shambles of the neighborhood of Forest Lake. "About 85% of all the debris has been removed, and that's enough to fill Bryant-Denny Stadium from the bottom of the field to the top of the lights three times. Everyone here is really looking forward to the season opener. Not only will it have an overall economic impact of bringing $17 million to the city, but it will also have a huge psychological impact. It will let us know that it's O.K. for us to live our lives again. For a few hours we can have some fun and enjoy ourselves."

Tinker had rehabbed in Birmingham with the renowned Dr. James Andrews, who declared the long snapper 100% healthy for preseason practice. And even in the drudgery of two-a-days, Tinker enjoyed himself, appreciating every drill as if it were a smell-the-roses moment. One afternoon at the end of practice, cornerback Dee Milliner caught up with Tinker; he knew that Carson had been speaking at churches, seeking to inspire others with his message of resilience. Milliner marveled at Tinker's irrepressible spirit. Reticent and soft-spoken by nature, Tinker often said that he didn't ask to be put in this position, but now that the storm had given him a voice, he felt obligated to use it.

"I couldn't do what you're doing," Milliner said.

"Dog," Tinker replied, "it could have been any of us."

On a Sunday evening, Aug. 14, the first day Nick Saban had given his players off since preseason drills had begun on Aug. 5, Tinker drove to Arab, Ala. Though weary from nine straight days of hard practice in the heat, and while most of his teammates were relaxing in the air-conditioned cool of their apartments and dormitories, Tinker felt energized. Dressed in a cream-colored blazer and open-collared white shirt, Tinker was introduced to the crowd of 900 at the Arab High School auditorium for a faith-based service called "A Community Event—Life After the Storm." With a wireless microphone in hand, Tinker recalled the moment his life was torn apart. "On April 27, God took everything from me," he said in a steady voice. "He took my girlfriend, he took my house, and he took my dogs. I remember as soon as I got out of the hospital, I was at my parents' house, and I remember thinking, O.K., God, where do we go from here?"

Tinker explained he'd found direction in the Bible, in the book of Luke, where he read verses about a woman who'd suffered a disease for years, desperate for a cure but unable to find one. "But she reached out and touched Jesus, and he healed her," Tinker told the crowd. "His power left him and touched her and healed her. If you reach out to Jesus, he will heal you. If he can heal this woman, I know he can heal me. . . . God has a purpose for everyone who was affected by the storm."

When Carson finished his speech, the audience rose in enthusiastic applause. He shook hands and shared hugs, then drove the two hours back to Tuscaloosa, looking forward to another brutal practice session in the morning.

Tinker had worried that when preseason workouts began, the coaches would treat him differently, deferring somehow to his grief. His fears were allayed at an early practice when he was yelled at for missing an assignment on special teams. The tongue-lashing felt good, like he was back, one of the guys again.

All his teammates knew the grim details of Tinker's tragedy, yet none ever heard him ask for any special treatment or to be excused from a workout or practice. He was just the same old Carson: quiet, determined—and grinning. "Carson walks around here with a smile on his face every day," said Brandon Gibson after an August practice. "He's an example of coming back and being strong. I can't tell you how important that is for all of us, seeing that nothing can knock Carson down. We draw on his courage and his strength. If you're struggling at practice, think of Carson. If you can get that extra rep in, think of Carson. He's an inspiration."

Saban could certainly see it, and he understood that Carson had both a reassuring and motivating effect on his teammates: If Tinker was O.K., then all the rest of us will be O.K.

"Knowing what Carson has been through in terms of loss personally, the players have a tremendous amount of respect for him for what he's done," Saban said after a practice. "It's very inspirational to a lot of us to see him overcome that kind of adversity and accomplish his goals." It was no wonder to the coach that the preseason practices were as intense and focused and sharp as any he could remember.

For Tinker, this was all part of the healing. "I've been looking forward to getting back out and playing another game for a long time," he said before the opener. "It's hard to put it into words how much it means to me. I know it will mean a lot to Tuscaloosa, and we're going to do everything in our power not to let this town down. They've certainly been there for me, and now we get a chance to be there for them and show them how much they mean to us. It's a huge motivation for all of us. I'm ready. The team's ready. And I know the town is ready."

At a candlelight vigil a month after the tornado, held on an outdoor stage behind City Hall, Mayor Maddox saw Tinker for the first time since the twister. They embraced tightly. Since the storm, Maddox had not yet allowed himself to cry, but as he held Carson, he came close. "I can't wait for that first game," Maddox said softly.

That evening at the vigil, at precisely 5:13 p.m., a video of the tornado was projected on a giant screen. Tinker sat with his parents and Ashley Harrison's grandparents. Behind them sat Shannon Brown and Ashley Mims. It was the first time since April 27 that Ashley had seen this footage, and she had to cover her eyes. It was still too soon.

At the conclusion of the video, following a moment of silence, the names of those lost were read aloud. When the ceremony was over, Ashley walked up to Carson. "I'm Loryn Brown's mama," she told him. The two spoke for a few moments, then Carson, misty-eyed, wrapped his arms around her, a long, tender hug. "You're so strong," Carson whispered in Ashley's ear. "I'm so sorry for your loss."

"I'm sorry for your loss, Carson," Ashley replied. "You're strong, so amazingly strong. But I'm not, Carson. I'm struggling."

"Yes, you *are* strong," Carson replied. "You are. I'm praying for you. Don't ever forget that."

The two parted, walking in separate directions. As Ashley climbed into her car to drive back to Wetumpka, she felt a curious connection to Carson. They were members of the same family now, Ashley reasoned. Loryn even looked a little like Ashley Harrison, with their long dark hair, dimpled cheeks, broad smiles. Meeting Carson had an unexpected effect on Ashley: She felt, for the first time, as if the pain was finally starting to seep away, even if only barely. From the abyss of a broken heart, a tiny light appeared.

It's time to suck it up and move forward, she told herself that night on the drive home. *I can do this. I can handle this. Let's go.*

THE FIRST call came in June, less than two months after the storm. An unfamiliar number kept popping up on Ashley Mims's caller ID, and she'd always let it go to voice mail, but no message was ever left. One morning at seven she heard the phone ring again. Ashley figured it was her mother-in-law calling because no one else would phone that early, so she let it go to voice mail. Seconds later as she listened to the message, the first four words caused her to sit straight up: "This is Nick Saban."

He was calling, he said, for Parker Mims, Loryn's 12-year-old brother. "I'm just calling to talk to Parker," the coach said on the voice mail. "I would love for him to call me sometime. This is my number. I'm going out of town, but call me anytime."

Ashley had watched her son struggle with the loss of his sister. There was an 8½-year age difference between Parker and Loryn, and she was as much a maternal figure to him as a big sister. It was Loryn who cried harder than Ashley at Parker's kindergarten graduation; she was always looking out for him and offering advice. He lovingly called her Sissy. After the tornado, whenever bad weather rolled through Wetumpka, Ashley would try to comfort Parker, telling him it would be O.K. "Mama, it wasn't O.K. for Sissy because she's not coming home," he would say, each time breaking Ashley's heart.

After hearing Saban's voice on the phone, she ran to Parker's bedroom and together they listened to the message again and again. Each time Parker's eyes shone with astonishment. That evening they returned Saban's call. Parker was so nervous he wasn't sure he'd be able to talk; Saban was a near-mythical figure to Parker, and now the Alabama coach wanted to talk to *him*? Ashley dialed Saban's number and handed the phone to her son.

The coach was on the line. "It's good to hear from you, Parker. . . . I'm so sorry about your sister," Saban said. "How are you doing? . . . Are you excited for the football season?" For more than 10 minutes Parker said barely a word as Saban spoke to him. For the first time since Loryn had died, Ashley saw Parker smile. All she heard her son say was "Yes, sir," as he responded to questions, but there was no doubt the talk was having a powerful effect on her boy.

In August they followed up on Saban's invitation to Parker to attend a practice and to visit with him in his office. Ashley had Dewayne make the trip to T-Town; she couldn't bring herself to go— too many memories. She couldn't quite fathom that Loryn would have been starting school at Alabama in less than two weeks.

Parker, along with his younger sisters Anna and Holly, joined Saban in his office for 30 minutes. The coach showed them his remote control that opened and closed his door—"Pretty cool, don't you think?" Saban said—and they talked about overcoming their troubles. "Whenever you feel bad, you should try to do something positive for another person," Saban told them. "That's what I try to do, and I've found that it really helps."

After saying goodbye to the coach, the kids, and especially Parker, were beaming. It was, without question, the greatest day of Parker's young life.

NICK SABAN stood in the darkness on the patio outside the Lakeside Dining Hall in front of Palmer Lake, nestled between two campus dorms. It was six days before the opening game against Kent State. Saban looked out at thousands of students and university employees who had come together on this evening to remember the six students who'd died in the storm. Without notes, and with only a faint light illuminating the outline of his figure, Saban gathered himself. If the crowd didn't yet understand how the tornado had impacted Alabama's head coach, they were about to learn.

"Each and every one of us," he began, "has some kind of memory in our heart and mind, as our family does, of Ashley Harrison. . . . Hopefully we all have gratitude for those memories but also have a deep appreciation of life itself and an appreciation for the lives that *we* have and what we can accomplish and how we can serve others. . . . These young students [who died] should also be an inspiration to us. . . . Life is very fleeting, and a lot of people put a lot of value on things that really don't have much value, but as you get older you put value on relationships. I'm so proud to be a part of a community that took advantage of creating tremendous relationships in response to a terrible tragedy to try to help other people. . . . We should help others. We should not need a tragedy to inspire us to try to help others. We should serve other people all the time. You cannot be a leader and affect other people if you're not willing to serve other people.

"Who was the greatest leader of all time? Was it Julius Caesar because he almost conquered the world, or Alexander the Great? I would think it was probably Jesus Christ, who had no army and had no power. All he did was serve other people and set an example. . . .

"Like the movie *Saving Private Ryan*. The last scene on the bridge when Tom Hanks gets shot and Private Ryan is holding him up. What did he say? 'Earn this. Everybody made all these sacrifices for you to live. Go live a good life. Be a good father. Help other people. Accomplish something of significance. Make a difference.' And that's my message to everybody here. Make a difference.

"The spirit of this is something that is special to our team. And we're really looking forward to this season for two reasons. I think the spirit that we have at this university, and the passion we have for football, can be a little bit of a diversion to what we all have to do to continue to rebuild our community. I also think it can create a tremendous awareness on a national level for everyone who comes to see one of our games of what they might be able to do to help and serve our community. . . .

"I really do believe that our spirit as a team—and we will wear a ribbon on our helmets in all our games to honor all of those we have memorialized as well as all those who have been affected and devastated by this storm—when you see that little ribbon on our helmet, that is the spirit of our team relative to what has happened to our community. We appreciate what you do to continue to support us. Hopefully we'll be able to do something to support this community that will be of significance and help everyone's spirit in a positive way.

"We are so happy and proud to be a part of the family at the University of Alabama. I am very happy and proud to be your coach at the University of Alabama. We're looking forward to a very exciting season. God bless you, and Roll Tide."

Alabamians routinely wonder how long their coach will stay in Tuscaloosa, but to those who heard Saban on this summer night, those who felt his emotion and his desire to do something special over the coming few months, those people understood that he wasn't about to leave anytime soon. He had become too invested in the community, too attached. Alabama was sweet home.

CHAPTER 14

Kickoff

THIS WAS the moment they'd all been waiting for. Under a perfect bluebird sky, thousands of fans stood outside Bryant-Denny, and just before 10 a.m. on Sept. 3, the three buses rolled to a stop on University Boulevard. From his seat in the first row of the lead bus, Saban looked out the tinted window at the shoulder-to-shoulder crowd massed before him. He rose from his seat, the door opened, and he stepped outside. In a full-throated roar, the fans thundered a hero's welcome.

Escorted by two state troopers and carrying a brown leather shoulder bag, Saban led his team through the crowd and across the plaza: the Walk of Champions. As he neared the bronze image of himself, he grinned awkwardly at the faces before him, trying to acknowledge the rising applause of the moment; but he simply had too much on his mind to conjure a full-blown smile.

Josh Chapman and Carson Tinker—in slacks and jackets, no tie— were directly behind their coach, their unsmiling faces tight with intensity. They slapped high fives with the fans as the noise around them grew. These diehards outside the stadium always raised a racket when the buses unloaded at Bryant-Denny, but this felt different. Football was back, but to the believers who lined the plaza, it was more than that.

Saban knew this season would be unlike any he'd ever experienced, and he had addressed the issue the night before the game. Standing in a large banquet room at the Hotel Capstone, where the team was staying, Saban articulated the high stakes to his players. "We all know that we are playing for something bigger than just ourselves," he declared. "We are all in this together—coaches, players and the fans. Let's win this game—let's win *every* game—for the city. This is our purpose. 2009 was to win a championship. But now it's about winning a national championship to help the city and the entire state of Alabama."

Saban kept moving now, past the statues and toward the stadium. After all he'd experienced over the previous four months, he understood not only what his team meant to the town but also the burden this imposed. He waved a few more times to the fans then, his stone face carved with mid-game focus, disappeared into the concrete catacombs of the stadium. It was time to put all those months of preparation to the test and face the first opponent of the season. And how oddly ironic that it was Kent State, his alma mater.

ON A spring afternoon in 1973, Saban, who was about to graduate from Kent State with a degree in business, was approached by the Kent State football coach, Don James. At the time, Saban had been looking into entering a General Motors program with an eye toward owning a car dealership. But now James asked him if he would stay on as a graduate assistant with the football team. Saban was thrilled. He and Terry had married during winter break of his junior year—their honeymoon consisted of an overnight stay at a Holiday Inn in Wheeling, W.Va., and a dinner at Bob's Big Boy topped off by strawberry pie—and now Saban was waiting for his wife to finish her degree at Kent State, where they lived in married-student housing. This coaching job would allow him to earn a little money while Terry completed her studies. Plus it would buy him some time to figure out how best to work his way into the car business.

Saban excitedly phoned his father to share the news. Neither of Saban's parents had attended college, and now here was their boy, a college grad, who was going to get a paycheck to be a football coach. Saban's parents, particularly his dad, couldn't have been more proud. Big Nick's son was on his way in the world.

That fall, on Sept. 22, 1973, the Kent State football team traveled to Ohio University to play the Bobcats. With Saban on the sideline as an assistant, the Golden Flashes beat Ohio 35–7. Saban wanted to share the news with his father, but more than that, he wanted to tell Big Nick that he genuinely believed that while standing on the sideline there in Athens, Ohio, he had realized his calling, his passion: He wanted to coach football. It was as if he'd resolved the biggest question of his life, and he couldn't wait to tell his dad. Before he boarded the team bus, he phoned home and then he called the gas station, but no one was sure where Big Nick was.

After riding the bus 200 miles back to the Kent State campus, Saban got a call. The news was knee-buckling. Big Nick, at age 46, had died of a massive heart attack.

In a fog of shock, Saban and his wife headed for West Virginia.

IN THE foothills of the Allegheny Mountains, a two-lane road snakes north-south the entire length of West Virginia, curling through the heart of coal country. Stretching 281 miles, Route 19 was a road Nick had traveled frequently in his youth—either in his dad's car or by hitchhiking with locals, a common practice for the teenage Saban, especially when he needed a ride to see his girl.

Now, driving with Terry on Route 19, south toward tiny Helens Run, the road was so familiar, yet so different. At age 21 and bewildered by grief, Saban was about to make the biggest decision of his life, and he had no idea what he should do. Should he quit his job at Kent State and return home to run the family service station? Or should he continue to coach? He reached the house and parked the car.

As Nick Sr. had neared his mid-40s, he'd become somewhat overweight. A family doctor suggested that he start jogging and stop coaching. Big Nick agreed to run but not to walk away from the sidelines. "I can't," he said to the doctor about quitting coaching. "I have to do that."

On the day he died, Big Nick and his wife were driving home when Nick asked to be dropped off; he'd already run some laps at a local athletic field, but he felt like he hadn't completed his workout. He told Mary to drive on home and he'd just jog the rest of the way. Within a few hundred yards of his house, he collapsed to the ground. He later died at the hospital.

It seemed as if every kid and every parent of every kid who had ever played for Big Nick showed up for his funeral. He was buried on a hill with a tombstone featuring two black diamonds and his epitaph: NO MAN STANDS AS TALL AS WHEN HE STOOPS TO HELP A CHILD.

On the family porch with his mother after the funeral, Nick announced that he'd made his decision: He would leave Kent State and return to Helens Run to handle the day-to-day business of Saban's Service Station. He had thought it over carefully and determined that he needed to help his family. That was what sons did in rural West Virginia when their fathers passed away. It was the way of things, an order as natural as spring following winter.

His mother reacted sharply: Never would she allow that. *Never.* Her son needed to make his own mark in the world, not pick up the pieces of what Big Nick had left behind. It was firm and final: Nick and Terry would return to Kent State and pursue their own dreams, whatever they may be. Mary Saban had spoken.

The young couple dutifully returned to Ohio. In 1975, Saban was promoted to part-time coach; he stayed at Kent State through the

'76 season, when he accepted the job of outside linebackers coach at Syracuse University, the second of what would be 13 stops in his coaching career. He was a full-time football coach.

LIKE HIS father, Nick Saban is a creature of habit. It gives him comfort to know the precise contours of each hour of each day. By adhering to a strict routine at Alabama, he eliminates the need to make trivial decisions—like what to have for breakfast and lunch—allowing him more time to spend on football.

On a typical day Saban will awaken at 6 a.m., flip on the Weather Channel and, sitting with Terry, drink his coffee and eat two Little Debbie cookies for breakfast. He'll devote the mornings at the office to football issues, down to the slightest detail. He'll ask the team nutritionist, for instance, what the body-fat percentage of a certain player is and, if too high, he'll want to know what can be done to lower it. At noon he'll have lunch, the same every day: a salad of iceberg lettuce and cherry tomatoes topped with turkey slices and fat-free honey Dijon dressing served in a Styrofoam container.

(In the off-season Saban organizes an early-afternoon pickup basketball game a few times a week at Coleman Coliseum. He is the league's commissioner. "I pick the teams, so I have the best players," he says. "I also pick the guys who guard me." And he chooses the referee—himself. Not surprisingly, Saban has never fouled out.)

The middle of his days are filled with meetings with coaches and players, and the late afternoons are spent on more football tasks, typically watching film of an upcoming opponent or breaking down his own team's practice film. And at some point every day he'll focus on recruiting—sometimes 30 minutes, sometimes an hour, sometimes several hours. Saban never stops recruiting; it's a 365-days-a-year endeavor, and he's relentless. "More than any coach in America, Nick understands that the jockey doesn't carry the horse, it's the horse that carries the jockey," says Phil Savage, Saban's longtime friend. "He knows he needs talent to win, and that's why he'll never get outrecruited by anyone." Saban typically leaves the office by 10 at night.

"I used to be able to work and not sleep," he says. "When Bill [Belichick] and I were with the Browns [in the early '90s], we'd stay up past midnight, get up at six and then do it again, day after day. I don't do that anymore. Get your work done by 10, get to sleep by 11 and then you can get your work done."

When Saban goes on vacation in early summer each year, he travels to his lake house in North Georgia. It is located on the shoreline of Lake Burton on the North Carolina border, not far from where the movie *Deliverance* was filmed. This is his escape.

The place has a calming effect on him. Saban has joked that he has only three outfits that he wears at the lake—three swimsuits to go with dozens of T-shirts. He spends hours on the water in his powered pontoon boat, pulling friends and family on inner tubes and listening to The Eagles, his favorite band, as he sits at the helm. "He could spend all day and all night on his boat with The Eagles blaring out of the speakers," says a family friend. "I think it's one of the few times he can be content with simply relaxing." Still, football is never far from his thoughts; even there at Lake Burton, in his time of tranquility, Saban stays in touch with his assistants.

IT IS visible from nearly 10 miles away, rising above the Tuscaloosa skyline the way the Colosseum towered over ancient Rome. Bryant-Denny Stadium is a place so holy to Alabama fans that hundreds—perhaps thousands—have secretly scattered the ashes of loved ones on its grass field. Upon entering the stadium on game day, one is greeted by the aroma of Denny Dogs, the stadium hot dogs wrapped in a foil bag with sauerkraut and a tangy brown sauce. The vast majority of fans hold shakers of crimson-and-white streamers, which they'll wave madly all game long, making the crowd look like some kind of gigantic living red-and-white organism. When the crowd reaches full boil, jumping up and down at their bench-style seats, the concrete walkways tremble. In the skyscraping top rows of the 101,821-seat stadium—seats that are 12 stories from the field—fans follow the game with binoculars and oversized headsets tuned to the familiar and comforting voice of Eli Gold, the Tide's longtime radio announcer.

From these seats in the highest reaches of the sold-out stadium, fans there for the Kent State season opener on this sunny early September afternoon could look out and see clearly the long scar of destruction from four months earlier, the stark detritus of lives shattered and painful evidence that the rebuilding of the city had only just begun.

On the field before the game, the Alabama governor, Robert Bentley, shook hands with the first responders to the storm—police officers, firefighters and medical personnel. Then the stadium fell silent as the tornado victims were remembered. Inside the locker room Saban told his players to gather around him and take a knee. Saban's pregame speeches never last more than a few minutes; this one was shorter than usual. He delivered a simple message. "This is when it all starts," the coach told his team. "How do you want to be remembered? Play hard and play smart. Let's do this for our city, our state and our fans."

The teams ran onto the field for the opening kickoff. Photos of the starters flashed on the scoreboard; when the picture of Carson Tinker appeared, the student section roared its loudest cheer of the afternoon, and it continued for 15 seconds, rocking the stadium. It wasn't just a salute to Tinker in recognition of all that he had endured, though it certainly was that; it was also a cheer for Tuscaloosa, a signal that the people and the city were on the mend. For the fans of the Crimson Tide, just watching this resilient young man run out of the tunnel and onto the field was almost like seeing a sick loved one heal before your eyes.

The teams lined up for the opening kickoff; as Tide kicker Cade Foster made his approach to strike the ball, a sudden gust of wind knocked it off the tee, a kind of mocking reminder from Mother Nature. An uneasiness rippled through the stands as Foster re-teed the ball and booted it into the air.

From box seats given to them by Kent State, Bob and Dana Dowling hugged at the sight of that ball in the sky. Dana's smile never left her face during the 3½-hour game, relishing a dominating performance by some of the young men who had helped build her house. Alabama won 48–7. It felt to the Dowlings like they'd regained something they'd feared they might never have again: the joy of feeling normal.

Mayor Maddox, watching from his seat, felt sheer relief that his city was now basking in football. As the Tide began to pull away, he was thrilled to hear nearby fans already wondering aloud if Alabama had the talent to win another championship. It all felt so familiar to Maddox, and so deeply good. "That first game didn't build one house, or bring a business back or a loved one back, but it gave us a sense of unity," Maddox said later. "And when I went to Washington and met with FEMA, the first thing they'd say is, 'Well, your team is pretty good.' Everybody knows us because of Alabama football. Our team keeps Tuscaloosa in the national eye, which I think is one reason we didn't have a problem getting help from federal officials."

SHANNON BROWN had considered attending the season opener, but the prospect of spending game day in Tuscaloosa without his daughter was too much to handle. He watched a few minutes of the game on TV, but he didn't get a lot of enjoyment from Alabama's easy victory. Ever since Loryn's death, a question had gnawed at him day and night: Why couldn't it have been me that God took instead of Loryn? A one-time devout Christian, he'd begun to question his beliefs. Yet each night, after turning off the lights and crawling into bed, he said a quiet prayer.

Midway through the game Ashley Mims walked away from the television in her Wetumpka home. She had awakened that morning with a paralyzing thought: This was the day that Ashley was supposed to sit in the stands at Bryant-Denny for the first time as an Alabama student. She tried to watch the game, but after a while, it was too difficult. She drove to a nearby Walmart and was aimlessly walking the aisles when she realized where she needed to be instead.

She drove to the New Home Baptist Church cemetery. Wearing an Alabama T-shirt, blue-jean shorts and a pair of houndstooth rain boots that had belonged to Loryn, she walked to her daughter's graveside. Just the day before she had placed a large bouquet of red and white carnations, shaped into a large A, next to Loryn's headstone. While the game in Bryant-Denny was moving into the fourth quarter, Ashley sat alone and wept. *You should be in Tuscaloosa*, she told Loryn. *This was supposed to be your big day.*

After an hour she returned to her car. Her time at the grave site with Loryn had helped, but she still felt empty. As Ashley drove home, the sky was cloudless, the sun was bright, and the wind was calm. It was a beautiful day for football.

CHAPTER 15

The Man With The Silver Tongue

JOSH CHAPMAN bounded out of the Alabama locker room 45 minutes after the Kent State game wearing an ear-to-ear grin. Still fueled by game-day adrenaline, he rushed toward the hundreds of Tide fans pressed against a wrought-iron gate. As soon as they spotted the starting noseguard, the fans began to applaud, the noise spreading outward and growing louder. Chapman signed autographs, posed for pictures, even shook the hand of a baby. He kept telling everyone, "We got this for you, we got this for you."

Chapman hugged his mom and his uncle. Even though the game was a blowout and the outcome never in question, he was as thrilled as he'd ever been after 60 minutes of football. He boarded the team bus and rode to Mal Moore. There he told his teammates he would throw a victory party in a few hours and encouraged everyone to swing by his town house. He jumped into his truck and drove home.

Chapman fired up his backyard grill and began piling on the meat.

Dozens of his teammates showed up. The after-dinner discussion moved to the inevitable topic: What would it mean to T-Town if the Tide were to win the national championship this season, in the Year of the Tornado? "The people need us," Chapman said to wide receiver Marquis Maze. "They need us to keep balling like our lives, and *their* lives, depend on it." Chapman felt a wholly new kinship with the locals. In the hardest, hottest hours after the storm, he'd been out there in the wasteland with them.

The Tuscaloosa summer of 2011 had been a blast furnace. Temperatures routinely pushed 100° or more, and the humidity was suffocating. When Chapman walked out of his air-conditioned town house, it felt just like walking into the locker room steam bath.

He'd spent the summer outside wearing a hard hat, jeans and boots. Along with his teammates Maze, Courtney Upshaw and junior linebacker Dont'a Hightower, Chapman worked for an emergency response contractor clearing debris in the area of 15th and McFarland. From six in the morning till six in the evening, with an hour break in the afternoon to get in a weightlifting session at the athletic facility, Chapman and his football friends moved street to street in the blistering heat. The work was exhausting and often heartrending. Over and over, nearly every day, they encountered scenes like this: A woman who recognized Chapman made a beeline for him. A fallen tree had crushed her house and she'd lost everything. "If there's one thing you can do," the woman pleaded, clutching Chapman's arm, "just win for the city. We need something to get us back on our feet and make us feel good."

"Yes, ma'am, we will," Chapman said. He put his big arms around the stranger, and she began to cry. One morning Chapman loaded several dozen Alabama football shirts into the back of his truck and gave them all away in less than two hours. He felt like he was handing out hope.

A redshirt senior, Chapman had lived in Tuscaloosa for four years. The most savvy among Tide fans held him in especially high regard because he was one of Nick Saban's first recruits at Alabama, one of the first building blocks Saban had acquired to construct his new football empire.

IN THE dim light of Saban's wood-paneled corner office—the shades are usually drawn as if to conceal secrets—the coach plies his trade. Whenever a recruit walks through the thick door of the office and enters this spacious inner sanctum, Saban will first lead him to a couch. The coach has a large desk on the far side of the room, but he prefers to speak to recruits in the more comfortable setting he has arranged between his desk and the door: an overstuffed brown leather sofa and a few upholstered easy chairs that surround a coffee table.

On the coffee table is a black case with a glass cover. Inside is Saban's 2009 championship ring, and even in the soft light of the office the diamonds sparkle seductively. It is eye-catching and the first thing anyone really sees upon entering the office. "I like to keep it there for recruits to look at," Saban says with a sly smile. "Some of them kind of think it's a pretty cool thing to have."

Saban will slide into one of the chairs, look the recruit squarely in the eyes and let loose his singular brand of a well-formulated hard sell: *We will win championships here. I will prepare you for the NFL. The best come here. You'll have to earn your way onto the field as well as your right to stay on it. We have a process here. It's an everyday thing. We focus on what is directly in front of us, not end results.*

One of the first recruits to walk into that office was Josh Chapman. As a senior defensive tackle at Hoover (Ala.) High, Chapman was one of the most coveted players in the South. Scholarship offers from around the country filled his mailbox. Growing up just 50 miles from Tuscaloosa, Chapman had long wanted to play for Alabama, but former Tide head coach Mike Shula never offered him a full-ride scholarship. In July 2006, the summer before his senior year, Chapman had made a decision that he said was ironclad: He committed to Auburn.

Not six months later, in January 2007, Saban landed in Tuscaloosa to begin the job at Alabama. Less than 48 hours after his arrival, Saban phoned Rush Propst, Hoover's head coach. "Do you think," Saban asked, "that Josh Chapman would have any interest in changing his mind?"

"I don't know," Propst replied. "But you can see."

Eager to sign Chapman, and perhaps even more eager to send a message to Alabama's cross-state rival by flipping a prized recruit, Saban invited Chapman to make an official visit to Tuscaloosa. The coach could share his vision of what was in store for the Crimson Tide program; then Chapman could make an informed decision about whether Alabama was the school for him. (Or, more pointedly, whether Auburn was not.)

"All I'm asking for is a chance," Saban said.

A few days later Chapman and his mom, Theresa, made the short drive from Hoover to Saban's office. Once they were seated on the couch, Saban told Chapman that he could be part of a new dawn in Tuscaloosa, that he could be a member of a recruiting class that would begin the turning of the Tide.

Saban explained the basics of his 3–4 defense and how he had developed dozens of defensive linemen who had gone on to play in the NFL. He told Chapman he envisioned him as a noseguard and explained how absolutely vital that position was in Saban's defense. "Everything we do starts right in the middle of the line," Saban said. "The nose needs to hold the point and demand double teams. That makes the whole thing go."

Chapman was intrigued. Saban, silver-tongued and earnest in the same breath, had charmed him.

In public settings, Saban often comes across as distant and distracted, aloof. But inside his office, when he talks football philosophy, he is a different personality. His face brightens, he sits on the edge of his chair, and he speaks with increasing animation, like an excited English professor teaching his favorite Shakespearean play.

When Saban gets a recruit into his office, each sell session he delivers comes off as the most important and urgent of his career. Chapman listened, somewhat thunderstruck: He saw Saban's excitement, felt his intensity and marveled at his knowledge. It didn't take long for Chapman to be convinced that Saban was very likely his best ticket to an NFL contract. Goodbye, Auburn.

"I was like, Wow, he really, really knows his stuff and really loves what he's doing," Chapman says. "My word is important to me, but playing for Coach Saban was something I couldn't pass up. So I changed my mind."

As a freshman, Chapman played only three games during the disappointing 7–6 season of 2007 because of a shoulder injury; he was awarded a medical redshirt. But even with Chapman's limited action it was easy to see that Saban had scored a recruiting coup and a centerpiece for his defense.

Unlike some college coaches who restrict the access of NFL scouts on campus, Saban encourages them to come to Tuscaloosa and watch Alabama's practices and games. (Saban temporarily banned NFL scouts from practices in 2010 because he wanted the NFL to address the issue of unscrupulous agents who were contacting his players; after he felt his point was made, he lifted the ban.) Saban *wants* his players to know that the NFL is watching; not only does it heighten the tempo and focus in practice, but it also generates additional buzz about his program. Saban wants the word to spread from the Carolinas to California that NFL scouts are fixtures on the Tuscaloosa campus.

Indeed, one of Saban's most important pitches to recruits is that Alabama plays NFL-style offense and defense. To recruits who play offense, Saban will remind them—repeatedly—that they'll spend three or four years at Alabama learning a system that they'll likely play at the next level.

But it is defense that is Saban's specialty, his primary passion. His 3–4 defense is as nuanced and varied and complicated as any in the NFL. When Saban was at LSU he began one season by naming his various blitzes after states, but he had to abandon that nomenclature because he ran out of states. At Alabama the defensive playbook is thicker than the Tuscaloosa phone book.

"It's an aggressive, attacking defense," says one NFL coach familiar with Saban's system, "that overloads sides and brings pressure from all sides. They change coverages and blitzes based on motions and formations. Most defensive coaches don't want to run that defense due to its exposure to potential big plays. But it punishes QBs and creates turnovers. It also allows defensive players to play with a chip on their shoulder. They can bring the heat on every play."

NICK SABAN didn't learn his frowning, exasperated visage from Bill Belichick, but shared football DNA can surely be found in the genetic codes of the two men. Perhaps the most important year in Saban's coaching life was 1991, when he left his job as the head coach at the University of Toledo to become the defensive coordinator for Belichick, who had just been hired as the new head coach for the Cleveland Browns.

Saban had become friends with Belichick in 1982 when Saban was an assistant coach at the U.S. Naval Academy, as was Steve Belichick, Bill's father. Nick and Bill, very close in age (and both, incidentally, of Croatian descent), were obsessed with the technical arcana of football and immediately clicked, forming a close personal relationship and developing an easy rapport that, outside their own friendship, was rare for either of them.

The day that Saban told his Toledo players he was heading to Cleveland, he cried for the first time since his father had died, 18 years earlier. "The opportunity to be a coordinator with an NFL franchise," he explained at a press conference to announce his departure, "especially one with the tradition of the Cleveland Browns, puts you in a position where the next step might well be consideration for a head-coaching job in the NFL."

When the then-39-year-old Saban arrived in Cleveland—it was

already his ninth coaching job—the Browns were preparing for the upcoming 1991 NFL draft. But unlike other teams that employed various scouts, each of whom had their own fixed ideas and their own vision of what made a good player, Belichick wanted to develop a consistent team system for evaluating talent. So before the coaches even considered any college players individually, they sought to define what physical attributes they wanted at each position. Debates ensued, notes were taken, and before the draft the Browns had identified the ideal height, weight and speed for every position on the field. At center, for example, the coaches determined that the desired size was 6' 3", 280 pounds, with a 5.19 40 time. A player was then evaluated against those measurables. Other important factors at every position were also considered, such as overall athletic ability, strength, playing speed and character. But always, when assessing any player, he was compared with the Browns' strict physical prototype. Saban learned not to look solely at a player's ability; rather he examined the player in the context of precisely what the team wanted at each position.

"It took a number of months to build that system, and we enlisted the help of [longtime Dallas Cowboys scout] Gil Brandt, but by the end we had a height-weight-speed template that really is the basis for what Saban and Belichick are still using today in evaluating players," says Phil Savage, who was an assistant with the Browns from 1991 to '93, working with Saban, and became the club's general manager in 2005. "Our quarterback needed to be 6' 3" or taller and weigh 218 pounds. If he met those requirements, he was considered 'clean.' If he didn't, we'd designate him on the chart with a red flag. But this system was particularly important on the defense side of the ball. We wanted tall corners, big safeties and big, strong linemen. If you look at Alabama today it's a height-weight-speed program. There are some outliers like Javier Arenas [who was a 5' 9" cornerback], and Nick has certainly made some modifications, but what he's doing today really started in Cleveland."

In his first season with the Browns, Saban revamped a defense that the year before had been last in the NFL in points allowed and transformed it into the No. 10 unit in 1992. Saban and Belichick would spend hours together in the football offices talking the finer points of defense, trading ideas about the 3–4 defense that they both believed in ardently, talking blitz concepts, presnap adjustments and different coverages based on down and distance. They debated—in often the bluest of language common in the Browns' offices—how best to scout, to motivate players and to prepare for an opponent. Into the wee hours, they matched minds. Unlike most coaches, the two wouldn't even use a chalkboard when they talked about complex schemes; they could both visualize all the X's and O's in their heads and communicate them with crystal clarity.

"I've never been around two coaches with higher football intellects than Nick and Bill," says Savage, "but the two really had different personalities. Bill is much quieter. He's steady, almost monotone, and he can be very sarcastic, and his criticism can be biting. Nick wears his emotions on his sleeve, particularly behind the scenes. He's much more animated in the hallways and in the meeting rooms. He won't tell you that you're doing a good job because he doesn't have time for that. But he will make it very clear to you if you're *not* doing a good job. Watching Bill and Nick work together on game day was as impressive as anything I've ever seen in football."

When Saban left Cleveland in late 1994 to become the head coach at Michigan State, he carried the Browns' positional specifications system with him and has used it ever since. So has Belichick, who has won three Super Bowls with the New England Patriots using the same core system. The two coaches have remained close, often talking on the phone and still tossing football thoughts at each other. Saban's four years at Belichick's side had two key effects: It refined the style of the 3–4 defense Saban would play throughout his coaching career, and perhaps most important, it sharpened his ability to scout talent.

ADJOINING SABAN'S office is Alabama's recruiting war room. Only key personnel are allowed inside the room. Covering an entire wall is a grease board and covering the grease board is a mass of information. To Saban, what takes place in this room every day is nearly as important as what happens on the field on autumn Saturdays at Bryant-Denny.

The Alabama recruiting system, born of the Cleveland system, is a position-specific approach. The Alabama staff compiles comprehensive reports on every prospective recruit, analyzing how accurately each fits the prototype the team is looking for at the recruit's likely position. No detail is extraneous—they'll assess ankle movement, hip flexibility and knee dexterity—but the core is still the height-weight-speed data. Only later, when a prospect has been qualified by those measurables, do they begin to examine his mental makeup: how he communicates to his teammates on the field, how he reacts to getting beaten or manhandled by his opponent, how he behaves once he has achieved success.

The war room grease board accounts for every player Alabama is targeting for the next *four years*, and the information includes each prospect's grade point average and the names of the college or colleges he is leaning toward at the time. The board undergoes constant revision.

"Recruiting with Coach Saban never stops," says Jim McElwain, Saban's former offensive coordinator. "Evaluating film, writing letters to players, writing letters to coaches—it's the lifeblood of the program. Nick doesn't care if a kid has 100 offers or zero offers; he just wants to know if he can fit in the Alabama program. No one at Alabama is concerned about star ratings or what so-called recruiting experts are saying about players. That's just background noise.

"The evaluation process Coach Saban has is incredibly exhaustive. If a player has the position-specific set of critical factors that's looked for in a high school player, the coaches feel that physically he'll have a chance to succeed at that position at Alabama. It's as much a scientific approach as is possible to what is ultimately a subjective matter. I don't think anyone in the nation can evaluate talent better than Coach Saban."

Even so, no matter how much personal contact Saban ultimately has with a recruit, he makes sure there remains a certain level of distance between player and coach. "A lot of coaches will try to become really close friends with recruits, but that's not Nick. He's matter of fact and all business," says Todd Grantham, a defensive line coach under Saban at Michigan State in the late '90s and now the defensive coordinator at Louisville. "When coaches do become buddies with the recruit, and then the recruit gets on campus and the coach is no longer his best friend, that's when problems can occur. But Nick just lays it all out there: 'Here's what we have to offer both academically and athletically. I'll launch you to an NFL career. Take it or leave it.'"

"Nick only hires coaches who have reputations for being good recruiters," says Curt Cignetti, Alabama's recruiting coordinator and receivers coach from 2007 to '10. "Every assistant recruits an area, so Nick wants assistants that have relationships with high school coaches in the specific area where he will be in charge of recruiting. Once there is film of the player, the position coach will evaluate it. He then passes his evaluation along to Nick. Then, if Nick decides to make an offer, he's very good at giving people attention, which is really what people want. He's good at developing and maintaining relationships. He's very, very smart; I think he could have been successful in any business he went into because he's the rare person who is intellectually gifted and extremely driven."

So relentless is Saban's recruiting that it led to the passage in 2008 by the NCAA of the so-called Saban Rule, which prohibits coaches from visiting recruits during the spring. The rule unofficially carries his name because of Saban's reputation for traveling so much during the spring to see recruits while most coaches are in their offices. Undeterred by this new restriction, Saban devised another way to connect early with prospects: videoconferences. The Saban Rule stipulated that he couldn't have direct physical contact with recruits during the spring evaluation period—*but* he could converse with them by attaching a camera to his computer and having the players do the same at their high schools. By May 2008, Saban had used that technology to reach 60 prospects. ("A picture is worth a thousand words," Saban said. "In my case, as ugly as I am, they probably don't like looking at me, but I like looking at them when I'm talking to them.")

Once again, Saban had the jump on his competition, sending his rivals scrambling to catch up. "He's ahead of the curve a little bit," Tennessee coach Phillip Fulmer said begrudgingly at the time. "If they're going to do it, we have to do it."

The Crimson Tide recruiting machine has been wildly successful, with Alabama's incoming classes sitting at the top of the annual rankings of such things for the past four years. It's the primary reason that Nick Saban, on his throne in Tuscaloosa, sits enviably atop the college football world.

He'd be the first to tell you, though, that it didn't start out that way.

CHAPTER 16

Decisions, Decisions

THE SILVER-HAIRED gentleman flew on a University of Alabama private jet bound for Miami, disappointment behind him and uncertainty ahead. It was New Year's Day 2007 and Mal Moore, the Crimson Tide athletic director since 1999, was desperate. Himself a former Alabama player, Moore sat now in a leather seat in the back of the plane and gloomily considered his circumstances. A month had passed since he'd fired head coach Mike Shula just nine days after Alabama had lost to Auburn for the fifth consecutive year, finishing the season 6–6. Since then Moore's search for a new coach had not gone well. He'd tried to seduce South Carolina coach Steve Spurrier into coming to Tuscaloosa, but his advances were rebuffed. He wooed West Virginia coach Rich Rodriguez, who ultimately said he wasn't interested. Alabama fans couldn't believe that the Tide were being rejected in favor of little brothers like the Gamecocks and the Mountaineers. Those high-profile rebukes were serious p.r. setbacks for Moore, who was being roasted on local sports talk radio for bungling the search for a new leader for the Tide.

Mal Moore knew he needed to score a touchdown of a hire or his own job could be up in smoke. Alabama fans were out of patience. They wanted a winner, and they lusted for one now like never before in the program's history. Only one championship in more than a quarter of a century was unacceptable, period. Moore understood. If he wasn't successful on his current mission, if he didn't lure Nick Saban, the coach of the Miami Dolphins, to Tuscaloosa, he may as well not return himself. Moore even told the pilots that if Saban wasn't on the plane with him on the return flight, they should just take him to Cuba. He was joking. Sort of.

More than a month earlier, rumors had begun to circulate in the media that Saban was Alabama's new target. Crimson Tide officials had indeed contacted Saban's agent, Jimmy Sexton, to express interest. On the afternoon of Nov. 27, in Miami, Saban told reporters, "When I was in college it was always about coming to the pros. This is the challenge I wanted. I had a good college job [at LSU]. Why would I have left that if I was going to be interested in those other college jobs?"

At the time the Dolphins were on a four-game winning streak and, at 5–6, still had designs on advancing to the playoffs as a wild card.

On Dec. 7, Saban was again asked about Alabama. "I'm flattered that they may be interested in me, but it never really progressed because we never let it progress." Then, two weeks later, Saban uttered the words that would cling to him like a bad odor for years to come, words he would later say he regretted as much as any he'd ever spoken: "I guess I have to say it," he testily declared on Dec. 21. "*I'm not going to be the Alabama coach.* . . . I don't control what people say. I don't control what people put on dotcom or anything else. So I'm just telling you there's no significance, in my opinion, about this, about me, about any interest that I have in anything other than being the coach here [in Miami]."

By then, with the season not yet over, the Dolphins' fortunes had begun to spiral downward. (Miami would lose its final three games to finish 6–10.) Saban was still fighting to win games and the possibility of his leaving for Tuscaloosa could only undermine his players' belief in him. But were Saban's eyes secretly wandering when he made those exasperated statements about Alabama? Moore admitted that Sexton had called him in the fall of 2006—midway through the college football season—to ask about a current member of the Alabama team. Near the end of their chat, Sexton mentioned that if Moore was considering making a coaching change after the season, Saban could possibly be interested. Sexton told Moore that Saban may want out of the NFL.

"When I got off the phone," Moore told the Montgomery Quarterback Club in September 2010, "I realized that was the purpose of the call, not the talk about the player."

In Saban's first season with the Dolphins, 2005, the players hadn't responded to his new schemes (he implemented the 3–4 defense) or his rigid discipline (players couldn't wear caps in meetings) or his heavy-handedness (he timed players in the 40-yard dash early in training camp to see who was in shape and who wasn't). In their minds, he was treating professionals like college players, and after a 22–0 loss to Cleveland in the 10th game of the season, Saban raged in the locker room with such vein-bulging fervor that even the veterans were left shaken.

The next day, when the players arrived at their training complex, they found a message taped inside each of their lockers: IF YOU CONTINUE TO DO WHAT YOU'VE ALWAYS DONE, YOU'LL CONTINUE TO GET WHAT YOU'VE ALWAYS GOTTEN, GUARANTEED.

The Dolphins responded by winning six straight games to finish the season 9–7. They missed the playoffs, but the future appeared bright. In the off-season Saban pursued free-agent quarterback Drew Brees, who was coming off surgery to his throwing shoulder; he was brought in for a tryout, and Saban badly wanted to sign him. But the Dolphins' medical staff intervened, saying Brees had flunked the physical. (Miami then traded a second-round pick for quarterback Daunte

Culpepper, who started the '06 campaign but would be benched after four games. Brees would go on to become the MVP of Super Bowl XLIV in 2010.) Saban had been promised full control of personnel when owner Wayne Huizenga lured him from LSU, but when it counted, the final say wasn't Saban's.

During the autumn of 2006, as the seasons of both the Crimson Tide and the Dolphins were rapidly falling apart, Moore sought to set up a meeting with Saban, but the coach indicated through Sexton that he had no interest in a face-to-face until the NFL season was over.

When Moore landed in South Florida early on that morning of Monday, Jan. 1, he did not even have a scheduled appointment with Saban. Over several hours he called Saban multiple times, but the coach didn't answer. Late that night Saban returned his call. Over the phone Moore spoke with Nick and Terry for an hour, trying to sell them on Alabama and life in Tuscaloosa. Near the end of the conversation, Saban finally opened up, telling Moore that he was frustrated with the Dolphins and already weary of dealing with professional players.

Moore, who had spent four seasons as an NFL assistant coach, sympathized. "I know," he said. "Nobody comes to see you. No one calls you. No one talks about the team. And the wife doesn't do anything. If you want a quarterback, you trade for one or you buy one. Same with a defensive end. You don't recruit."

Saban said he'd call Moore the next day and they could meet for lunch. Moore hung up the phone, feeling hopeful. By noon the following day, however, Moore had yet to hear from Saban. Wilted with disappointment, he packed his bag and ordered the driver to take him to the airport, convinced his mission had failed. On his way to the jet, Moore's phone rang. It was Sexton, who told him that Saban needed more time and that Moore should stay another day in South Florida.

The next day Saban met with Huizenga, who told Saban he needed to do what was best for himself and his family. Meanwhile

Moore, out of patience, had driven to the Sabans' house. When he approached the sprawling mansion, he saw TV crews set up nearby and a helicopter hovering overhead; rumors had been running rampant. Undaunted, he knocked on the door and was greeted by Terry; Nick was still at the Dolphins' headquarters.

For an hour Moore turned on his extensive Southern charm—he had a Tom Wolfe quality about him—and chatted with Terry in his dripping-honey drawl. Moore knew well that Terry played a vital role in her husband's success and is his most trusted adviser. As he courted her, the phone rang. It was Saban.

"I don't think I'm even going to talk to [Moore] tonight," he told Terry.

"Oh, Mal's already here," Terry said. "We've been talking for an hour."

Saban arrived home soon thereafter. He told Moore, "Mal, when I go to work, I feel like I'm working at a damn factory." After about an hour Moore rose to leave—still without an answer from Saban—and said he would fly back to Tuscaloosa the next day. As she led him out, Terry grabbed Moore's arm and whispered, "We've got to get him on that plane tomorrow."

The next morning Moore arrived back at the Sabans' house, and Saban told Moore that he would take the job. Moore couldn't contain his giddy smile. "We need to get out of here as soon as possible," Moore said. Both men knew that they were leaving behind, in Miami, an understandably angry city of fans and media who felt scorned by the coach who had promised to stay.

At the airport Moore and the Sabans boarded the Alabama jet, and within minutes they were bound for Tuscaloosa. By the time the plane landed just two hours later, Saban was already looking forward, not back. As they were about to deplane, he turned to Moore and said, "Well, Mal, I guess you think I'm a hell of a coach."

"Yes, I do," Moore replied.

"Well, there's something you need to understand," Saban said. "I'm not worth a damn without players."

Moore nodded. "Thank God you realize that," he said.

TONY MCCARRON, who grew up in Mobile, is a Crimson Tide fan down to the marrow in his bones. Tony is AJ McCarron's father, and a widely reported story tells of how Tony missed the birth of AJ's younger brother, Corey, to attend the 1992 national championship game between Alabama and Miami in the Sugar Bowl. The story isn't true, though it might have been if circumstances were different. "He was at the hospital," says Dee Dee Bonner, AJ's mother. "But if he'd had tickets, I'm sure he would've gone in a heartbeat."

While AJ was growing up, Tony watched every Tide game on TV with white-knuckled intensity. He'd yell at the Alabama quarterback whenever he made a mistake, and he'd scream at the television whenever a Tide receiver dropped a pass. Young AJ would wrinkle his face in confusion; he couldn't understand why his father got so upset. Besides, unlike his dad, AJ didn't pay much attention to the Crimson Tide. He was a Miami Hurricanes fan.

Tony and Dee Dee divorced, and Tony bounced from apartment to apartment. It wasn't easy for AJ and his brother. "I grew up in a trailer park for a lot of years," AJ would tell *Sports Illustrated*. "Both parents worked two or three jobs to put food on the table. Grandparents had to take care of us. Sometimes the power would be on, but we couldn't pay the cable bill. Other times the phone didn't work. People always robbed our house, taking what little we had. It was hard for us to catch a break." For years, a typical dinner for AJ was a grilled-cheese sandwich.

One thing AJ could always afford was to go to a local park with his little brother and throw a football, hour upon hour. By the time AJ reached St. Paul's Episcopal School, he was a quarterback, the starter as a sophomore, a gunslinger type who loved to fire a pass to a receiver even if the window was tight and he was double-covered. As a junior he threw for 2,532 yards, 26 touchdowns and, somehow, only three interceptions. Top football schools from all over the nation offered McCarron a scholarship. He narrowed his list of potential colleges to three: Miami, Oklahoma and Alabama.

Saban personally recruited McCarron, flying to Mobile and bringing AJ to his office in Tuscaloosa. He didn't promise McCarron playing time or guarantee a national championship, but he laid out his vision for the next four years, step by step, telling him how he would grow the program. He explained precisely what he wanted from his quarterbacks—and it wasn't the free-wheeling style that McCarron played in high school. At Alabama, Saban said, the number one responsibility of the quarterback was to take care of the ball, which meant no winging it 50 yards on third-and-two.

Though McCarron liked most of what he heard, he wasn't convinced. He informed Sooners quarterbacks coach Josh Heupel that he would commit to Oklahoma. When McCarron broke the news to his parents, his mother wept. Like Tony, Dee Dee was a lifelong Alabama fan, and she had hoped to watch her son play at Bryant-Denny. Tony understood that his son wanted to make a name for himself in another state but warned that neither he nor Dee Dee would be able to attend all of AJ's games in Oklahoma because of the financial strain of travel.

That night, as McCarron lay in his bed in Mobile, he kept thinking about Saban, how the man had been so supremely confident that his plan would work, how he had seemed to take such a deep interest in McCarron and how he had promised to help mold him into a man. McCarron couldn't put his finger on precisely what it was, but something about Saban was hard to resist. The next morning AJ told his mom that he'd changed his mind: He was going to Alabama. Dee Dee cried again, this time with delight.

In his first intrasquad scrimmage at Alabama, McCarron was put on a team of walk-ons. Playing against the first-string defense, McCarron had no time to throw and was sacked several times. He was the only quarterback Saban signed in 2009, but the coach wasn't showing him any red-carpet treatment. Irate, McCarron, with his cleats still on, stomped into Saban's office after the scrimmage.

"I need to talk to you," he demanded.

"O.K.," said Saban, shuffling paperwork.

"You want me to show you what I can do, how I can play?" McCarron said. "Well, I can't do shit when you put me with walk-ons who can't even block. I don't understand why you don't put me with the starters."

"Why?" Saban said, hardly lifting his head to McCarron. "Because today we were testing your leadership. And you failed miserably."

TWO YEARS after that confrontation, McCarron, wearing a coat and tie, stepped off the team bus outside Beaver Stadium in State College, Pa., on a sun-dappled autumn afternoon. He looked as if he were in his own faraway world, oblivious to the Alabama fans on either side of him screaming his name as he strode coolly toward the massive stadium. He was about to make just the second start of his Alabama career, and first on the road, against a very good Penn State team in one of the largest, loudest venues in the country. Yet if there was one attribute above all others that Saban liked about McCarron, it was his ability to remain calm in the midst of chaos. He glided now toward the visitors' locker room, the master of his emotions, looking not the least bit concerned about the looming challenge in front of him.

Like every player on the roster, McCarron had felt the extraordinary impact of the tornado. Minutes after the twister had passed through Tuscaloosa, McCarron made his way to 15th Street to see what he could do to help, to look for survivors in the rubble. He had spent the summer building houses and spending time with victims. Inevitably the 20-year-old had gained a new perspective. "It's just a game," he often said to curious fans during that summer. "Real life is what happened out in the streets of Tuscaloosa."

Saban coaches the defensive backs and oversees the defense, but he spends time each week during the season with his quarterbacks and his offensive coordinator. On Tuesday mornings he typically stops by the office of his offensive coordinator to talk about the upcoming opponent, to pass along a few ideas about how that defense should be attacked. On Friday afternoons, usually for 30 minutes, Saban meets with his quarterbacks and his offensive coordinator to review play calls in different circumstances.

"Coach Saban does not like to be surprised by anything," says Jim McElwain, the former offensive coordinator, "so he wants to know what you have in mind going into the game, what you're going to do in certain situations. I truly believe he would have been just as successful as an offensive coordinator as he's been on the defensive side of the ball. He has an impressive offensive mind to say the least."

Against Penn State, McCarron, playing in front of a crowd of 107,846—the largest ever to watch an Alabama game—confidently led the Tide on an 11-play, 69-yard scoring drive in the first quarter that ended with a five-yard touchdown pass. In the second quarter he hit five of seven passes on a 50-yard drive capped by a Trent Richardson touchdown plunge. That score put the Tide up 17–3, and Alabama coasted to a 27–11 victory. After the game it was clear that Saban, who hadn't even named his starting quarterback before the opener against Kent State, had found his signal-caller of the future.

"AJ did a really good job today, managing the game and taking care of the football," Saban said afterward. "He needs to take what the defense gives us, so he's not forcing the ball down the field and making bad decisions."

"That's what Coach preaches—check-downs are touchdowns," McCarron said. "I'm not going to force it. It's about living for the next play."

In the course of a few hours, life had changed for McCarron. For the rest of his time as Alabama's quarterback, he would not be able to go anywhere in Tuscaloosa—a bar, a restaurant, a grocery store—without being recognized. Alabamians especially love their quarterbacks when they are homegrown, when they have been raised to appreciate every Crimson Tide flag that flies on a front porch or a pickup truck. Alabama fans like to see a bit of themselves in their quarterback, and now, needier than ever, they fell fast and hard for the young man wearing number 10.

CHAPTER 17
Two Daughters

THE GAME wasn't the same anymore for Shannon Brown—any football game, football itself, but especially an Alabama game. He'd honestly never known a more devout Crimson Tide fan than Loryn. Alabama football had been their bond, their common ground; a conversation about the Tide felt like its own happy language. But with Loryn gone, so was much of Shannon's interest in his team. He had flipped on the television to the Penn State game and took in a few plays, but he couldn't watch for long. It did nothing but remind him of his daughter.

A few weeks after the tornado, and after laying Loryn to rest in the graveyard in Wetumpka, Brown had traveled to Tuscaloosa for a reunion of Tide players who had played for coach Gene Stallings. Brown had attended with great reluctance.

Stallings and the players spent a day helping to clean up the town of Holt, just outside Tuscaloosa. Brown met the foreman of the operation and was assigned to operate a towering excavator with oversized tires and an articulated boom, at the end of which was a large steel-toothed bucket. His job: scoop debris from home sites and move it to the street.

Under a fireball sun, sweat flowing, Brown maneuvered that prehistoric praying mantis of a machine among the mountains of remains. Brown had yet to talk to anyone there about the aching sadness that still consumed him. But as he worked, an odd thing happened: He began to feel good. Attacking what the tornado had left behind was therapeutic, as if he were somehow fighting back. At the end of the day he said to a friend, "I let a lot of frustration out in that machine."

That night Stallings hosted a dinner in an expansive lounge inside the north end of Bryant-Denny. Midway through the evening, Stallings greeted Brown. "Hey, man, come over here," Stallings said. "Let's talk."

They moved to a table and sat alone together. Three years earlier Stallings's son, John Mark, had died at age 46 from complications of a congenital heart defect, related to his Down syndrome. John Mark had often stood by his father's side at practices in Tuscaloosa, happily holding a ball in his hands with a beaming smile on his face. Brown had known him well.

"We are in a fraternity that no parent should be in," Stallings said. "How are you doing?"

"I don't know, Coach," Brown replied. "I just really don't know."

After a pause, he continued. "I feel like people are waiting for me to wig out and lose it. But I just don't talk about it. I can't."

"Hey, man, just cry," Stallings said. "I've cried buckets and buckets of tears over John Mark. There's nothing wrong with that. You're not weak if you cry."

After all these years, Stallings was still coaching. The two spoke a few more minutes, embraced, then went off to join others. Brown knew he'd been given valuable advice. Still, he didn't—couldn't, wouldn't—cry.

IT WAS a call she knew she had to make. Ashley Mims had exchanged a few emails with Darlene Harrison, the mother of Ashley Harrison, but the two hadn't yet spoken over the phone, and it was now a few months since the day of the tornado, the day their daughters had been taken from them.

She made the call, and for 20 minutes the two mothers connected. They talked of all that their daughters had in common: their love of Crimson Tide football, of living in Tuscaloosa. They talked about how the two girls had dressed alike, even looked alike, sharing expressive brown eyes and easy smiles. Each mother wanted to know everything about the other's daughter, her hobbies, her eccentricities, her dreams for the future.

They talked about how they, the two mothers, had for weeks struggled to simply rise out of bed. Both were tortured by nightmares, detailed and exhausting. They could empathize, understand the other's torment, the emotions that few parents could ever comprehend. As they spoke, it was as if they knew what the other was going to say before words were spoken. It was an awful bond they shared, but it felt good to vent and to cry with someone who understood, precisely, the pain.

They were hundreds of miles apart—Ashley in Alabama, Darlene in Texas—but for those 20 minutes they were unquestionably close. Still, soon after Ashley hung up the phone, the grim reality set in again: Her daughter would never come home, and no amount of talking or commiserating would change that. In Texas, Darlene was pierced by the same feeling.

Neither Ashley Mims nor Darlene Harrison, nor Shannon Brown, took much notice on Saturday, Sept. 17, when Alabama beat North Texas 41–0 in the third game of the season.

CHAPTER 18

The Process

THE WORD was out, and it traveled at warp speed: Nick Saban was the new head coach at Alabama, and he was on his way to Tuscaloosa, though nobody knew exactly when he would arrive. At 11 a.m. on that Wednesday, Jan. 3, 2007, the first wave of fans, buzzing with anticipation, was already arriving at the Tuscaloosa Regional Airport, crowding into the BAMA Air terminal used by private planes. The throng swelled past 200, everyone eagerly scanning the sky as if waiting for God himself to appear. It was a long wait. At around 3:45 the jet finally landed on Alabama ground. (As some would say, it was the Tide's biggest touchdown in years.) When the door opened, Terry Saban stepped out first, waving to the crowd with an oh-my-Lord look on her face. Then Saban appeared, in a gray suit and lavender shirt; as he walked toward the fans he was greeted by shouts of "Roll Tide!"

Saban signed autographs as he slowly made his way through the narrow terminal. One well-lubricated woman kissed him on the face; other fans pounded him on the back. He and Terry eventually climbed into one of the cars in a cavalcade of five that slowly pulled away from the terminal. But the fans wanted more. Some continued to run alongside the vehicle. (The Sabans would laughingly recall later that when they had flown into Baton Rouge after Nick had been hired away from Michigan State, only the LSU equipment manager was there to greet them at the airport.) After being in Alabama for mere minutes, they understood instantly how drastically things had changed. They were now public property.

The next day, in a large conference room teeming with television cameras and nearly a hundred reporters, Saban, suited and wearing a red tie, stepped to the podium and laid out his plan for the Crimson Tide. "Everybody should take the attitude that we're working to be a champion, that we want to be a champion in everything we do," said the new coach. Camera flashes popped in his face. "Every choice, every decision, everything that we do every day, we want to be a champion. Everyone take ownership for what they need to do relative to their role, whatever it is, whether it's being a fan, a booster, be a good one. . . . Everyone take ownership that we support each other so we can have the best possible football program that Alabama has ever had."

The print reporters in the room scribbled in their notebooks. They had the bullet point for their stories: *We can have the best possible football program that Alabama has ever had.*

Saban went on to speak for nearly 45 minutes, rambling from topic to topic. He described his approach: "We're not going to talk about what we're going to accomplish; we're going to talk about how we're going to do it." He set forth his expectations: "We want a big, physical, aggressive football team that is relentless in the competitive spirit we go out and play with week in and week out. What I would like for every football team to do that we play is to sit there and say, 'I hate playing against these guys. I *hate* playing them.'"

Eventually he got around to his sudden departure from Miami: "My commitment to the [Dolphins], and it was premature not to stay there, all right, but I knew—Wayne [Huizenga] and I talked about this—that my heart was to go back to college. . . . I gave my best effort for two years. . . . It was premature to leave. At the same time, if I knew my heart was someplace else in terms of what I wanted to do, I don't think it would have been fair to the organization if I had stayed."

In answer to a final question from a local reporter about how soon fans could expect a national championship, Saban said, "I can't make any predictions, nor will I ever, about when something's going to happen. I like to keep working on it, making it better, making it better than everybody else has, then all of a sudden you have a chance to do that."

In the days that followed, Saban went straight to work, intent on giving Alabama a positive return on its substantial investment. Saban had signed an eight-year, $32 million contract, making him one of the highest-paid football coaches in college or the NFL. His contract featured several plums that were the envy of his college peers across America: two cars, a country-club membership and 25 hours of private use of the university's jet.

AFTER SPRING practice one day in 2007, Saban sat in his office and elaborated on his methods, again emphasizing what had become his central theme, all about staying and playing in the moment: "I got on our guys in a team meeting. I said, 'I'm tired of hearing all this talk about a national championship when you guys don't know how to get in and out of the rain, don't know what to do in the classroom.' It's like you've got little kids in the backseat saying, 'Are we there yet?'

"The journey itself is important, not just the destination. You have to follow direction. Discipline, off-season recruiting, conditioning, practice, more recruiting, player development, classroom development. I'm not interested in what should be, could be, was. I'm interested in what *is*, what we control. And when we lose—and we will, one game, two or more—we have to have a trust that what we are doing will work, trust and belief in who we are. And you get where you're going one mile marker at a time."

Saban refers often to "the process" at Alabama, the system that governs everything in his football program. So celebrated has it become that it is often popularly dubbed, in capitals, The Process. It is rigid and it is pervasive; it guides recruiting, conditioning, practice, game preparation and play on the field.

The Process did not start at Alabama. It first sprang to life in the fall of 1998, and like so much innovation in football, it was born more of desperation than inspiration. Saban was in his fourth season as head coach at Michigan State when he took his 4–4 Spartans to Columbus in early November to play undefeated and No. 1–ranked Ohio State. During practice that week, knowing his team was overmatched, Saban had opted to try something new: He told his players not to focus on winning the game. Rather, they should treat each play, in practice and in the game ahead, as if that play alone was an entire game and concentrate only on what needed to be done during *that* play to be successful. And as soon as the whistle blew to end each play, it was to be wiped from memory like it never happened; all that mattered was the next play and what needed to be done in order to "win" that next play.

To his delight, Saban discovered during the week that his players were sharper in practice—both physically and mentally—than they'd been all season. It seemed that by limiting their focus to only what was immediately in front of them, Saban had eliminated extraneous mental clutter, most especially their worry over end results. A four-touchdown underdog, Michigan State went into Columbus and upset the Buckeyes 28–24. As Saban jogged off the field that day in Ohio, he felt like he'd discovered something significant.

It was the beginning of The Process.

If the system were as simple as that, of course, it would be the mantra of every football coach in America—take it one play at a time, boys. But what makes the philosophy work for Saban is the full-blast, crank-it-up-to-10 intensity of the man who espouses it. "When you work for Nick, you always feel like it's fourth-and-one on the goal line and the Super Bowl is on the line," says Phil Savage. "He's the pacesetter. Players at Alabama today will swear to you that they've never seen him close his eyes in meetings. He's got a lot of firepower in that engine. You feel like if you don't get something done, then you're letting him down. It's intense with him. Meetings, practices—everything is intense. That's one reason why Alabama plays so well in big games, because it's almost easier and more relaxing out there on the field in the game than it is with him at practice and in the building."

"Nick knows every part of the program and every person who touches the program," says Jim McElwain. "From the equipment guys to the janitors to the lawn guys to the players to the coaches, the message is the same: Work hard today to be a champion tomorrow. That message never changes. Never. It's not for everyone because it requires so much sacrifice and hard work. But that's the price for success he demands. And if you're not willing to buy in, you won't be around very long, guaranteed. If you're with Nick, you have to give maximum effort, all day, every day."

No detail is too small. By the time an incoming recruit first steps onto the football field, Dr. Lonny Rosen has written an extensive psychological profile on him. A professor of psychology at Michigan State, Rosen has been an adviser to Saban since his days as head coach in East Lansing; Saban considers Rosen's profiles to be fundamental to the development of both talent and character in his players. As Curt Cignetti, the former recruiting coordinator, has described them, "The profiles help to figure out the best way to help the player. They show what the best way to reach him is, what he responds to and what will turn him off."

At Alabama, Saban has also brought in instructors from The Pacific Institute, a leadership-development consultancy based in Seattle. At a price tag of around $40,000, instructors from the institute would meet with the players for 12 sessions that last between 30 and 45 minutes. In these sessions the players chant various affirmations, each intended to promote team unity and strengthen commitment to each other. Some examples, as cited in a *Birmingham News* story:

"We are a team that's committed to excellence. It's represented in everything we do."

"Our team is a family. We will look out for each other. We love one another. Anything that attempts to tear us apart only makes us stronger."

"Our defense is aggressive. We fly to the ball seeking always to cause big plays on every down. We intimidate our opponents."

During preseason practice Saban also has Dr. Kevin Elko speak to his team. An expert in sports behavior, Elko first worked with Saban in 2003 when he met with the LSU players several times during the Tigers' run to the national title. Since then, Elko and Saban have remained close, talking on the phone several times a week. Elko has been instrumental in helping Saban shape The Process—"It was something we constantly talked about at LSU, focusing only on what was in front of you," Elko says.

When Elko (who also worked with the Green Bay Packers when they won the Super Bowl in 2011 and the Miami Hurricanes before their 2001 national title) prepared for the first time to speak to the Crimson Tide players in August '08, a few trainers suggested to him that he keep his speech short and sweet. Overhearing this, Saban stepped in. "Go as long as you want, man," he told Elko. "This is important."

For 45 minutes Elko addressed the team. "You have to have a vision for where you're heading," he said. "Know where you want to go and know what it will take to get here. You also have to eliminate the mental clutter from your life. Get rid of it. It does you no good to be thinking of how you're having trouble with your girlfriend when you're on the practice field. And remember that there is a process to becoming a champion. There's a process to how you play the game and a process to how you prepare. The process is the price you pay for victory."

He continued: "If you see a little on the field, you see a lot. If you see a lot on the field, you see nothing. If you're a wide receiver and trying to catch a football, you should just see a little and focus on that ball and nothing else. If you see a lot at that moment the ball is coming and your eyes wander around the field, you won't make the catch. Same with blocking. If you are an offensive lineman, keep your eyes focused on what your assignment is, not what's happening to the guy next to you. Just remember: You see a little on the field, you see a lot. You see a lot on the field, you see nothing."

Saban frequently repeats other Elko phrases: "Don't worry about accepting failure, worry about the process of preparing." Or, "Pain instructs."

Still, no amount of pigskin philosophizing replaces for Saban the importance of his central tenet: Work harder than everybody else.

Tuscaloosa has its own little-known film festival; it takes place every day inside the Mal Moore building, and often the only attendee is Nick Saban. Sitting in the cool dark of his office, remote control in his hand and reading glasses resting low on his nose, Saban watches tape. Nothing breaks the intensity of his viewing; a mundane run up the middle for a two-yard gain is studied with the same laser focus as a 40-yard touchdown pass, always searching for a secret to be revealed.

During every week of the season Saban watches as much as 50 hours of film of the upcoming opponent, painstakingly looking to find the tiniest vulnerability he can exploit. Many, from rival coaches to prying reporters, have sought to explicate Saban's "football genius." In truth, the reason for his success is rather rudimentary: He's single-minded and driven like no one else, and he will not allow himself to be outprepared or out-game-planned by anyone. "I'm really not a complicated person," Saban says. "I just work hard."

One of his favorite sayings is, "Right is never wrong." This means, in Saban's uncomplicated world, that there is only one way to do everything: the correct way. The guiding energy of The Process can be boiled down to the application of that principle: Right is never wrong.

TERRY SABAN would surely not choose to be called a part of The Process, but Saban's wife is a vital, and not-so-secret, weapon in his coaching arsenal. Miss Terry, as everyone at Alabama—including Saban himself—calls her, is elegant, refined, a natural conversationalist and as warm as a winter campfire; she is the maternal figure for the entire program.

When a prospect makes an official visit to Tuscaloosa, he and his family will typically spend time with Miss Terry. She hosts a recruiting party after the A-Day game each spring at the Sabans' home. While Nick works the backyard grill and talks X's and O's with the recruits, Miss Terry will gracefully move from family to family with the skill of a royal. In many ways she's Saban's ultimate closer—the person who assures recruits' parents that their children will be well cared for in Tuscaloosa. And once the players arrive on campus, Miss Terry spends countless hours with them, making sure they are making the needed adjustments to life in college and to life as a Crimson Tide football player.

"Terry does a fantastic job," says her husband, "of being very supportive, not only in the things we do, or try to do, in terms of recruiting, but getting to know and develop relationships with people that are important to feel comfortable with when they come to our university." What's more, she's not shy when it comes to talking football. Says Saban, "She's quick to tell me when we're running it too much up the middle, when we're not passing enough, when we don't blitz enough on defense. I get lots of feedback on all those things. So I would say that she's probably as big a part of the program as anyone in terms of her time and her commitment."

"Because Nick is so relentlessly single-minded about football, it would be tough for him to do his job the way he wants to do it without Terry," said Phil Savage. "She does the bills, takes care of the cars and makes sure their personal house is in order. Nick just doesn't have time for that. They have a true partnership. She makes it so he doesn't have a lot of distractions. Her role in his career has just been enormously important."

In 2011 her job, like her husband's, was more demanding than ever.

IN THE fourth week of the 2011 season, at Bryant-Denny, Alabama beat Arkansas 38–14. The Tide, 4–0, were now ranked No. 3 in the nation. Tuscaloosa was continuing to rebuild, and the team was doing its part to revive spirits.

Three days after the win over the Razorbacks, the coach walked through his office and slid behind his huge mahogany desk into his high-backed leather swivel chair. Even though his team was undefeated, playing inspired football and manhandling every opponent so far, Saban was on edge, worrying and fretting like a man afraid of losing his job. More than a few national writers had come out with stories in recent weeks suggesting that this could be Saban's best team ever. The coach thought all the bouquets being tossed to his team were, to put it nicely, unwarranted.

"I always worry," Saban said, leaning forward to pin a visitor with his eyes. "We've got *so far to go* to get where we want to be. I mean it's not even funny."

A trip to Gainesville to play the 12th-ranked and undefeated Florida Gators was 72 hours away.

CHAPTER 19

A Punishing Defense

A FEW DAYS after the tornado, Lee Henderson instructed his employees to meet at his Smoothie King on The Strip, which had been untouched by the storm. "Even though one of our stores has been wiped out," he told them, "we'll make sure that everyone will have a place to work, even those of you from the store that's gone. We're not going to open this store for the next three or four days because I want everyone to go out into your communities and do whatever you can to help. We're lucky. We're all alive. We need to roll up our sleeves."

Three months later he was still trying to find the answer to the question, What's next? He had made some basic decisions: It was determined that the Smoothie King at 15th and McFarland would not be rebuilt. He had received a check from his insurance company for the lost franchise and was trying to decide his next move. Should he open another Smoothie King in a new location? Maybe. Or should he find a new kind of business to start? He knew he wanted to be an active part of the regrowth of Tuscaloosa; he just wasn't sure where to plant the next seed.

FOR FIVE MONTHS Bob Dowling had toiled sunrise to sunset, working for a general contractor that specialized in debris removal following major disasters. Yet he still couldn't shake the chillingly vivid memory of the moment that twister had stared him in the face, and he knew how close he'd come to dying. He may have been suffering from symptoms of post-traumatic shock; still he climbed out of his bed each morning, walked out of his new house built by Alabama football players and went to work.

In the past Dowling had sometimes left his family for months at a time to work on different disaster relief projects and never thought twice about doing it. But now it was difficult for him to be away from home for more than a few hours. And whenever storm clouds gathered, Dowling would grow highly apprehensive.

The Dowlings had a seven-year-old Chihuahua named Taco, and even the dog suffered aftereffects from the tornado. Each time the storm sirens cranked to life now, Taco bolted into the Dowlings' safe room in the interior of the house, as if he knew somehow that he would be protected there. Taco, like every other living creature in Tuscaloosa, would never again hear those sirens the same way.

Bob and Dana, with their daughter Marilyn, had attended the Alabama season opener on Sept. 3—Kent State had given the family tickets—and since then had watched every Tide game on television. For the Dowling family, like so many others in T-Town, the games were a kind of group-therapy session, a chance to come together and release their emotions for three hours and soak themselves in the sweet ecstasy of Alabama football. Marilyn Dowling, who had so enjoyed the teenage thrill of giving out orders to Tide players like AJ McCarron and D.J. Fluker, now had the fun of seeing them on TV. "I know that guy!" she'd shout to her parents. "He was on our roof!"

On Saturday night, Oct. 1, the Dowlings, like most every other family they knew in T-Town, were gathered in front of the TV for the Florida game, the biggest contest of the season so far.

THE ALABAMA defense huddled near the 30-yard line during a timeout, standing in a circle around their coordinator Kirby Smart and Saban. It was 9:21 on this warm fall night in Gainesville, and the Swamp, packed with orange-and-blue fans, was at full volume. Smart yelled instructions to his defense. The Gators had the ball on their own 14-yard line, first-and-10, trailing 17–10 with 8:44 remaining in the second quarter. Smart told his players that now was the time to seize control of the game, to puncture the hopes of the home team. He implored them not to give any ground at all.

The Bama defenders jogged to the line of scrimmage, taking their positions in the usual 3–4. As the Gators broke the huddle, Saban paced the sideline, squinting into the lights. At moments like these, he looks as if he wants to put a fist through the nearest wall, yet these are the moments he lives for.

On first down Florida quarterback John Brantley dropped back to pass, but Josh Chapman hit Brantley as he released the ball, forcing a harmless throw. On second down defensive lineman Damion Square steamrolled running back Chris Rainey for a one-yard loss. On third down Brantley fired a 25-yard strike to wide receiver Andre Debose, but when safety Will Lowery delivered a rattling hit, the ball fell to the grass, incomplete. On fourth down, as the noise in the stadium dwindled, the Gators punted.

Ten plays later McCarron dived into the end zone for a one-yard touchdown, and the game was essentially over. The Alabama defense had already so impressed all observers that there was talk that this D had a chance to be remembered as one of the best in college football history. A two-touchdown lead was plenty. Never mind that Florida had led the SEC in total offense heading into the game.

In the second half the Gators scored zero points, had 32 yards rushing, 14 yards passing and made just two first downs. The final was 38–10. It was an unmerciful beating. Said Florida's Rainey afterward, "Just call it a punch in the mouth."

The Tide defense had indeed been spectacularly good through five games, leading the country in points allowed per game with a puny 8.4. "We come to punish people," said Courtney Upshaw, who meant it—his brutal sack had knocked Brantley out of the game near the end of the second quarter. "But everything we do," he hastened to add, "starts with Coach Saban. Everything."

An offensive coordinator whose team had lost to the Crimson Tide earlier in the season put it this way: "Their linemen are monsters. Their linebackers look like linemen. Their safeties look like linebackers. Their corners are big. And all of them on that D are incredibly fast—NFL fast. On top of that, they are the most disciplined, gap-sound team I've ever faced, which means they're never out of position. Saban is as good of a defensive mind as I've ever come across."

It was team defense, yes, but if there was one player more essential to its success than any other, it was junior linebacker Dont'a Hightower, a 6' 4", 260-pound force of nature who'd once been a relatively unheralded recruit from Tennessee—until Saban took an interest in him.

THE ITINERARY was ambitious: On a spring day in 2007, Saban and recruiting coordinator Cignetti left Tuscaloosa at 7:30 a.m. in a private plane and flew to Huntsville, Ala., to check out a few players. Then they jetted to Nashville to see more recruits, then swung by Lewisburg, Tenn., to watch a kid Saban was curious about before they would return to Nashville to watch another potential recruit compete in a track meet; all in all, more than 12 hours in the air and on the road. Ambitious but, for Saban, typical.

By the time they arrived at Marshall County High in Lewisburg, the team was in the indoor practice facility for the first day of spring practice. As Hightower performed various drills with no pads, he noticed a guy on the sideline following his every move. He asked a teammate, "Is that one of our new coaches?"

"No."

"Then who is it?"

"That's Alabama coach Nick Saban," the teammate replied. "Um, he's here to see you."

What Saban saw excited him. Hightower wasn't rated by most recruiting services as a blue-chip player and had only two scholarship offers at the time, from Ole Miss and Vanderbilt. But Saban likes his linebackers big—he reminds his coaches repeatedly that "heavyweights knock out lightweights"—and Hightower fit the mold. He also could run a 4.6 40.

After just a few minutes, Saban turned to Cignetti. "What do you think?" he asked.

"We need to offer him," Cignetti replied.

Later that night Saban called Hightower's home. Though he had not seen Hightower play in a game (except on tape), he offered him a scholarship on the spot. Saban trusts what he sees. "What I saw that day in the indoor practice facility at his school was probably the most athletic linebacker in the country," Saban recalled later. "I was blown away. I knew right away he could be a perfect fit for what we want to do."

As the two coaches walked off the plane that night at the BAMA Air terminal, Saban looked at Cignetti, smiled and said, "Just another day in the NCAA." To Cignetti's eye, Saban looked absolutely blissful.

AFTER THE game clock expired in Gainesville, Hightower was one of the last players to leave the field, high-fiving dozens of Alabama fans leaning out of the stands before he disappeared into the locker room. Ever since the summer months working cleanup in Tuscaloosa, Hightower had grown to savor his interactions with fans; after the final whistle of each game he typically lingered on the field longer than his teammates, walking the base of the stands to share some time with the Alabama faithful.

This evening Saban followed close behind Hightower. As the coach jogged into the tunnel, he saw Terry, wearing a crimson-colored scarf and leaning against a concrete wall. He gave her a quick kiss—their postgame custom—before continuing to the locker room. Even seeing Terry, his scowling expression never changed, the same dour face he wore on the sideline all game. The big win over Florida only meant it was time to worry about the next game.

After his postgame press conference in a cramped space near the visitors' locker room, Saban walked outside into the Florida night. He was the last one in the Alabama program to board the bus. Moments after taking his front-row seat, Saban was scanning some notes.

Next up was Vanderbilt, a home game; in fact, it was homecoming weekend in Tuscaloosa. For Saban, just another football game. But it would be a game—and a day—that the parents of Loryn Brown would never forget.

CHAPTER 20

Homecoming

IF THERE were a statute of limitations on grief, Shannon Brown would have welcomed it.

Six months after his daughter's death, he still caught himself searching for her face in a crowd, still turned expectantly when he heard her voice come out of thin air. He was now intimately acquainted with the pain of losing a child: For the most part it smoldered just beneath the surface, then every so often it would be fanned into flame, and it felt to him like an inferno of sadness in the middle of his chest. Six months, and it still consumed him.

Too often Shannon would be hit by a maddening recurring thought: If Loryn had only been 25 yards to the right or to the left when that twister arrived on April 27, she'd likely still be alive. The *what if* notions haunted him; he so deeply wished the specter of regret would vanish, but it simply would not.

On the day before Alabama's Oct. 8 game against Vanderbilt, Brown packed an overnight bag at his home in Madison and began the 2½-hour drive to Tuscaloosa. Traveling this same road had once been charged with anticipation; now it was a mess of conflicting emotions. He really didn't like spending time in T-Town anymore; invariably he would be stricken by the image of himself identifying Loryn's body. But he also missed seeing his teammates; the five years he'd spent playing football at Alabama were some of the best of his life, and even now there was some comfort in remembering those days with his buddies, recalling the whole-body shiver of excitement that came with running out in front of 80,000 roaring fans. As he neared Tuscaloosa now he just felt scared—scared that the bad memories would simply overwhelm the good ones.

During Shannon's junior year at Alabama, when Loryn was four, he and his wife Ashley had divorced; they'd married so young, too young, and it wasn't working anymore. But they shared their devotion to Loryn, and whenever Alabama had an open date during the season, Shannon would take his daughter to the zoo or jump on a trampoline with her or even join her to play with her Barbie dolls. For the rest of his college career he spent every other weekend with his daughter.

Now he checked into the Hotel Capstone—the same place he used to stay with his teammates before games—and after dropping off his bags he walked to the Quad to meet up with several of his former teammates and friends for a barbecue under a tent on this cool, bright afternoon. The old stories flowed in a steady stream even as dusk settled and the temperature dropped. To Brown, it felt almost like being with the guys back in the locker room again.

Almost. Several of Loryn's friends stopped by the tent. They hugged Shannon tight, and each time he didn't want to let go; each time it gave him the sensation that he was embracing his daughter. The girls talked about everything they missed most about Loryn: her great laugh, her sassiness, her kindness. No one could comprehend that she'd been gone for nearly six months now.

Ashley Mims had also come into town for homecoming weekend,

and Loryn's friends visited with her as well. Mary Jean Traylor, one of Loryn's closest friends, told Ashley about a text message she had received after the tornado. Traylor explained that her phone seemed to have a mind of its own, and sometimes a new message would pop up days or weeks after it had been sent. A few days after the storm, she was working on a cleanup crew in Tuscaloosa when a text appeared. Traylor gasped. It was from Loryn. She read the message and started to cry. It said, simply, *Good job.* It had, of course, been sent before Loryn died, but Traylor felt now that it was Loryn talking to her, telling her she was doing a good thing by helping the victims. When Traylor showed the message to Ashley, they cried together.

Over the years Ashley had grown close to many of Loryn's friends; she recalled driving some of them to Atlanta to see 'N Sync and another time to a Backstreet Boys concert. It felt good to Ashley to be with them again; she began calling them "my Tuscaloosa kids." They were helping to fill the void.

Ashley had struggled to sleep ever since the death of her daughter, and on many of those sleepless nights, long after Dewayne and their three children had gone to bed, Ashley would slip out to the garage and open up the boxes that were full of Loryn's belongings. She wasn't sure, though, what she was looking for.

One night she found a sketch pad; it had been in Loryn's house in Tuscaloosa, and after the tornado it had been pounded by rain. The pages were brown and moldy. Ashley carefully leafed through it and, after a few minutes, she had what she calls a "God Stop" moment—something that causes you "to slam on the brakes and pay attention to the Higher Power."

On the only page in the sketch pad that was perfectly white and unsoiled by the rain, Ashley found a pencil drawing by Loryn of an angel standing on a cloud. The angel had dark curly hair, like Loryn. Ashley stared at it for a good 10 minutes before raising her head to the heavens and smiling. She believed with all her heart that her daughter had just sent her a message.

ON THE Saturday morning of the Vanderbilt game, 300 people filled the theatre-style seating of Moody Hall at 10:00. Shannon and Ashley walked onto the stage and were presented with a certificate from the University of Alabama Alumni Association. It stated that the Loryn Alexandria Brown Memorial Scholarship had achieved endowed status that would carry on in perpetuity. Shannon and Ashley had worked diligently to raise money, getting generous donations from alumni, friends and family, for a scholarship that would cover the cost of a student's freshman year; it had brought them closer than they'd been in almost two decades.

On the stage, Shannon said, "It feels so good to know that Loryn is now forever at Alabama. We had so many wonderful times together here. This would mean so much to her."

"This is such a wonderful thing," Ashley added. "It's like Loryn's hopes, dreams and aspirations will be carried on. Her name will always be at Alabama, the place she loved so much."

AFTER THE ceremony Shannon strolled over to Denny Chimes where, 15 years earlier, he and his little girl had knelt down and pressed his hand into the wet concrete. A breeze ruffled the orange and yellow leaves on the grand oaks that shaded the Quad. It was difficult being here at the Chimes, reminding him as it did of what would never be again, but he also felt the presence of Loryn. He stayed until it was time to go to the stadium.

He entered the A-Club, a lounge inside Bryant-Denny open only to Alabama's lettered athletes. Shannon shook hands with old friends. Many didn't know what to say other than "I'm so sorry for your loss" or "I'm thinking of you, buddy" or "I love you, man." Shannon had by now become accustomed to these awkward greetings. They didn't bother him much anymore.

Thirty minutes before kickoff he rode an elevator down five stories and stepped onto the football field. It was approaching 5:30 p.m.

Five minutes before kickoff the stadium was full, and Shannon walked onto the field. He had been named an honorary team captain for this game, and as he waited now on the sideline for the coin toss ceremony to begin, running back Trent Richardson came over and shook his hand. Shannon said, "Hey, buddy, good luck. Don't ever underestimate this experience."

"No, sir, I won't," Richardson replied. "I thank the good Lord every day."

Shannon trotted out to midfield, where he joined Alabama game captains Dont'a Hightower, Mark Barron, Marquis Maze and Alex Watkins for the coin toss. He shook hands with the Tide players and then the Vandy captains. Before the referee flipped the coin, the P.A. announcer introduced Shannon Brown and told the crowd that his daughter, Loryn, had died in the tornado. The introduction brought 101,000 fans to their feet, and they clapped and whistled, a resounding salute. Shannon had a familiar sensation, the back-of-the-neck hair-raising rush he'd felt so often on this field as a football player. He stepped forward in his houndstooth sport coat and red tie and lifted his right arm to acknowledge the crowd. But there was no smile.

After the coin toss he returned to the sideline, where several players and coaches ran to Shannon and grabbed his right hand. Nobody may have known precisely what to say, but the handshakes and hugs from players present and past felt warm and comforting, at least for as long as it lasted.

FOR THE first time since the tornado, Ashley Mims walked into Bryant-Denny and took a seat. Before kickoff, as she watched her ex-husband being honored below, she thought, of course, of Loryn sitting in her lap in her cheerleading uniform as they rooted for Daddy down on the field.

Ashley now wore a red dress with a houndstooth bow. It was the same dress, same bow, that Loryn had worn a year earlier for Alabama's 2010 homecoming game against Mississippi. Loryn had texted her mom that day, sending pictures of her with friends tailgating on the Quad in that spectacular red outfit.

By halftime Ashley had to leave. "It's just too hard," she told a companion. "As exciting as it is being back here, it's too much. I just can't stay. I can't."

She walked out of the stadium and into the evening. She could hear the fading rise and fall of the crowd noise as she moved toward her car. The sound was so familiar, loosening more bittersweet game-day memories of her little girl. At this moment Ashley didn't know if she could ever bring herself to attend, or even watch, another Alabama game.

FROM THE Alabama sideline, Shannon could feel something different about this team. Shannon had gone through training camp in 1996 with the Atlanta Falcons before a knee injury ended his career, but he had been around the pros long enough to know that those players never had the look in their eyes that these Alabama kids did. Everyone on this Tide team exuded a passion and an intensity that Shannon had never before seen, not even on his squad that won the national championship in 1992.

Shannon turned to a friend on the sideline. "These players," he said, shaking his head in admiration. "These players are reminded every day, just by all the destruction they drive past, of how lucky they are to be alive and how much their city is hurting. They are going to win the national championship. *They are going to do this.* You can sense it down here. Even in the way they warm up. They want this more than any team I've ever seen want to win. It's really incredible."

After watching the Crimson Tide build a 14–0 halftime lead—that defense again—Shannon left the stadium. With his family, he wandered past Denny Chimes one more time. It had been a good day, but he needed to get out of Tuscaloosa.

CHAPTER 21

Doomed, Redeemed

JOSH CHAPMAN went bug-eyed at the sight: an endless expanse of Alabama and LSU fans, heads bobbing along in every direction as far as he could see. As Chapman rode the team bus from the Hotel Capstone to Bryant-Denny on Nov. 5, the streets and sidewalks and parks in Tuscaloosa were swarmed with fans, still two hours before the 7 p.m. kickoff. Looking through the tinted windows of the bus, as a golden twilight washed over the city, Chapman felt as if he were witnessing the biggest party he'd ever seen, a fall Mardi Gras in Alabama. "Oh, my goodness," Chapman kept muttering, over and over, as he took in the scene. According to local police, more than 50,000 fans without tickets stood or sat within a mile of Bryant-Denny before kickoff just to be close to the impending event: the game between the two top-ranked teams in the nation.

After beating Vanderbilt 34–0 at homecoming, second-ranked Alabama pounded Mississippi 52–7 on Oct. 15 and, seven days later, dismissed Tennessee 37–6. This set the stage for what was clearly the biggest game of the 2011 season: No. 2 Alabama versus No. 1 LSU in Tuscaloosa on the first Saturday in November. It was the first time in the history of the SEC that two conference teams had played each other in the regular season ranked one and two, and the first time the country's top two teams had squared off in the regular season since 2006 when No. 1 Ohio State beat No. 2 Michigan. An estimated 20 million people would watch this Tide-Tigers matchup on television, the largest audience for a CBS college football game in more than 20 years.

What a day it was in Tuscaloosa: Sunny and 60° four hours before kickoff, with a whisper of wind from the west. The RVs and campers and pickup trucks, as well as the BMWs, first began streaming into T-Town three days before the game and now, as kickoff approached, the Quad overflowed with tailgaters grilling everything from chicken to pigs feet to alligator. In SEC country the 60 minutes of game action is only a piece of the grand experience of a football Saturday. "We don't just play games in the SEC," says Georgia coach Mark Richt. "We host all-day events." In Tuscaloosa the tailgating epicenter is the Quad, where more than 1,000 tents, set up on Friday nights, cover virtually every inch of its 21 acres.

Six hours before a Bryant-Denny kickoff, as many as 15,000 fans—the women decked out in bright sundresses, many of the men in ties and slacks, and the diehards in full houndstooth—transform the Quad into a college football mecca. They lounge on their hauled-in couches in front of flat-screen TVs, and they listen to music on speakers big enough to have been stolen from a dance club. Here, amid mounds of chicken wings and coolers overflowing with Dixie's drink of choice, Bud Light, the fans celebrate all things Tide. These parties, post 4/27, were an affirmation that Tuscaloosa's collective sense of greatness hadn't been blown away. Today, more than ever, the future felt rich with possibility.

ON THE brick plaza in front of the north end of the stadium, the bronze statues of the five Alabama coaches were each guarded by a stern, square-jawed police officer. A hundred fans surrounded the likeness of Bryant, nearly a thousand clustered close to the bronze Saban. Fans pulled out their iPhones to video the nine-foot version of the current head coach as if it might suddenly spring to life, yell "Roll Tide" and jog into the stadium.

More than a thousand members of the media had requested credentials for the game—an unofficial college football record for a regular-season game. Longtime sportswriters who had covered multiple Super Bowls, World Series and Olympics swore they had never witnessed more pregame buzz than what was happening today outside of Bryant-Denny.

Six-and-a-half months earlier this scene in T-Town had been unimaginable. Not even Mayor Walt Maddox, a category-five optimist at heart, had ever envisioned this kind of celebratory atmosphere so soon after the tornado. His wildest dreams didn't reach that far.

Lee and Leigh Henderson squeezed into a jammed restaurant on The Strip to watch the game. The Dowlings gathered around the TV in their new home five miles from the stadium and prepared to take in the action together. Shannon Brown settled onto his living room couch and turned on the television, confident that his Tide would carry the day once more. For the next three hours, for all of them, the storm didn't matter. Only football did.

THE GAME was an old-fashioned defensive struggle, the kind the Bear would have loved—though he'd surely have growled about the Tide missing four of six field goals. With the score tied 6–6 with 52 seconds to play in the fourth quarter and Saban holding two timeouts, the Tide had the ball on their own 20-yard line. Alabama fans clamored for a last-minute scoring drive, but Saban elected to let the clock run out and take his chances in overtime. Beleaguered Bama kicker Cade Foster stood alone at the end of the Alabama bench as he watched the time tick away. His helmet was off, his mouth was open, and his eyes were full moons. He looked spooked, as if hearing voices.

On the first possession of overtime, the Tide offense began at the LSU 25-yard line. This was the kind of moment AJ McCarron had played out in his dreams ever since he was a boy playing catch with his younger brother in the public park in Mobile. In the games he'd imagined, he always engineered the last-minute scoring drive. But now, facing into the student section in the southeast corner of the stadium, McCarron threw incomplete to Trent Richardson on first down. Before the ball was even snapped on second down, Alabama was flagged five yards for a substitution infraction. On second-and-15, McCarron again tried to hit Richardson down the right sideline, but the ball was overthrown. On third down McCarron, looking as rattled as he'd been all season, was sacked by defensive end Sam Montgomery for a five-yard loss back to the 35.

Foster lined up for a 52-yard field goal attempt. It wobbled into the air but never had a chance, falling short and left. As the ball bounced meekly onto the field, it sounded as if thousands of Crimson-clad fans were about to be sick as they let out a collective *ohhhhhhhhh*. Foster, reaching the sideline, put his hands on his helmet and looked up despondently toward the night sky.

LSU took over. After four plays the Tigers had gained 17 yards, and kicker Drew Alleman split the uprights from 25 yards for the game-winning points. LSU had beaten Alabama 9–6. Lee Henderson dropped his head in disappointment, Bob Dowling slapped his knee in frustration. And in Madison, Shannon Brown sighed deeply and went to bed. The too-good-to-be-true story line of a tornado inspiring a national title had come to a sad and sudden end.

The last two Alabama players to walk off the field were Trent Richardson and Chance Warmack. Richardson put his arm around the big left guard, who had tears running down his cheeks. Warmack, like so many of the Tide players, felt as if he had failed their town, letting everyone down. Football had been the miracle drug in Tuscaloosa. The chase for a national championship had become the narrative of hope. And now, Warmack believed, that quest—and all that it would mean to T-Town—was over. The loss hurt Warmack more, far more, than any other in his college career. Richardson tried to console his teammate.

"It's O.K., it's O.K.," Richardson said as the two slowly walked into the concrete tunnel. "We'll be back. We'll be back."

Forty-five minutes later several hundred Alabama fans stood outside the stadium in the chilly darkness, waiting next to the Alabama team buses. As the Tide players trudged out of the locker room and toward the idling buses, the crowd cheered as if they were greeting conquering warriors.

"You can still do it," a voice yelled.

"Keep going!" a woman shouted.

And so it went for a half hour, voices from the dark pleading for the Tide to keep fighting. The players heard every word as they filed on board. Dont'a Hightower stared out a window, bewildered. "Damn," he said to a teammate, nodding toward the mass outside. "They still believe in us."

THE NEXT night, some 24 hours after the loss to LSU, McCarron called his father, Tony, a fireman; it was midnight, and Tony had been asleep in his dorm room at Station No. 11 in Mobile. AJ was still upset, still replaying the game, frame-by-frame, snap-by-snap, in his mind. Yes, he'd thrown for 199 yards against the Tigers, but he'd also tossed an interception and appeared indecisive for much of the game. The agony of losing for the first time as a starter was sharp. As a native son he understood perfectly what the Tide meant to the legions of fans. That night he made a promise to his father: "Daddy, I will never play another game where I allow the other team to dictate how I play. I was so worried about losing the game for my team, I didn't go out and win it."

How he wished for one more shot at LSU. He would be a different player, he vowed. Just one more chance was all he wanted.

There had been a national consensus in the weeks before the

Alabama-LSU game that these were the two best teams in college football and that their showdown was a de facto championship game. The tight overtime result did little to dispel that notion; still, Alabama fell from second to third in the BCS rankings with the loss. The Tide would need help to advance to the BCS title game in New Orleans on Jan. 9. For Alabama to have a shot at winning the title, as the majority of analysts had it figured, Oklahoma State, Oregon (which beat undefeated Stanford on Nov. 12) and Oklahoma would all have to lose a game in the last month of the regular season—with Alabama, of course, not losing again. The chances of that happening seemed about as likely as Saban throwing a surprise Christmas party for the local beat writers.

The coach, however, appeared to be undaunted. During practices after the LSU loss, Saban repeatedly told his players to focus only on what they could control—on the field, in the weight room, in film study. In other words, stay with The Process. "It's not over for us yet," Saban told his team. "Trust me on that. Just trust me."

THEY SAT on their beds at the Hotel Capstone. The Tide players had just finished a team meeting on the evening of Nov. 18 in preparation for the next day's game against Georgia Southern. Barrett Jones and tight end Brad Smelley flipped on the TV to check out the game between No. 2 Oklahoma State and Iowa State. The Cyclones were 27-point underdogs.

In the bathroom, center William Vlachos had finished showering when he heard yelling and pounding on the walls. He ran into the room to find Jones and Smelley whooping and high-fiving. In the biggest upset of the season, the Cyclones had defeated Oklahoma State 37–31 in overtime. It was the first domino to fall in Alabama's unlikely scenario for reaching the title game.

Dozens of the players bolted out of their rooms at the hotel and into the hallways, bellowing and literally bouncing off the walls, waking every soul in the place. Even so, the Alabama coaches allowed their players to celebrate. "We're going to get another chance at LSU!" Hightower yelled. "I can feel it!"

Moments after the Iowa State fans stormed their field in Ames, Alabama fans on The Strip poured out of restaurants and bars to celebrate in the street. They hugged and howled and blared *Sweet Home Alabama* from car stereos. Within minutes the main drag through campus had been blocked by human traffic and the street was shut down. Not even the police officers minded.

After the Crimson Tide beat Georgia Southern 45–21 the following afternoon, the unexpected good fortune continued. That night, with all the players fixated on their TV sets, Alabama's path to New Orleans cleared with startling speed: No. 4 Oregon missed a last-play field goal against USC and lost 38–35; less than an hour later Baylor upset No. 5 Oklahoma 45–38 on a 34-yard touchdown pass by quarterback Robert Griffin III with eight seconds left on the clock. Immediately after the Sooners' loss, fans rushed again out onto The Strip, marveling at their luck and baying at the moon in happiness.

Such a scene: students, players and locals slapping high fives and partying a few hundred yards from Bryant-Denny and less than a mile from the ugly swath of destruction carved into their town. The survivors of the storm danced in the cold together, united and uninhibited. It felt like magic.

Of course, if Nick Saban had been out there in that joyful mob, he would have reminded them sternly that they hadn't achieved anything yet. The Crimson Tide would have to win their way to a title or all this happy circumstance would count for nothing. And, he might have added, there was another game next week—and it was against archnemesis Auburn.

CHAPTER 22

Passion
And
Poison

CARSON TINKER jogged onto the field at Jordan-Hare Stadium and glanced into the stands, trying to spot friends and family. Kickoff for the 76th edition of the Iron Bowl between Alabama and Auburn was still 45 minutes away. But Tinker, in his white road jersey and carrying his helmet, was unsmiling, jaw clenched and eyes narrowed. He was game ready.

Since the first day of preseason practice, football had been Tinker's escape. Out on the field he was just one of the guys, not the player known throughout the state, and even across the country, as the guy whose girlfriend was killed in the tornado. Football let him unleash his emotions—the bruising contact felt good. His teammates were his lifeline; they were constantly checking in on him, telling Tinker they were a phone call away if he wanted to talk, if he needed anything at all.

Saban had spoken to Tinker several times. When he was first summoned to the coach's office, Tinker worried that he had done something wrong on the practice field. Instead Saban quietly asked Tinker to sit down, then asked him how he was holding up. Saban is much more a cool taskmaster than a warm avuncular figure, but his relationship with Tinker had grown into something different from any other Saban had experienced in his coaching career. He had been with Tinker in his worst hours following the tornado, sitting at the young man's bedside in the hospital. He'd stayed in close touch with Tinker in the days and weeks that followed. It was not the kind of thing that Saban would ever say, but even before the tragedy of the storm, the gritty, strong-willed Tinker had become one of the coach's favorite players on this team.

Even the Auburn fans admired Tinker. In the aftermath of the tornado, a group of Tigers fans calling themselves Toomer's For Tuscaloosa had traveled to the shredded city and helped in the cleanup. Within days of the storm the group's number of "likes" on Facebook swelled from 50 to 80,000, enough supporters to nearly fill Jordan-Hare. And now as Tinker ran back toward the tunnel that would take him to the cramped visitors' locker room in the northeast corner of the stadium, many of the Auburn fans rose to their feet and applauded him. In the blood feud that is the Iron Bowl, this may have been the first time that a Crimson Tide player had been shown such affection on Auburn's home turf.

THE IRON BOWL is a year-round obsession in Alabama. With many of the other biggest rivalries in college football—Texas-Oklahoma, Ohio State–Michigan—the schools aren't located within the same state. And because there are no major professional sports teams of any kind in Alabama, every sports fan in the state has to answer a single question: *Do I support the Tide or the Tigers?* There really is no alternative. Usually the decision is made at birth; typically parents will dress their newborns in either Alabama or Auburn clothes before they've left the crib.

A poll in the *Mobile Register* several years ago indicated that 90% of the state's population described themselves as college football fans, and 86% of those rooted for either Alabama or Auburn; just 4% said they supported any other team. This meant that in the God-fearing state of Alabama, there were more avowed atheists than there were football fans who didn't believe in either the Tide or the Tigers.

What makes the annual Alabama-Auburn game unique is that fans of the teams grow up with each other, go to high school with each other, work together, socialize together, go to church together, go hunting together and—in many cases—get married. It's repeatedly said that the state's most recognizable figures are, in this order: 1) the Alabama coach, 2) the Auburn coach, 3) the Crimson Tide's starting quarterback, 4) the Tigers' starting quarterback. The governor is a distant fifth.

During the past two decades the rivalry has been fanned to white heat by the Paul Finebaum radio show out of Birmingham. (The show went national and moved to Charlotte in 2013.) For four hours, five days a week, Finebaum rarely strays far from talking about Alabama and Auburn. The week of the Super Bowl? The talk on the Finebaum show is about college football recruiting. During March Madness? The topic is the spring football games.

The Paul Finebaum Show is a caller-driven circus in which he is the ringleader. Finebaum influences public opinion like no other sports media figure in the South—Robert Bentley claims he wouldn't have been elected governor of Alabama in 2010 if not for his appearance on Finebaum's show—and heaven help the coach who comes into Finebaum's crosshairs. A former columnist for the now defunct *Birmingham Post-Herald*, Finebaum, 58, combines an acerbic, sharp-tongued style with the interview skills of a Charlie Rose. He's become a polarizing figure in Dixie, but even those who loathe him can't help but be entertained by the deep-fried fanaticism of callers that go by handles such as Legend, Jim From Tuscaloosa, and Phyllis—all household names in Alabama.

It doesn't take long while listening to the show to discern the extreme stereotypes each fan base in the Alabama-Auburn war continues to project on the other. Alabama is seen as the state's flagship school, where the upper class send their children to rub shoulders with other rich kids. There they learn the fine arts of cocktailing and riding about in expensive cars gifted them by their parents. When they earn their degrees, they'll either go to law school or medical school or move back to the hometown to take over daddy's business. Generation after generation, Alabama grads ensure that the family cycle of charmed life won't end. The University of Alabama is the state's high society, the cultural elite. It is, according to the stereotype, where winners go.

Auburn, located in the small, rural town of Auburn in the eastern part of the state near the Georgia border (and about 160 miles from Tuscaloosa), is portrayed as a "cow college," as Bear Bryant once dubbed it. Founded in 1856 it was, for many years, the Agricultural and Mechanical College of Alabama. Its students, the stereotype holds, hail from middle- and lower-class families. Auburn students spend their time analyzing soil samples and bovine infections. Auburn, says the stereotype, is where the underdogs go.

The first football game between the two schools was played on Feb. 22, 1893. That morning special steam-engine trains from Tuscaloosa and Auburn clickety-clacked into a station near Lakeview Park in Birmingham. Once the wheels of the iron horses screeched to a halt, fans poured out of the rail cars and walked through the chill of the winter afternoon to the park to watch the University of Alabama versus the Agricultural and Mechanical College of Alabama. By 3 p.m., thirty minutes before kickoff, thousands of fans filled the small grandstand and surrounded the field, some standing 10 deep.

The Alabama players ran onto the field, wearing red stockings and white sweaters with the red letters "UA" emblazoned across their chests. The A&M team then appeared, outfitted in white pants, blue stockings and blue sweaters with a bright orange "A" on the front. It didn't take long for the crowd to become impassioned. At one point an A&M back took a direct snap and ran 65 yards down the field. After he was tackled at the Alabama 35-yard line, Tigers fans exuberantly stormed the field. The two officials needed help from police to push the fans back to the sidelines.

A&M won the game 32–22. The team from Auburn then gathered in front of a festively decorated carriage, where, according to John Chandler Griffin's book, *Auburn vs. Alabama,* a Miss Delma Wilson was waiting to present a silver cup to the captain of the winning team, Thomas Daniels. Wilson rose to her feet and exclaimed, "Gallant and victorious captain, in the name of the city of Birmingham, I present this cup. Drink from it and remember the victory that you have won this day. May you and your team live to see many more victories." The Auburn fans cheered, the Tuscaloosa fans sulked, and so began a rivalry like no other in sports.

ON THE morning of the 75th Iron Bowl, in 2010, the intensity seemed to have reached a new peak. The tailgating around Bryant-Denny Stadium was in full swing even earlier than usual. The Quad, under a cold, overcast sky, was jammed by eight.

Alabama had already lost two games that season, with no title hopes, but the possibility of knocking undefeated Auburn out of the BCS race was a delicious prospect. And in so doing, the Tide might also punch a hole in the Heisman Trophy hopes of Tigers quarterback Cam Newton, whose story added a powerful undercurrent to this game.

Newton had barely spoken publicly in the few weeks since it had been alleged that during his recruiting his father, Cecil, a pastor in Newnan, Ga., had asked Mississippi State for as much as $180,000 in a pay-for-play scheme. As the bloodhounds from the SEC, NCAA and even the FBI followed the scent of scandal, Auburn stood by its star quarterback, while Alabama fans—and many in the media—suggested that something nefarious *must* have occurred that led Newton to sign with the Tigers. Outside the stadium before kickoff, vendors sold $CAM NEWTON T-shirts. When the quarterback ran onto the field for pregame warmups, the sound system at Bryant-Denny tauntingly blared the songs *Take the Money and Run* and *Son of a Preacher Man* (which would result in the firing of the person responsible).

Among the Alabama rooters sitting in the stadium that day was Harvey Updyke Jr., a 62-year-old hard-core Crimson Tide fan. Updyke especially despised Auburn. The season before, during most game days, he had worn a shirt that read, IF YOU SEE ME IN A TURBAN & SANDALS AU IS PLAYING IRAQ! He had attended his first Alabama game in 1970, at the Astro-Bluebonnet Bowl in Houston, and had made a lasting impression when he ran onto the field during the third quarter, one hand brandishing two rolls of toilet paper on a broom handle and the other holding a box of Tide detergent. His message: Roll Tide.

Several years later he had a daughter and named her Crimson Tyde. He then had a son whom he named Bear Bryant. He wanted to name another daughter Ally Bama, but this time his wife—his third wife—put her foot down. The girl was named Megan.

After retiring on disability in 1988, after a career as a Texas state trooper, Updyke and his wife had been renting a small, cinder-block cabin on Lake Martin near Dadeville, Ala., located, ironically enough, a mere 30 miles from Auburn. That proximity, it seemed, had only served to stoke his hatred of Alabama's rival.

As the Cam Newton story unfolded just a half-hour's drive from his home, Updyke seethed. Every day he heard locals talking about how wonderful Newton was; every day he'd tell them that the Tigers were cheating and that Auburn would be put in its rightful place once it played Alabama. Most afternoons Updyke would listen to the Paul Finebaum show, where accusations against Newton and Auburn grew and festered, where venom was spewed by both sides of the rivalry as the Iron Bowl approached. "We are going to stomp that butt coming up in T-Town," yelled one caller, the Alabama fan known as Legend. "It's frigging war. I ain't got no love for those West Georgia coon dog buzzards, in-bred toenail lickers!"

On the day of the 2010 Iron Bowl, before the game, Updyke and a friend strolled the Alabama campus. Upon nearing the stadium they saw, according to Updyke, that someone had put a Newton jersey on the statue of Bear Bryant. Updyke, a zealous worshipper of the Bear since he'd been an awestruck 10-year-old, was infuriated.

Updyke appeared to be vindicated when Alabama built a 24–7 lead at halftime. Then, on the second play of the third quarter, Newton lofted a long, tight spiral down the center of the field. Alabama safety Mark Barron appeared to have coverage and a shot at an interception, but Auburn's Terrell Zachery slid just past him, caught the pass and sprinted 35 more yards for a touchdown, making the score 24–14.

The game had changed. Newton led Auburn to touchdowns on two of the Tigers' next three possessions. The crowd fell into a what-is-happening silence. When the final whistle blew, the scoreboard read Auburn 28, Alabama 27. As Saban and his players walked off the field, downcast and in disbelief, Newton ran a clockwise victory lap, holding one hand over his mouth, as if to prevent himself from saying, "I told you so." He had essentially just won the Heisman, and he'd done it on enemy soil.

Later that night the Tigers' team buses rolled into Auburn and paused at the intersection of Magnolia Avenue and College Street, where two oak trees, now 30 feet tall, have framed the main entrance to the Auburn campus for 130 years, a place called Toomer's Corner. (Sheldon Toomer, a halfback on the Tigers' very first team, in 1892, built a drug store there in 1896, across the street from the campus entrance, and the trees have long been known as Toomer's Oaks.)

For more than 50 years, Auburn fans have gathered here at this corner to scream "War Eagle" and celebrate victories. In 1972 a Tigers running back named Terry Henley promised to "beat the number 2" out of second-ranked Alabama; minutes after the Tigers won the game 17–16, Auburn fans hurled rolls of toilet paper into the oaks. "Rolling Toomer's Corner" has been a revered tradition ever since.

As soon as the 75th Iron Bowl was over, a throng of Auburn students flocked to the intersection and began papering the oaks. As the buses carrying the Tigers' team now paused at Toomer's Corner, every Auburn player was delighted at the sight of hundreds of rolls of toilet paper hanging like streamers from the branches. Several players pulled out their iPhones and snapped pictures.

FROM HIS seat near midfield at Bryant-Denny, Updyke had felt his blood boil as Auburn mounted the greatest comeback in the history of the Iron Bowl series. He and a companion had planned to stay in Tuscaloosa, but they canceled their hotel reservation and drove through the night back to his home in Dadeville. Updyke was so despondent that he didn't say more than a few words during the three-hour trip.

On Jan. 27, 17 days after Auburn beat Oregon to win the national championship, Updyke called the Finebaum radio show. He identified himself as "Al from Dadeville." (His middle name is Almorn.) He told Finebaum about seeing Newton's jersey on Bear Bryant's statue and also said that a friend had sent him a newspaper clipping describing how Auburn fans had rolled Toomer's Corner after Bryant had died—which Finebaum correctly pointed out had never happened. The end of the on-air exchange went like this.

Al: Let me tell you what I did. The weekend after the Iron Bowl, I went to Auburn, Alabama, 'cause I live 30 miles away, and I poisoned the two Toomer's trees.

Finebaum: O.K., well that's fair.

Al: I put Spike 80DF in 'em.

Finebaum: Did they die?

Al: Do what?

Finebaum: Did. They. Die?

Al: They're not dead yet, but they definitely will die.

Finebaum: Is that against the law, to poison a tree?

Al: Well, do you think I care? I really don't. Roll damn Tide.

Finebaum and his producer initially dismissed Al as a crank caller seeking attention, but Finebaum grew more concerned when he was told that the federal government was investigating the incident because of the possibility of groundwater contamination underneath Toomer's Corner. Auburn officials later announced that the amount of poisonous herbicide found in the soil was 500 times the amount necessary to kill the trees.

Updyke was eventually charged with four felonies—two for each tree, actually—and he pleaded not guilty by reason of mental defect. Updyke admitted to calling the Finebaum show but not to poisoning the trees. During a later call to Finebaum he said that he would get what he deserved, but he did not confess. "I just had too much Bama in me, all my life," Updyke said. "I know they [Auburn fans] don't feel sorry for me." Later he tried to point the finger at an unnamed man in his 30s who, he said, had been sitting beside him at the Iron Bowl; during the game, claimed Updyke, the man had told him he planned to poison the trees.

(On March 22, 2013, Updyke agreed to a deal with Lee County prosecutors in Opelika, Ala. He pleaded guilty to criminal damage of an agricultural facility and was sentenced to three years in prison. Under the terms of the plea, Updyke was required to spend at least six months in jail—he was credited for 104 days previously served—and was to be placed on five years of supervised probation, during which time Updyke would have a 7 p.m. curfew and be banned from setting foot on the Auburn campus or attending any college sporting event. He also was prohibited from talking to reporters. The two sickened trees were removed in April 2013.)

For Updyke, the worst punishment was the way Alabama fans turned on him. They sent him messages strewn with profanities on his Facebook page, and he was eviscerated on the Alabama message boards that Updyke read every day. There are hundreds of Alabama fan sites, which are populated by posters who go by handles such as Alabama Slamma and King Nick, and they all trashed Updyke. He felt like he'd been cast out of the village.

Embarrassed Crimson Tide fans raised $50,000 to help save the oaks, but that didn't prevent a certain amount of nationwide scorn from being directed at the Alabama fanhood, many commentators declaring that Updyke was representative of a larger problem of out-of-control Tide fans with a twisted devotion to their team.

Saban, for his part, said that the tree poisoner "does not represent

our institution, our program or our fans in any way." But com-
bined with his team's historic collapse in the Iron Bowl, the Updyke
episode marked the low point of the Nick Saban era at Alabama.

In many ways, the stain of Harvey Updyke Jr. would linger in Tuscaloosa, and upon the Alabama football program, until, perversely, it
was wiped away by the tornado. Within days of the storm, as images
of the devastation were broadcast across the country, the national
perception of the Tide and their legion of followers began to soften
and change. Fans from around the country called the Finebaum show
to say that though they never had before, they were now rooting for
the Crimson Tide because they were rooting for the desolate people
of Tuscaloosa. Some said they thought that Alabama had become
"America's College Team."

And the Auburn fans, of all people, showed sympathy too, which
was why, now, at the ensuing Iron Bowl, the 2011 edition, they were
cheering Carson Tinker as he left the field following pregame warmups.

Even so, there was a game to be played, and it was Auburn that
now stood in the way of Alabama's revitalized quest to advance to the
national title game.

DATING BACK to the beginning of the year, the Tide players had
adopted the slogan Never Again in reference to their astounding
collapse in the previous Iron Bowl. That defeat had stung Saban
like no other in his coaching career; it was the biggest blown lead
in Iron Bowl history. And now this game had taken on enormous
added importance.

A few hours later it was done, and redemption was total. The Tide,
riding the speed and strength of Trent Richardson (a career-high
203 yards rushing), executed a ruthless 42–14 dismantling of Auburn.
Midway through the fourth quarter, with the ball on Alabama's
27-yard line, Richardson produced a Heisman-worthy highlight.
Running to his left, the 5' 11", 224-pound Richardson twisted, turned
and stiff-armed to break four tackles, sprinted down the sideline and

then across the field before finally being taken down after a 57-yard gain. As it would turn out, Richardson didn't win the Heisman—he would finish third behind Baylor's Robert Griffin III and Stanford quarterback Andrew Luck—but his punishing runs against Auburn made certain that the Tide didn't implode as they had 12 months earlier. And made sure that the Alabama title dream lived on.

An hour after the game, Richardson was still following his lead blocker, a police officer who tried to clear a path through a swarm of fans outside of Jordan-Hare. Richardson waited patiently until he saw an opening. Darting past the officer, he jogged toward the idling team bus 50 feet away.

"Go get LSU, Trent!" a fan wearing an Alabama jersey yelled as he reached the bus. "Get the damn Tigers! They'll never beat us twice!" Richardson stopped. For a few heartbeats he smiled to himself as it hit him: The Tide were now virtually assured of a spot in the title game. Alabama was on the cusp of gaining something exquisitely rare in sports—a second chance.

The whole team, of course, shared his mood. "I told everyone [after the LSU game], This ain't over, this is *not* over," said cornerback Dre Kirkpatrick. "I'm pretty sure LSU was watching us tonight. I hope they're saying, 'Come on, come on.' "

"In my mind," said Richardson, "our game against LSU still isn't over. Give us four more quarters, and we'll see what happens. Four more quarters."

"That was a game of inches, literally," said William Vlachos. "We are so closely matched with them. But we feel like we've definitely improved the last three weeks."

Indeed, while the Alabama defense had continued to smother its opponents to finish out the regular season—the Tide led the nation in virtually every significant defensive category—the offense had become more potent because of the development of one player: AJ McCarron. The sophomore had been a different quarterback ever since making that late-night call to his father after the LSU game. McCarron had his finest game of the season against Auburn. Throwing a mixture of short, medium and long balls, McCarron completed 18 of 23 passes for 184 yards and three touchdowns. "The running game is not all we've got," said McCarron afterward. "But it's nice to have the best player in the country, Trent Richardson, lining up behind me."

When Nick Saban was running off the field after the Auburn win, some 5,000 Alabama fans who had gathered directly above the tunnel chanted, "LSU, LSU, LSU!" Saban thrust his right index finger into the air, for him a wildly flamboyant display of showmanship. For a coach like Saban, who thrills to the tiniest details and the most intricate strategies of the game, what could be better than a rematch with the team that had beat him?

Eight days later the final regular-season BCS standings made it official: Alabama would play LSU for the national title in the Super-dome on Jan. 9, 2012. A little more than eight months after Tuscaloosa had been torn apart, the Crimson Tide would have another chance to bring everyone together.

CHAPTER 23

Game
Ready

TWO WEEKS before leaving for New Orleans, Barrett Jones sat in the Alabama football offices. Just a junior, Jones was already deemed by analysts to be as versatile and valuable as any lineman in Alabama's football history. In the title game, from his left tackle position, he would be charged with protecting McCarron's blind side, as he had all season.

The Alabama-LSU rematch had moved squarely into the hot center of the national sports spotlight and the Alabama players with it. It was no surprise that besides the usual media inquiries—How will this game be different from the first? What offensive changes has Coach Saban made? Can you protect your quarterback from the fierce LSU rush?—there were questions about Tuscaloosa and the tornado and what impact it might have had on the team. By now the players had become not only passionate on the subject but also increasingly articulate. It mattered to them greatly, and they were happy to make that clear.

Jones was now explaining again what those days after the storm had meant to this championship quest. "When we as a team," he said, "went out there into the community of Tuscaloosa and did everything we could to lend a hand in the recovery from the tornado, it *definitely* made us closer. It gave us the opportunity to know each other in a different way. It strengthened our bond as teammates. And it *definitely* made us want to do something special on the field for our town."

Chance Warmack echoed his linemate's thoughts. "It did something to all of us when we went out into town as a team, as brothers, as citizens," he said. "We gave shoulders for others to cry on. The amount of devastation we saw—even movies aren't that bad. It changes you. We always want to win, but going through all we did made us want to do that extra rep in the weight room or that extra play in practice, just so we could do everything we could to not let the people of Tuscaloosa down. I've never been more motivated than I have this season, and that's all because of April 27."

If motivation alone could win a national championship, then this title game, it seemed, would be no contest.

A FEW days after Christmas, at the same time the Crimson Tide players were practicing and preparing for their showdown with LSU, Lee Henderson was at home reading a magazine when he noticed an advertisement for a chain of sandwich shops called Which Wich. The name caught his eye and his ear—he liked it. And the timing felt epiphanic; in recent days he had been feeling, finally, that it was time to get on with the next step in his life. At last he felt ready— emotionally, physically, intellectually—to take on the next challenge.

More than that, Henderson wanted to be a part of the new Tuscaloosa. New businesses were starting to open in even the areas hardest hit by the tornado, like flowers blooming on barren ground, and now Henderson was inspired to join in. Over the next several months he would travel to 13 locations in three cities to visit Which Wich stores, working out his plan, a kind of reclamation project to replace what had been taken from him by the storm, to replace it with something new.

But first things first: On Jan. 7, Henderson and his wife, Leigh, packed a few bags into the car and headed for New Orleans. They didn't even have tickets to the game, but nothing was going to stop them from being a part of Alabama versus LSU in the Big Easy. Their plan was simply to watch the game from the team's hotel and be in the lobby waiting for the players afterward to congratulate them. It would be their "thank you" for all the team had done for Tuscaloosa. As Henderson put it, "They came back, and we're coming back."

FAR FROM New Orleans, an assistant coach for one of Alabama's rivals in the SEC was sitting at a desk in a dark, windowless room in his school's football complex. A 10-foot-by-15-foot screen stretched from ceiling to floor on the far side of the room. The coach had been asked by a reporter to break down tape from the Nov. 5 Alabama-LSU game, to shed some light on what might be expected in the coming rematch. He knew these two teams all too well. "I *hate* these programs," the coach said, "but man, they are far and away the top two teams in the nation. Every starter on this field has the ability to play in the NFL. Every. Single. One." (He would be proved nearly correct; an extraordinary 31 players from that BCS championship matchup would be selected in the next two NFL drafts, unprecedented for a single title game.)

Holding a laser pointer in one hand and a remote control in the other, the coach pushed the play button. For the next 90 minutes he examined every play on the tape, frame by frame, block by block. At one point he leaned back in his chair and, as if to cut to the chase, declared, "They have the top two defenses in the country, and both offenses are loaded with big-time athletes. It's going to be a hell of a title game."

He continued: "The extended time to prepare for the game is a huge advantage for Saban. LSU doesn't do anything fancy on defense. They line up and say, 'Beat us.' But Alabama plays an

NFL-type of scheme. They say, 'Not only will we beat you with our athletes, but we're also going to outscheme you.' Saban has more blitz packages than any coach in the country. And it's a very complicated scheme, with more shifting based on the presnap motion of the offense than any other team. If one guy on the Alabama defense doesn't get lined up correctly, you can burn them for a long play. But these Alabama players are so smart and sound, it's truly amazing. I don't know if I've ever seen a smarter defense. They'll study like crazy and, based on LSU's tendencies, they'll know what's coming a good deal of the time."

Having spent hours dissecting the two teams, the coach believed two things: LSU would have more overall talent on the field, but Alabama would win. Why? "It's almost unfair to give Saban so much time to prepare," he said. "Alabama generally outplayed LSU the first time, but the scoreboard didn't say that. I think they'll do it again, but this time the result will be different."

BOB DOWLING drove his black Jeep through the empty streets of Tuscaloosa on Jan. 9, straining to hear the pregame discussion over the static on the radio. As he delivered pizzas for Papa John's on this cool winter night—he was heartbroken that he couldn't watch the game on television, but he needed the work—he grinned every time a name such as D.J. Fluker or Barrett Jones was mentioned. They'd been part of his work crew.

With game time approaching, he delivered a pizza to a house near campus. When the door opened, he caught a glimpse of the television inside. The teams were on the field, preparing for the championship showdown. Dowling was invited inside and offered a cold beer, but he regretfully declined; he had more addresses to reach, more tips to earn. Yet Dowling, 300 miles from the Superdome, could still feel the thrill of anticipation as kickoff neared. That was what Alabama football did for him now: it kept him looking ahead, rather than at the tragedy behind.

SHANNON BROWN decided to throw a party, albeit a small one. Even the smallest steps were moving him in the direction of healing. So Brown invited a few of his close friends to come to his house on the night of the title game to watch it with him. There was zero doubt in his mind that Alabama would win the game, and with relative ease, he thought. The Tide had been given a second chance against LSU, and Brown understood exactly what that would mean to the team. "The tornado made this season personal to the players and to Saban," Shannon told his friends. "I saw it in their eyes when I was on the field for the homecoming game. They knew they could make a difference and give Tuscaloosa something to be proud of. There is *no way* they're going to let Tuscaloosa down."

His friends, of course, wanted to know how he was holding up. Shannon still hadn't sought professional help, but there were signs of improvement. Best of all was being around his two other children, both younger than Loryn. As for his oldest daughter, he told his friends, "It's not easy. It will never be easy. I just hope no one has to go through what Loryn's mother and I have gone through."

He settled into a living room chair and waited for kickoff. For three hours he could lose himself.

THIRTY MINUTES before kickoff, Ashley Mims turned on all four television sets in her house. She and 13-year-old Parker crawled onto the bed in the master bedroom, their favored viewing spot for Alabama games. Ever since he'd visited Saban in his office, Parker's mood had brightened. Saban had told him that whenever he missed Sissy he should "do something good for someone"; Parker, hearing instruction from the coach he idolized, had taken it to heart, helping his mother around the house with chores like the laundry and the dinner dishes. For that, for Saban's influence, Ashley was thankful.

Now Parker, wearing a Tide jersey and overamped with excitement, was jumping up and down on the bed. Loryn had always done the same thing. Ashley remembered how, during the '09 title game against Texas, Loryn insisted on briefly changing the channel when the Longhorns mounted a second-half comeback. When Alabama prevailed 37–21, Loryn boasted that by changing the channel, she had personally turned the game in favor of the Tide.

"Can't you just feel Loryn right now?" Ashley asked Parker moments before the Alabama players ran onto the Superdome field. "I really can feel her. She's with us. She's here. And she's happy." She looked at her son and smiled a genuine smile. "She's so happy."

It felt like a real party. Ashley was ready to cheer on the Tide again.

ALONG WITH hundreds of other fans decked out in everything crimson, the Hendersons stood in the lobby of the Marriott Hotel on Canal Street, cheering and clapping as the Alabama players walked down a flight of stairs and toward their three team buses. The ground seemed to tremble, especially as the enormous linemen lumbered by—*whomp, whomp, whomp*. Even the Hendersons, veteran loyalists, were struck by how *big* these guys were.

Wearing a crimson bow tie with tiny white Alabama logos, AJ McCarron marched past the Hendersons. Only a sophomore, and though he'd played his worst game of the season against LSU two months earlier, McCarron was a picture of calm confidence. As much as any quarterback to play for Saban, McCarron was an extension of his coach, an obsessive film junkie who knew exactly what his job was when he stepped on the field. As McCarron passed the Hendersons, his face was creased with a knowing half-moon smile.

Scott Cochran, the Tide's strength coach, approached, and Lee Henderson grinned as he strode by; the blond, blue-eyed Cochran had given Lee a spirited high five in the lobby the day before. Cochran was a 32-year-old supercharged, in-your-face coach known throughout Tuscaloosa for his screams of *Yeah, yeahh, yeah-hhhh!* played on the big video screen in Bryant-Denny before the start of every fourth quarter. His voice typically hoarse at the end of every day, Cochran constantly challenged the Alabama players—at the top of his lungs—to do an extra rep in the weight room or run an extra wind sprint at the end of a conditioning session. To keep the internal motors of his charges revving, Cochran liked to dig into a computer file that contains more than 2,000 pages of inspirational quotes, then deliver chosen nuggets to his players. Cochran, who spends more one-on-one time with the players than anybody in the Alabama program, is universally admired by freshmen and veterans alike. He is forever asking about family members, classes and grades, life away from the field. He is the good cop to Saban's bad cop. As he passed by the Hendersons, Cochran was radiating such intensity, it looked as if he could glow in the dark.

Lee Henderson leaned into the ear of his wife. "They're really going to do this," he told her. "There's no way they're losing tonight."

After the buses pulled away and headed for the Superdome, the Hendersons found seats in the hotel lobby in front of a large flat-screen TV. In a few hours, as they planned it, they would greet the team here in the lobby upon their return as national champs.

CHAPTER 24

This
One Was
Different

THREE DAYS before the biggest game he'd ever played, Carson Tinker had stood inside the empty Superdome. His big, brown eyes gazed up into the highest reaches of the vast dome as if he were looking to heaven. He was remembering those crowded hours of happiness he had spent with his Ashley, how simply sitting on the couch with her, watching TV, had filled him with such peace.

The tornado. It had changed everything. For him and for his team. In the eerie quiet of the Superdome, as he walked slowly along a sideline, Tinker spoke softly to a reporter walking with him. "It's been hard, very hard," he said, "but I just try to smile and be an inspiration and share my story with anyone who wants to hear it." He turned to look out at the field. "We became a different team on April 27 because we knew we were playing for something more than just ourselves."

The message, the mantra—*Let's play for Tuscaloosa*—had been repeated again and again, by the players, the coaches, everyone associated with the Crimson Tide program. There had grown a powerful sense that it was their *duty* to bring solace to a place that had been visited by so much horror. Something strong—unquantifiable but as real as a clenched jaw—roiled inside every Alabama player and coach. They had been living with the haunting aftereffects of that tornado every single emotional day for the past eight months. *Let's play for Tuscaloosa* was a reminder of everything that was at stake for the Crimson Tide, all rolled together in a single football game.

HE WALKED onto the Superdome field, flanked by two state troopers, the intensity, as always, glimmering in his dark-brown eyes. When he reached the south end zone, about 50 minutes before kickoff, Nick Saban gathered his Alabama players around him in a cluster, clapping his hands sharply. In a voice loud enough that each could hear him clearly, he told them that now was their time—time to seize the moment, the night, the national title. He was a picture of steely resolve. It was, Saban would later admit, the most important game of his football life.

He moved briskly to midfield, where he paced with his arms folded, silent now and deep in thought. He watched closely as his players—in crimson jerseys, white pants, crimson helmets—went through their warmup routines. Three, four, five minutes, Saban strode back and forth across the BCS national championship logo painted at midfield. He looked almost miniature among these armored football giants, but his players, with no more than a quick glance in his direction, knew he was there in full, a commanding presence, assessing, analyzing, plotting.

He shook hands with LSU coach Les Miles, offering only a tight smile and a few words of greeting before the two men quickly parted. From the back pocket of his khaki pants, Saban pulled out a piece of paper, about the size of the folded lineup card a baseball manager carries in his uniform pocket. Written there were Saban's "field notes," as he calls them, prepared earlier in his suite at the Marriott, carefully created reminders of what he had learned in the more than 200 hours of film study of LSU games he'd reviewed during the previous 43 days. He was preparedness personified, and now as he stepped across the field with the clock ticking closer to kickoff and his players in the final stages of their meticulously scripted pregame regimen, Saban's eyes scanned his notes one more time, shorthand for all that he hoped to accomplish on this night. He scribbled a few added thoughts, then slipped the paper back into his pocket, out of sight but never out of his busy mind.

He spoke briefly with AJ McCarron before heading across the field. Saban could not stand still; his eyes swung sideline to sideline, watching, watching, watching. Bear Bryant had been known for the way he would always lean against a goalpost before a game, passively regarding his team during warmups, as if his job of preparing his players were done and done well, nothing more he could add. But Saban walked and worried, still working, frenetic even in these final minutes.

TINKER BENT forward in his number 51 jersey and fired one long snap after another between his legs, each one expertly hitting the outstretched hands of the punter, then the field goal holder, all part of his pregame routine. Tinker had been near perfect in his two seasons as Alabama's starting long snapper. In 242 punt, field goal and extra-point attempts, Tinker had misfired only twice. In this 2011 season he was 119 for 119.

When the warmup session was done, Tinker began a slow jog around the stadium. Surely, in the long history of college football, there had never been a long snapper—a specialist player seldom out on the field—who had been the emotional heart and soul of an elite team. But that was what Tinker had become. Every Alabama player believed him to be as integral to their team as anyone else on the roster, and they most certainly believed he was their spiritual leader. In the waning minutes before kickoff, as he trotted around the field, Tinker high-fived his teammates and shouted words of encouragement. His mere presence was a reminder to each of them of how lucky they had been just eight months earlier.

Just before warmups, inside the locker room, Tinker had carefully pulled out his Louis Vuitton wallet from his back pocket and placed it in his locker. Like almost everything else he owned, the wallet had been lost in the tornado, snatched by the wind; but it was recovered several days later—the cash and credit cards gone—and eventually returned to him. Now the leather wallet was among his most cherished possessions. Inside it, still intact after the storm, was a note from Ashley, who had given him the wallet as a Christmas gift with the note inside. It was signed "Ash" and she had adorned it with a hand-drawn heart. Now, back in the locker room with kickoff only minutes away, Tinker thought once more about that note, thought once more of Ashley, just as Saban called his players together.

He stood before his team. Saban is rarely lyrical in his pregame speeches; he typically reminds his players of football fundamentals in flat, businesslike language. But now even the coach was moved by the magnitude of the moment, and his most basic instructions were tinged with his passion. He spoke of the need for everyone to do their jobs, to focus on their particular responsibility each play, and to finish strong. As always, it was a call to adhere to The Process. More than ever, he said, paying close attention to every detail was paramount. He ended his speech with a loud shout: "We fight, we fight, we fight!"

The players ran onto the Superdome field, sure that their long days of preparation would give them the edge. Defensive coordinator Kirby Smart felt that the LSU offense was about to fall into a trap. On Nov. 19, Georgia Southern had rushed for 302 yards against the Tide in Alabama's 45–21 victory. The Eagles had primarily used the option attack, and now Smart figured that the Tigers would try to employ that offensive plan. He wasn't worried, he would later say, because LSU was not an option-based team, and "you can't learn the option in a few weeks."

What's more, Saban and Smart had designed several new blitz schemes during their six weeks of preparation. In the new packages the blitzers would come primarily from the right side of LSU quarterback Jordan Jefferson because game film revealed that the righthanded Jefferson struggled with his accuracy when forced to move to his left. As Saban and Smart conferred on the sideline in the minutes before the players took the field for the opening kickoff, both felt comfortable with their plan.

LSU received the kickoff. On first down from his 28-yard line, Jefferson handed the ball to running back Michael Ford, who was leveled by the Alabama line. On second down Jefferson completed a six-yard pass to wide receiver Rueben Randle, who was run down on the left sideline by linebacker Courtney Upshaw—and no doubt some of the 20,000 who had made donations in exchange for Upshaw's autograph were up there in the stands cheering his effort. On third-and-two Jefferson scanned the defense, audibled to a new play and then fumbled the snap for a two-yard loss. Tide defenders surrounded the quarterback, pumping their fists in an overflow of emotion. It would be a defining image of the game.

Alabama's first drive stalled and the Tide punted. When the Tigers faced a second-and-12 from their 19-yard line, Jefferson, as Saban and Smart had predicted, tried to run the option and was drilled by Upshaw after a two-yard gain. On the next play Jefferson audibled at the line for another option, to the left. After running a few strides, he pitched to Spencer Ware, who was banged to the turf, again by Upshaw, no gain, fourth down. The Bama players were seeing the game develop just as their coaches had told them it would, and their confidence soared. The Tigers had run only six offensive plays, and the scoreboard still read 0–0, but on the Alabama sideline it already felt as if the Tide had an insurmountable lead.

The Tigers punted. Wide receiver Marquis Maze fielded the ball at Bama's 25-yard line. With a few jukes, he returned the ball up the right side of the field, LSU defenders lunging at air; Maze was finally pushed out-of-bounds at the LSU 26-yard line, a 49-yard runback. McCarron completed two of three passes to move the ball to the six, where Jeremy Shelley, now the Tide field goal kicker, kicked a 23-yarder, his first of five in this game. With five minutes left in the first quarter, Alabama was up 3–0.

The remainder of the game belonged to the Bama defense and to McCarron. LSU would gain only five total first downs as quarterback Jefferson was thoroughly confused by Alabama's presnap shifts and all the motions and blitzes Saban had spent weeks designing and perfecting. McCarron would play brilliantly, in a rhythmic groove all evening, completing 23 of 34 passes for 234 yards.

With 4:44 remaining in the fourth quarter and Alabama up 15–0, all points scored on field goals, McCarron handed the ball to Trent Richardson, who darted around the left edge, down the sideline and sped 34 yards into the end zone to score the first touchdown either of these teams had scored against each other in nearly eight quarters. The score clinched the game for Alabama. As the clock ran out, the scoreboard told the story: Alabama 21, LSU 0.

McCarron ran to Saban, wrapped his arms around his coach and lifted him off his feet. Hightower, Chapman and Upshaw grabbed each other tightly and yelled, "We did it! We did it! We did it!" They then pointed into the stands at the delirious Alabama fans.

Nearby Richardson raised his right index finger in the air, hoping his No. 1 sign could be seen all the way back in Tuscaloosa. "There's so much talent on this team, it's ridiculous," Richardson crowed to a group of reporters on the field. "And just like the town of Tuscaloosa, we proved that we can overcome anything."

A few yards away Carson Tinker gazed in the direction of Darlene and David Harrison, who had made the trip from Dallas. Ashley would have turned 23 at midnight—only 90 minutes away—and she'd promised Carson that this game, this victory, would be the beginning of her birthday party. Accompanied now by a reporter, Tinker walked along the field, tears in his eyes, his mind on Ashley.

"There's not a day goes by that I don't think of her," he said as he looked up at the still-cheering Alabama fans in the stands. "We've been through so much this year, and I'm at a loss for words to describe what I feel. Just happy. . . . I do hope the people of Alabama can feel this joy tonight." Moments later a few Alabama players grabbed Tinker, hugging him hard and bellowing: *This one was for you!*

In the stands Darlene cried, emotionally overwhelmed. Saban had asked Mal Moore to make tickets available to Ashley's parents, and before the game the Harrisons had attended a tailgate party hosted by a friend who was an LSU fan. Dressed in Alabama crimson, Darlene and David at first had been playfully ribbed by the Tigers faithful, mostly strangers to them, but when Darlene explained the circumstances, that they were attending the game for Ashley, the LSU fans had embraced her as if she were a blood relative.

As Darlene watched Tinker and the Alabama players celebrate on the field, she was warmed by a comforting thought: This was all a gift from Ashley. This was the way it should be. It had been a difficult 3½ hours for the Harrisons—memories of Ashley and her love of Crimson Tide football inevitably flooded back—but they both keenly felt their daughter's presence on this night, as if her spirit were seated next to them. They lingered in the stands as Tinker and his teammates lifted the BCS trophy above their heads.

IN TUSCALOOSA, Bob and Dana Dowling felt only joy. Bob had finished his pizza deliveries by halftime and, sitting next to his wife and two children, watched the second half of the game in their new house. Dana felt like those were her boys out on that field; she and Bob pointed at the TV screen whenever one of their players, the house builders, made a play. "This is just like a dream coming true," Dana said as the game neared its end. "It's payback for everything we've been through."

The celebration was more subdued in Madison, where Shannon Brown was fast asleep when the game ended. His friends had left his house early in the fourth quarter, and Shannon, with 10 minutes left in the game and confident of a Tide victory, turned off his television, brushed his teeth and climbed into bed. There was something deeply satisfying about Alabama winning the national championship, but still, Shannon wasn't in a mood to celebrate. It was a great story, yes, the Tide winning for Tuscaloosa, yet ultimately it didn't change the waking reality of his life. He was proud of this team, and he felt as good as he had in months; still, for him, the game was only a game, the title only a title. . . .

In Wetumpka, Ashley Mims and Parker had dissected every play as if they were coaches on the sideline. "Why did they run that?" Ashley would ask after LSU was stuffed again on an option play. "Doesn't Les Miles realize that it isn't working?"

Midway through the fourth quarter, Ashley had turned to Parker. "It's just so nice," she told her son. "This game is like our football therapy." She checked her Facebook page and was overjoyed at what she found: more than 20 messages from Loryn's friends, telling her that Loryn would be so happy right now that Alabama was winning and that they were feeling Loryn's presence tonight.

After the game she read more messages. "Your daughter would be so proud right now!" wrote one friend. Said another, "She's dancing in heaven! I just know it!"

Her tears felt warm—less of grief than of happiness. Finally.

THIRTY MINUTES after the final whistle in the Superdome, after the celebration on the field had subsided, Saban and his players crammed into the tight locker room. As soon as everyone was inside, the door was shut. The players each took a knee as they surrounded their coach, many still with tears rolling from reddened eyes. They had won their second national title in three seasons, but this one was different, and they all knew it. Saban raised his right hand, and the locker room fell perfectly silent. The coach waited, his eyes slowly scanning one by one the faces around him, then he finally declared in an emphatic voice, "We buried the pain tonight."

The players showered, filed out of the stadium, passed a swarm of cheering Alabama fans held back by police barricades and climbed onto the buses. Darlene and David Harrison stood in the crowd, wanting a last glimpse of the team, to feel connected one more time to this emotional night. Darlene checked the time: It was a few minutes before 12. The Harrisons had determined earlier that they wanted to be by themselves at the moment Ashley would have turned 23, so they turned together and walked away.

At exactly midnight Darlene's cellphone chimed with a text message. It was from Carson.

Happy Birthday Ashley, it said.

CHAPTER 25

Roll Tide

OTHER THAN the sports-writers on deadline hunched over their laptops high up in the press box and a smatter-ing of yellow-shirted stadium workers picking up trash in the aisles, Saban was alone now inside the Superdome. After speaking to his players in the locker room, he had returned to the field, taped a television interview, then, for a few lingering moments, meandered through the vast, vacant stadium, his mouth still locked in its customary frown. Even with his new national title in hand, he looked worried.

He had just become the first coach since Tom Osborne of Ne-braska in 1997 to win three national championships—and the ninth three-time winner since the advent of the wire-service polls in 1936. His defense had just limited LSU to 92 yards of offense, and he had overseen the first shutout in the 14 seasons of all BCS bowls. But when you're in the business of dynasty building, there's no such thing as being satisfied.

With his team up 21–0 late in the fourth quarter, an Alabama defender had jumped offside. It was the first and *only* penalty of the game for the Crimson Tide, but Saban reacted like he was ready for a bar fight the way he ranted and stomped on the Alabama sideline. For a coach like Saban, the devil of imperfection is always lurking.

Still, there was every reason, even for Saban, to feel good. In three of the previous four years, according to scouting services, Saban had landed the nation's top recruiting class. He had won two of the previous three national titles. A new standard of excellence had been set. He had raised his own bar.

The Superdome was quiet. The coach needed to get on the bus so that his players could be set free to celebrate on Bourbon Street. But for several more seconds he remained on the field. The insatiable Saban has never been accused of stopping to smell the roses, but here in the silence, alone, he cracked the thinnest of smiles. It was as close to satisfaction as Nick Saban was going to get.

He left the field and, with two state troopers by his side, walked briskly out of the stadium and onto the bus.

IN THE lobby of the Marriott, the Hendersons were awaiting the return of the champions. They had been joined now by about a thousand Alabama fans, who flooded the hotel and the street outside. The buses rolled to a stop. Saban was the first one to step inside the hotel, and thunderous shouts of "Roll Tide!" greeted him. AJ McCarron followed close behind, and the quarterback flashed the No. 1 signal with his left hand and slapped high fives with his right. The rest of the players filed in behind them, stepping into the warmth of a standing ovation. The Hendersons were right there, clapping enthusiastically as each player passed by.

"It's like it was meant to be," Lee said to his wife. The next morning, weary and happy, they would climb into their SUV and begin the journey home to Tuscaloosa, where they would soon start a fresh chapter in their lives.

THE PLAYERS, all of them dressed in their Alabama warmups, strutted through the smoky, boozy haze of Bourbon Street, where thousands of giddy Alabama fans continued to shout "Roll Tide!" into the small hours of the morning. McCarron, his face fixed in a championship smile, posed for photo after photo with wide-eyed admirers. Trent Richardson slapped every hand that was thrust his way as he moved through the crowd that clogged the street. Other players raised their right index fingers, while necklaces of Mardi Gras beads rained down like glittery ticker tape from the balconies above. It was a celebration that the players and the fans had been working toward together for eight months, and now they were primed to party till the sun rose over the Bayou.

"One of the best nights of my life," McCarron later pronounced. "It was like, finally, the tornado was behind us."

EARLY THE next morning Ashley Mims drove to Academy Sports in Prattville, where she purchased a championship commemorative T-shirt. The store was packed aisle to aisle with Alabama fans, none of them happier than Ashley. To the bottom of her heart, she felt that the team had won for her daughter.

After returning home, she changed into workout clothes and went jogging. Alone, she ran from her home for two miles, passing through the entrance of the New Home Baptist Church cemetery. She ran past one towering pine tree after the next as she neared Loryn's grave.

When she reached the site, breathing heavily, Ashley took a few moments to catch her wind, then sat cross-legged on a black slab that faced Loryn's headstone. For the longest time, motionless, she stared at her daughter's name carved into the stone and let memories of her sweet Loryn flow through her.

At last Ashley whispered. "They fought for us, baby," she said gently into the breeze.

Epilogue

THE BELLS tolled at 5:13 p.m. on April 27, 2012, one year to the minute that the deadly funnel first hit Tuscaloosa; 53 times they tolled at dozens of churches throughout the city. In three-second intervals—the typical delay for gun salutes to the fallen—the chimes reverberated, their somber echoes heard for miles.

At a memorial service in Coleman Coliseum, the students sat together surrounded by several thousand residents of T-Town. The names of the 53 victims in the Tuscaloosa area were slowly read aloud as their images appeared on a huge video screen.

"In time, hearts will begin to mend and the destruction will slowly fade," Mayor Maddox told the crowd, "but what will never vanish is who we are and what we have become following the days and months since April 27. . . . We are Tuscaloosa, and we will come back."

Yet even 12 months later, despite massive rebuilding efforts, the physical marks of the storm remained imprinted on the landscape. In places such as Alberta City, only a few miles from downtown Tuscaloosa, block after block of damaged buildings had been left untended. In more fully cleaned areas such as Forest Lake, empty, weed-strewn fields were the only remnants of once vibrant neighborhoods.

And for so many students at the university, the sheer fright of that day was still emotionally vivid and raw. Many spoke of ongoing nightmares; one young woman, now a senior, said she had to start sleeping with a mouth guard. Others talked of breaking into tears at the sound of sirens. Many said they were still haunted by survivor's guilt, a feeling that just wouldn't go away. And, of course, many were still mourning dead friends.

On the day of the one-year anniversary, a letter written by Darlene Harrison appeared in *The Crimson White*, the Alabama student paper.

"Ashley is our love and always our light," Harrison wrote. "Her smile will forever be your beacon of light and reminder of her huge heart to the many who befriended and loved Ashley there in Tuscaloosa.... To Carson Tinker, a survivor of the storm along with his roommate, Payton Holley: what love can we give to two such brave and courageous men. Carson, a UA senior and Alabama football player, had to go through enormous healing of his own and contributed to a successful season and a BCS National Championship victory. Still, he has never stopped finding ways to cherish the memory of Ashley.... We have no doubt Ashley is so very proud of each and every one of her friends for finding the courage to move on past this storm, remember the lives that were lost forever, find peace within themselves to grow and we know she, as well as we, are so deeply thankful for all these generous hearts expressing their love and kindness to her memory."

In the vacant grass field across from where Tinker's house once stood, Darlene and David Harrison held a small memorial for their daughter that day. They had traveled from Texas to be there, at the place where Ashley's body was found. Prayers were softly spoken and stories of happier times were shared. Yet the anguish remained penetrating and pervasive. It was a feeling felt all over town. On this day, Tuscaloosa was the broken heart of Dixie.

NICK SABAN called Carson Tinker to his office on Aug. 20, 2012. It was less than two weeks before Alabama would kick off its new season, and Tinker felt more than a little anxiety as he opened the thick wooden door. He and Saban had grown close since the tornado, but there must be something he'd done wrong to get this summons.

Saban waved an arm toward a chair in front of his enormous desk. Tinker sat obediently. "You know," Saban said, "we have an extra scholarship available. We'd like you to have it. You deserve it. You've worked hard, and you really deserve it." Tinker was speechless.

A scholarship had seemed a distant, elusive dream ever since he'd walked on in the summer of 2008. Saban tiptoes along the line of the NCAA limit of 85 scholarships. He has been criticized in the past for "oversigning" recruits, meaning he'd promised more scholarships to players than he had available, forcing him to "grayshirt" one or more recruits. (Grayshirting is the practice of delaying enrollment for a recruit until the second semester of his freshman year to prevent his eligibility clock from starting to tick.) With scholarships so precious to him, Saban had very rarely awarded one to a walk-on, much less a long snapper.

Tinker stood up from his chair and wrapped his arms around his coach in an emotional embrace, a hug of relief, joy and fulfillment.

Soon after, Tinker called his parents to tell them that they wouldn't have to send any more tuition checks to the University of Alabama. It was a phone call he could not have fathomed 16 months earlier when the tornado slammed his body to the ground. Sharing this news with his father and mother felt impossibly good.

THE ALABAMA football machine continued to hum with ruthless efficiency. In the 2012 season the Tide won the SEC championship, defeating Georgia 32–28 on Dec. 1 in Atlanta to earn a spot, again, in the BCS national championship game, this time to be played in Miami. On Jan. 2, 2013, the coaches and players left the gray winter chill in Tuscaloosa and landed in the bright afternoon sunshine of

South Florida. In five days, at Sun Life Stadium, the Tide (12–1 with a single loss to Texas A&M and ranked No. 2) would play top-ranked Notre Dame (undefeated at 12–0). Saban led his team off the chartered plane at the Miami airport and approached a group of waiting reporters. In the span of four minutes he was asked twice about his dramatic departure from the Miami Dolphins after the 2006 season.

Ever since walking away from the Dolphins, Saban had been repeatedly eviscerated in the South Florida media. *Miami Herald* columnist Dan Le Batard had called Saban "a loser" and "a gasbag" and "a weasel." Now, six years later, Saban faced a gaggle of Miami reporters for the first time as Alabama's head coach. "We all learn things about ourselves as we go," he responded. "Some things we all would like to do differently. I just think we all make mistakes and would like to do things differently. You know, you don't get the opportunity to get it back."

Saban then turned and walked to a waiting team bus. He understood that he had mishandled the situation in 2006—he later described it as one of the great regrets of his life—but Saban isn't one to hit the rewind button. He is not given to personal reflection or introspection or apologizing for the past. He lives obsessively in the present; it is vital to his intensity of focus. The Process, with its pounding emphasis on the here and now, is built on it.

The hype and media attention for this title game had been off-the-charts, two legendary football schools, the two best teams in the country. The Alabama players surrounded their coach in the Sun Life locker room, each on one knee, listening to Saban's final words before kickoff against the Fighting Irish. "Give your teammates the best opportunity to be significant," Saban said. "Play for your teammates, don't play for yourself." His speech was brief, and his team filed confidently out of the locker room. Alabama was a 10-point betting favorite, and not a single Crimson Tide player believed that even the luck of the Irish would be able to help Notre Dame on this night.

The Bama players charged out of the west end zone tunnel behind

Saban, dressed in white jerseys with crimson numbers and white pants with twin crimson stripes on the side of each leg. Barrett Jones, his face looking like a man possessed, jogged onto the field. On the flight to Florida, his left foot had been in a walking cast; now he was moving forward without a trace of a limp. Near him was Tinker, who peered into the stands and kept nodding his head at the Alabama fans, as if to say, No worries, we got this for you. Saban grabbed a headset, fitted it on his head and glowered toward the field.

Notre Dame won the coin toss but elected to kick. Irish kicker Kyle Brindza put his foot into the ball, sending it to Alabama's Christion Jones, who gathered it at the one-yard line and ran it to the 17. On first down AJ McCarron handed the ball to Eddie Lacy, who gained one yard. On second down McCarron fired a deep out to Kevin Norwood on the right sideline for 29 yards. Then Lacy and T.J. Yeldon rushed on three consecutive plays to the left side, behind guard Chance Warmack and Jones; the last was a bruising 20-yard touchdown run by Lacy. Notre Dame hadn't allowed a touchdown drive of more than 75 yards all season, but in just two minutes and 57 seconds, the Tide had marched 82 yards with startling ease.

After the Fighting Irish went three-and-out, the Tide took possession on their own 39-yard line. Again pounding the left side of the line with running plays, Alabama methodically moved down the field. Lacy rushed for three yards on the first play, then eight, then five, then five again, then 20. It was Football 101, beat the hell out of the man in front of you, precisely as Saban and his staff had drawn it up during their five weeks of preparation: Use our strength and size advantage in the trenches and wear them down. The 10-play second drive was capped when McCarron hit wide-open tight end Michael Williams over the middle for a three-yard touchdown. Less than 10 minutes into what had been one of the most anticipated clashes in college football history, the game felt like a mismatch. Alabama won 42–14, earning its third national title in four years.

The streets of Tuscaloosa had been virtually vacant for four hours, as the city hunkered down in front of television screens. Near the end of the fourth quarter, Bob Dowling, working his pizza delivery job, drove past Academy Sports on Skyland Boulevard. Dozens of fans already were lined up outside the store's doors, waiting for it to open the moment the game ended so they could buy their freshly minted 2012 national championship T-shirts, caps and jerseys. While listening to the game on the car radio, Dowling watched the happy fans standing in the cold winter night and once again marveled at how much joy the Tide pumped into this town.

Dana Dowling, watching the end of the game with Marilyn, leaned back on her living room couch at 4214 5th Street and grinned a winning smile. Alabama had now won two consecutive national titles since her house was built from the ground up by many of the Bama players she saw celebrating on the field. She fully appreciated the connection of one to the other.

IN THE fall of 2013 Alabama had a chance to become the first team since the advent of the AP poll in 1936 to win four national championships in five seasons, a feat that would cement its status as a football dynasty. (Sadly, the man who had gotten it all started, Mal Moore, was not there to watch, having died of a lung condition less than three months after the Notre Dame game.)

Alabama was ranked No. 1 in the nation when the team traveled to Auburn for the Iron Bowl on Nov. 30. With one second left in the fourth quarter and the score tied at 28, Alabama redshirt freshman kicker Adam Griffith attempted a 57-yard field goal. The kick was short and to the right. The Tigers' Chris Davis, standing in the back of the end zone, caught the ball and ran 109 yards for a game-winning touchdown. It was a stunning play and a shocking conclusion, instant history—the Kick Six, it was dubbed—that would be rolled in the taped highlights over and over and over, into the night and after.

The Auburn fans, joyous and in wild-eyed disbelief, stormed past security guards onto the field—dozens of students cannonballed into the prickly holly bushes that ring the sidelines. They wouldn't leave the field for an hour. Some re-created Davis's astonishing touchdown sprint, others carved up pieces of the field with pocket knives and plucked holly twigs for souvenirs. One devotee even dumped the ashes of a loved one near the Tigers' sideline.

The celebration moved to Toomer's Corner. The two cherished old oak trees had been removed, but fans, players and even coaches hurled rolls of toilet paper over wires that had been installed just for this purpose and into the limbs of dozens of other trees still standing at the school's entrance.

Among the revelers was Auburn alum Charles Barkley, the ex-NBA star who had given a pregame locker room pep talk to the Tigers. He joined the thousands at Toomer's Corner before taking his celebration to Hamilton's restaurant two blocks away, where he bought a $1,000 round of drinks for fans. Barkley would later voice the sentiment that most every Auburn fan was feeling: "It was a payback moment for poisoning our damn trees," Barkley said. "And man, it was sweet. One of the great moments in my life."

One football fan who was not there to witness the Auburn victory was Harvey Updyke Jr. After spending six months in the Lee County jail, Updyke was released on June 10, 2013. He was ordered to pay $796,731.98 in restitution to Auburn; there is little chance that Updyke, unemployed and living in Albany, La., will ever pay his debt in full. At Toomer's Corner, replacement oaks were scheduled to be planted in early 2015.

THE CITYWIDE party in Auburn was still raging when the three Alabama team buses rolled out of town. The Tide's quest for a three-peat was over, and Saban and his team would have to settle for a date with Oklahoma in the Sugar Bowl. Though there was only disappointment inside those buses, dispassionate statisticians could say there was little cause for shame, considering what the Crimson Tide had achieved over the previous five years. In that span the Tide had won 60 games, matching Nebraska (1993–97) for the most victories during any five-year stretch in major college football history. Since the start of the 2008 season, Alabama had been ranked No. 1 in 40 of the 95 weekly AP polls, a remarkable 42.1% of the time. Perhaps Saban and the players would take pride in that, if not comfort, in the days and weeks ahead. But not now.

As the buses cruised down Interstate 85, Dawn Ward, a 40-year-old Tide fan from Cullman, Ala., was driving along the same route, outside of Montgomery. She had watched the Iron Bowl from the upper reaches of Jordan-Hare Stadium and was heading home, still proudly sporting her crimson cowboy boots with script A's, an Alabama sweatshirt and a houndstooth scarf. Flashing blue lights appeared in her rearview mirror, and she pulled over to the shoulder. She watched as first the police escort and then the Alabama team buses passed by her. Unexpectedly, she began to cry. "I'm just so proud of them," she explained to a passenger. "So proud of everything they've done for this state since the tornado."

Three weeks before the Sugar Bowl, Nick Saban signed a contract extension that would pay him $7 million a year through 2020, making him the fourth-highest-paid coach in the U.S. in any sport. Before arriving at Alabama, Saban had never stayed at one school longer than five years. Entering his eighth season at UA in 2014, Saban seemed almost certain to finish his coaching career in Tuscaloosa.

THEY ALL watched the Sugar Bowl on Jan. 2, 2014. Carson Tinker, now the Jacksonville Jaguars' long snapper after making the team as a long-shot undrafted free agent, watched the game from his off-season home. Life has moved forward for Tinker—he is engaged to Annie Bates, a UA graduate, and they plan to marry in 2015.

Barrett Jones, a fourth-round pick of the St. Louis Rams in 2013, felt the old game-day rush of adrenaline as the Tide took the field in the Sugar Bowl; he sat in the Superdome stands with his parents, there to support younger brothers Harrison and Walker, both on the team. Dont'a Hightower watched the game as a member of the New England Patriots; picked 25th in the first round of the 2012 draft by the Pats, Hightower had 97 tackles in 2013 as a starting linebacker. Hightower's close friend D.J. Fluker tuned in three days before his San Diego Chargers took on the Cincinnati Bengals in a playoff game; the 11th overall pick, by the Chargers, in the '13 draft, Fluker started 15 games at tackle and was the cornerstone of an offensive line that powered San Diego's prolific offense.

Josh Chapman watched the Sugar Bowl from his condo in Indianapolis. The defensive leader of the 2011 Tide squad, Chapman was picked by the Colts in the fifth round of the 2012 draft. The noseguard missed his rookie season with a knee injury, but in 2013 he became a regular contributor late in the season. He still spends his off-seasons in Tuscaloosa. Javier Arenas watched the game from his house in Phoenix; after spending three seasons with the Kansas City Chiefs, Arenas was traded in May 2013 to the Arizona Cardinals and in March 2014 signed with the Atlanta Falcons, where he's a returner and defensive back.

Mayor Walt Maddox tuned into the Sugar Bowl game from his in-laws' house in Nokomis near the Florida state line. In June 2013, quelling local rumors that he would make a bid for the U.S. Senate or the governor's mansion, Maddox announced he would seek a third term as mayor. A liberal-leaning politician in a city that's heavily Republican, Maddox remains a revered figure in T-Town. His boots-on-the-ground, door-to-door leadership in rebuilding the city has been hailed by politicos from coast to coast. The reconstruction plan he oversaw has served as a model for the cities of Joplin, Mo., which was hit by a tornado in 2011, just a month after the Tuscaloosa storm, and Moore, Okla., which was leveled by a huge twister in 2013. Empty fields and vacant lots across Tuscaloosa remain as visible scars, but the rhythms and beats of normal, prestorm life have returned to the college town.

Lee and Leigh Henderson sat in the stands at the Sugar Bowl; their eyes followed Saban as he led his team through pregame warmups. In January 2013, Henderson opened a Which Wich sandwich shop on University Boulevard in downtown Tuscaloosa. Six months later he turned on the lights at another new Which Wich at 1800 McFarland Boulevard, less than two blocks from where his Smoothie King once stood; Lee often fuels his car at the new gas station that now occupies his former lot. "We're making great strides in the redevelopment of Tuscaloosa, but we still have work to do," Lee says. "Every time I drive by where my old store used to be the memories come back. Mostly, I'm just grateful that we were spared and didn't have any fatalities."

Bob and Dana Dowling watched the Tide from the living room of their home on 5th Street. Beneath their television was a framed poster-sized display of some of their precious mementos: ticket stubs from the 2011 Kent State game given them by the Sabans; a card from Terry Saban congratulating them on their new house (she noted how much she loved the cabinetry); and a deflated football signed by many of the players who built their home. Bob recently landed a job doing electrical work at the nearby Mercedes factory—"He sticks close to home now," says Dana—and Marilyn Dowling, 15, a freshman at Bryant High, is taking extra engineering classes at the Tuscaloosa Center for Technology. In the summer of 2013 she traveled with a group to Waco, Texas, to build new homes and now hopes to become an engineer, to design and construct houses and apartment complexes. "Nick Saban and the Alabama players changed Marilyn's life," Dana says. "They didn't just build us a home, they also gave Marilyn inspiration to help others."

ASHLEY MIMS watches all the Crimson Tide games, usually from her favorite perch in her Wetumpka bedroom. In Madison, Shannon Brown still takes time on Saturdays to cheer on his old team. But almost three years since Loryn's death, Ashley and Shannon still suffer many difficult days, with some interludes of peace. It is a matter of coping, and it won't ever be easy.

"I choose to remember the good times and the smiles," Ashley says. "I'll never be the same, but that's the only way I can keep living."

"Loryn will always be in my heart, and I miss her dearly," Shannon says, "but you have to come to terms with things if you're going to be able to get up in the morning. Our good times together are what fill my thoughts."

Darlene and David Harrison know that the deep-rooted grief of losing a child will never go away. Even three years since that awful day, the memories are sometimes frighteningly harsh. "It is so difficult to see your child on a morgue table," says Darlene, her voice strained with emotion. "No parent should ever have to experience that. They don't wake up. No matter how much you shake them or talk to them, they don't wake up."

Their pain has been mitigated only by the generosity of others on behalf of their daughter, Ashley, and for that they are grateful. "For us," says Darlene, "our legacy is to keep her legacy alive."

The flow of generosity began within hours of the initial news of Ashley's death. Donations in her name began to pour into the university. A number of people made proposals to start scholarships in Ashley's name. Her leadership fraternity, Delta Sigma Pi, reached out to the Harrisons immediately about funding a scholarship, as did the University of Alabama. More offers came from people at home in Dallas. It was overwhelming to two grieving parents still in shock, but the wheels continued to turn. Today there are five different scholarships and funds operating in Ashley Harrison's name, including one from her high school, Ursuline Academy of Dallas, and one that sponsors a child to attend the St. Mark's School Summer Camp, also in Dallas. The University of Alabama scholarship was endowed at close to the same time as the scholarship in the name of Loryn Brown.

There is even an Ashley Harrison Memorial Pet Fund in honor of Josey and Ms. B, Carson's and Ashley's dogs. Sponsored by the Dallas veterinary clinic that has cared for the Harrisons' dogs, the fund helps people who cannot afford medical care for their dogs. "There are beautiful people out there," Darlene says. "We're just blessed to have people who loved Ashley. She touched so many lives."

Darlene goes to Tuscaloosa several times a year. Sometimes she takes people with her, sometimes she prefers to go alone. Each time she visits the field where Ashley died. The place looks different these days. A year after the tornado the Harrisons and a large group of friends and family planted trees, flowers and rose bushes there. "We planted mostly pink roses," says Darlene. "Ashley's favorite color was pink." They planted a Christmas tree, a blue spruce. Darlene decorates the tree every November.

The owners of the property and their neighbors, who live adjacent to it, take care of the field. "They are just amazing," says Darlene. "The owners planted trees everywhere, all over. They bought the most gorgeous dogwood tree, and he put in an irrigation system just so everything could be taken care of. Forever."

ON THE last play of his college career, in the fourth quarter of the Sugar Bowl, with less than a minute to play against Oklahoma, AJ McCarron was sacked, and the ball popped loose. A Sooners defensive end scooped up the fumble and returned it eight yards for a touchdown, capping Oklahoma's 45–31 win. McCarron walked off the field with an empty stare. His eyes were pointed in the direction of Saban, but he wasn't actually looking at him. He walked past his coach without saying a thing. This was how the McCarron-Saban era ended—stunned and wordless, after two straight losses.

McCarron, eye-black smudged over his face, undressed in front of his locker. The player who had led Alabama to more wins, 36, than any other starting quarterback in school history, pulled off his number 10 jersey and set it on the carpeted floor for the final time. Before he headed to the shower, a parade of teammates, assistant coaches, police officers, a bus driver and a janitor approached, each extending a hand. Everyone said a version of the same thing: Thank you.

Acknowledgments

THIS WAS an emotional book to report and write. Asking mothers and fathers to recount the worst moments of their lives was a heart-wrenching undertaking. This book would not have been possible without the brave honesty of Ashley Mims, Shannon Brown, Darlene Harrison and Carson Tinker. Words cannot adequately express how greatly I admire their courage and strength. Photographs of Loryn Brown and Ashley Harrison were mounted above the laptop in my home office in Birmingham as I wrote; the inspiration of these two beautiful young women—neither of whom I ever met—influenced every word.

So many others shared with me their memories, often painful, often uplifting: Bob and Dana Dowling; Lee and Leigh Henderson; Mayor Walt Maddox; Alabama players Javier Arenas, Josh Chapman, D.J. Fluker, Brandon Gibson, Dont'a Hightower, Barrett Jones, AJ McCarron, Trent Richardson and Courtney Upshaw, among others. All were exceedingly generous with their time and their help.

Over the past five years I've spent a good amount of time, one-on-one, with Nick Saban. He has always been gracious, thoughtful and patient with me. While I'm very much aware of the difficulties that some other reporters, especially those who cover Alabama football on a daily basis, have had in dealing with Saban, my experiences with him have been positive. I remain steadfast in my belief that the primary reason Saban will remain as Alabama's coach until he retires from the game is the impact of the events of April 27, 2011, and the months that followed.

The editor of this book, David Bauer, has been my mentor at *Sports Illustrated* for nearly two decades. His vision for the narrative and his pitch-perfect edits reinforced what I already knew: He is, put simply, the best in the business. During the painstaking process of fact-checking the book, Elizabeth McGarr McCue, a writer-reporter at *Sports Illustrated*, engaged in critical, emotionally draining interviews; always, her big heart shone and comforted. SI copy editor Pamela Roberts and her eagle eyes examined every word, improving this book with every subtle change. SI's Stefanie Kaufman expertly oversaw the entire project. Jim Childs and Michele Bové at Time Home Entertainment Inc. supported this book from the beginning, as did *Sports Illustrated*'s Paul Fichtenbaum and Chris Stone. I'll always be indebted to the many SI staffers (present and past) who have supported me over the years, especially Rich O'Brien, Hank Hersch, Richard Deitsch, Mark Beech, Simon Bruty, B.J. Schecter, Richard Demak, Mark Bechtel, Trisha Lucey Blackmar, George Dohrmann, Terry McDonell, Larry Burke, Steve Madden, David Sabino, Kelli Anderson and Gene Menez.

Cary Estes, a Birmingham-based writer and SI.com contributor, deftly reviewed an early version of the manuscript. Amy Bickers, a former editor at *Southern Living*, made sure this Nebraska-raised writer was schooled in the Southern vernacular. Allyson Angle, a former student of mine at the University of Alabama who currently works at *Cooking Light*, helped me report the original *Sports Illustrated* story on the Tuscaloosa tornado and offered valuable ideas throughout the book-writing process. Gordy Bratz, a retired Army colonel and my stepfather, read various drafts and improved the final product immeasurably with his concise, cerebral additions.

My literary agent, Scott Waxman, helped shape this project before a word was written, and his feedback on the book proposal was invaluable as always; I'm beyond grateful that Scott is in my corner. Two of my closest cohorts in Birmingham—ESPN's Paul Finebaum and musician Taylor Hicks—were always a phone call away when I needed them. So too were Marie Craig, Matt Crane, Michelle Crunk, Sean Kelley, Andrew Salser, Mary Brunson Salser and Brian Shinnick.

And finally, I'm unfathomably lucky to have April Nicole Anderson by my side. On 4/27/11 in Birmingham, before we'd ever met, an early-morning twister blew past her house and took down an 80-foot oak tree in her yard; the tree landed near her bedroom, where she trembled in a corner clutching her dog. She knows the terror of a tornado. Yet one look into her blue-sky eyes always reminds me of my good fortune and that fully experiencing the present is what truly matters.

Lars Anderson
Birmingham
Spring 2014

(To contribute to scholarship funds, send donations to these addresses: Loryn Alexandria Brown Memorial Endowed Scholarship, P.O. Box 861928, Tuscaloosa, AL 35486-0017; and Ashley Harrison Memorial Scholarship, P.O. Box 180098, Dallas, TX 75218.)

Bibliography

BOOKS

Barra, Allen. *The Last Coach: A Life of Paul "Bear" Bryant*. W.W. Norton & Co., New York, 2005.

Benedict, Jeff and Keteyian, Armen. *The System: The Glory and Scandal of Big-Time College Football*. Doubleday, New York, 2013.

The Birmingham News, The Huntsville Times, Press-Register. Day of Devastation: Photos & Stories of Alabama's Deadliest Tornado Outbreak. The Birmingham News Multimedia, Birmingham, 2011.

Bowling, Lewis. *Wallace Wade: Championship Years at Alabama and Duke*. Carolina Academic Press, Durham, N.C., 2010.

Chambers, Catherine. *Tornado*. Heinemann Library, Chicago, 2002.

Dougherty, Terri. *Anatomy of a Tornado*. Capstone Press, Mankato, Minn., 2011.

Dunnavant, Keith. *Coach: The Life of Paul "Bear" Bryant*. Thomas Dunne Books, New York, 1996.

Ford, Tommy. *Tornado to National Title #14*. Whitman Publishing, LLC, Atlanta, 2012.

Fradin, Judith Bloom and Fradin, Dennis Brindell. *Tornado! The Story Behind these Twisting, Turning, Spinning, and Spiraling Storms*. National Geographic, Washington, D.C., 2011.

Gibbs, Chad. *God & Football: Faith and Fanaticism in the SEC*. Zondervan, Grand Rapids, 2010.

Glier, Ray. *How the SEC Became Goliath: The Making of College Football's Most Dominant Conference.* Howard Books, New York, 2012.

Griffin, John Chandler. *Auburn vs. Alabama: Gridiron Grudge Since 1893.* Hill Street Press, Athens, Ga., 2001.

Kazek, Kelly. *A History of Alabama's Deadliest Tornados: Disaster in Dixie.* The History Press, Charleston, S.C., 2010.

McNair, Kirk. *Tide Rolls: Alabama's 2011 National Championship Season.* Triumph Books, LLC, Chicago, 2012.

Saban, Nick with Curtis, Brian. *How Good Do You Want to Be? A Champion's Tips on How to Lead and Succeed at Work and in Life.* Ballantine Books, New York, 2005.

Sports Illustrated. Alabama Football. Time Home Entertainment Inc., New York, 2010.

St. John, Warren. *Rammer Jammer Yellow Hammer: A Road Trip Into the Heart of Fan Mania.* Crown Publishers, New York, 2004.

NEWSPAPERS, MAGAZINES AND WEBSITES

Athlon Sports. "Kent State's Terrific Trio in 1972: Nick Saban, Jack Lambert and Gary Pinkel." Oct. 24, 2011.

Bachman, Rachel and Cohen, Ben. "How Saban Turned the Tide." *The Wall Street Journal,* Aug. 28, 2012.

Bradley, Mark. "Bama–Notre Dame? A Big Game. Nick Saban? Even Bigger." AJC.com, Jan. 6, 2013.

Bragg, Rick. "In the Nick of Time." *Sports Illustrated,* Aug. 27, 2007.

Burke, Monte. "The Most Powerful Coach in Sports." *Forbes,* Aug. 14, 2008.

Casagrande, Michael. "Alabama Football: Nose Guard Josh Chapman is Unsung Key to Crimson Tide's Top-Ranked Defense." *Ledger-Enquirer,* Columbus, Ga., Dec. 23, 2011.

Casagrande, Michael. "Nick Saban's 'Process' Was Born 15 Years Ago Today with a Stunning Upset at Ohio State." AL.com, Nov. 7, 2013.

Crossman, Matt. "Football Plays Vital Role in Tuscaloosa's Healing from Tornado." *Sporting News,* Sept. 9, 2011.

Crossman, Matt. "The House that Bama Built Gives Life, Hope to Fervent Tide Fans." *Sporting News,* Jan. 10, 2012.

Edwards, Mark. "Family and Football." *The Decatur Daily,* Jan. 4, 2007.

Gast, Phil. "Fans Will Cheer Both Teams at Alabama's First Game Since Tornado." CNN.com, Sept. 3, 2011.

Gattis, Paul. "The First Nick Saban." *Huntsville Times*, Aug. 26, 2007.

Hogan, Nakia. "Alabama Player's Girlfriend Dreamed of Seeing Him Play for BCS Title in Her Hometown." *The Times-Picayune*, Jan. 8, 2012.

Layden, Tim. "Right Place, Right Time." *Sports Illustrated*, July 3, 2006.

Marvez, Alex and Hijek, Barbara. "A Brother To All." *South Florida Sun-Sentinel*, Feb. 27, 2005.

Mason, Carolyn. "At Home with the Sabans." *The Tuscaloosa News*, Oct. 4, 2008.

McCready, Neal. "Big Catch For Bama!" *Mobile Register*, Jan. 4, 2007.

Murphy, Austin. "Staying Power." *Sports Illustrated*, Jan. 18, 2010.

Murphy, Austin. "Absolutely Alabama." *Sports Illustrated*, Jan. 16, 2012.

O'Keefe, Brian. "Leader of the Crimson Tide." *Fortune*, Sept. 24, 2012.

Selk, Jason. "What Nick Saban Knows About Success." *Forbes*, Sept. 12, 2012.

Solomon, Jon. "Team Motivation Comes Off the Field. Tide Takes it to Classroom to Learn Decision-Making." *The Birmingham News*, Aug. 10, 2008.

St. John, Warren. "Nick Saban: Sympathy for the Devil." *GQ*, September 2013.

Sunseri, Jaclyn. "Barrett Jones Spends Spring Break Lending a Helping Hand in Haiti." Rolltide.com, March 26, 2010.

Tankersley, Mike. "Montgomery Quarterback Club: Moore Relives Moments of Luring Saban." *Montgomery Advertiser*, Sept. 22, 2010.

Thompson, Wright. "The Life and Times of Harvey Updyke." ESPN.com, May 24, 2011.

Tierney, Mike. "Teamwork Continues in Honoring a Coach." *The New York Times*, Jan. 4, 2013.

Tomlinson, Tommy. "Something Went Very Wrong at Toomer's Corner." *Sports Illustrated*, Aug. 15, 2011.

Wertheim, L. Jon. "Underrated." *Sports Illustrated*, Nov. 25, 2013.

Whisenant, Charles. "900 Turn Out for Post-Storm Community Service." *The Arab Tribune*, Aug. 17, 2011.

About the Author

LARS ANDERSON worked for *Sports Illustrated* for 20 years and is the author of five books, including *Carlisle vs. Army* and *The All Americans*. He is an instructor at the University of Alabama. He lives with his wife, April, in Birmingham, where the April 27, 2011, tornado passed five miles north of his house.

No Longer Property of

ANYTHINK LIBRARIES/
RANGEVIEW LIBRARY DISTRICT